Second
Edition

Governmental
Accounting
Made Easy

Second Edition

Governmental Accounting Made Easy

Warren Ruppel

WILEY

JOHN WILEY & SONS, INC.

Library of Congress Cataloging-in-Publication Data:

Ruppel, Warren.
  Governmental accounting made easy / Warren Ruppel.—2nd Ed.
    p. cm.
  Includes index.
  ISBN 978-0-470-41150-6 (hardback)
  1. Finance, Public—United States—Accounting. 2. Finance, Public—Accounting I. Title.
HJ9801.R86 2010
657'.835 00973—dc22

                                                          2009028342

Printed in the United States of America

V10012443_072419

Contents

Preface

When I first began discussing the concept of a book on governmental accounting for nonaccountants for the first edition of this book, the publisher, John Wiley & Sons, Inc., asked a good question: "Who would be interested in a book on governmental accounting who is not an accountant?" The quick answers were obvious—bond underwriters and investors, lawyers, elected officials, financial and other managers working in government, labor unions, and so forth. On second thought, anyone who is impacted by a state or local government (this includes virtually everyone in the United States) might have an interest in understanding what at times seems like the overly complex and confusing world of governmental accounting. Being able to more intelligently read and understand the financial statements prepared by governments and understanding some of the key accounting concepts that underlie those financial statements can help nonaccountants better understand the financial affairs of governments.

The goal of this book is to provide a broad range of information about governmental accounting and financial reporting that will be useful to people who either have no (or very little) accounting background or have some accounting knowledge in the commercial or not-for-profit accounting areas, but do not understand governmental accounting. Governments have recently implemented a new financial reporting model that has resulted in a radical change in the way that governmental financial statements are presented. Frankly, even after several years of experience with the new model, there are very few people who actually understand what these financial statements are trying to communicate. This tries to make sense of these financial statements for the casual reader.

The information in this book is presented in as simple and as understandable a format as possible. This book will not make a governmental accountant out of you, nor will it give you all of the information that you would need to prepare a set of financial statements for a government. If you want to be a governmental accountant or prepare financial statements for a government, you might be interested in the current year's edition of *GAAP for Governments*, also published by John Wiley & Sons, Inc. and written by me.

The sequence of chapters in the book is designed to gradually build an understanding of governmental accounting and financial statements. Chapter 1 describes what is meant by governmental accounting and to what types of entities it applies. Chapter 2 discusses some basic accounting concepts underlying all governmental accounting and financial reporting, while Chapter 3 discusses fund accounting. Chapter 4 describes the basic financial statements prepared by governments under the recently implemented financial reporting model mentioned above, including the government-wide financial statements and the fund financial statements. Chapters 5 through 9 examine some of the more specific and complicated accounting issues often found in governmental financial statements such as defining the reporting entity and accounting for revenues, capital assets, and pensions. Finally, Chapter 10 discusses some of the upcoming changes that are expected to impact governmental accounting and financial reporting in the near future as a result of the issuance of new accounting standards and pronouncements.

I would like to thank John DeRemigis of John Wiley & Sons, Inc. for his steady direction of the project, as well as Judy Howarth for her editorial assistance. As always, I am truly lucky to have a supportive family—my wife, Marie, and sons Christopher and Gregory.

Warren Ruppel
Woodcliff Lake, New Jersey
August 2009

About the Author

Warren Ruppel, CPA, is a Partner at Marks Paneth & Shron LLP, New York, where he serves in the firm's nonprofit and Government Services Group and also is a leader in its Professional Practices Group. He formerly was the assistant comptroller for accounting of the City of New York, where he was responsible for all aspects of the city's accounting and financial reporting. He has thirty-five years of experience in governmental and not-for-profit accounting and financial reporting. He began his career at KPMG after graduating from St. John's University, New York. His involvement with governmental accounting and auditing began with his first audit assignment—the second audit ever performed of the financial statements of the City of New York. From that time he served many governmental and commercial clients until he joined Deloitte & Touche in 1989 to specialize in audits of governments and not-for-profit organizations. Mr. Ruppel has also served as the chief financial officer of an international not-for-profit organization.

Mr. Ruppel has served as instructor for many training courses, including specialized governmental and not-for-profit programs and seminars. He has also been an adjunct lecturer of accounting at the Bernard M. Baruch College of the City University of New York. He is the author of four other books, *OMB Circular A-133 Audits, Not-for-Profit Organization Audits, Not-for-Profit Accounting Made Easy,* and *Not-for-Profit Audit Committee Best Practices.*

Mr. Ruppel is a member of the American Institute of Certified Public Accountants as well as the New York State Society of Certified Public Accountants, where he serves on the Governmental Accounting and Auditing and Not-for-Profit Organizations Technical Committees and is a trustee of the Foundation for Accounting Education. He has also served as the Chair of the Society's Audit Committee. He is also a past president of the New York Chapter of the Institute of Management Accountants. Mr. Ruppel is a member of the Government Finance Officers Association and serves on its Special Review Committee.

CHAPTER 1

Introduction and Background

This chapter sets the stage for understanding governmental accounting by explaining some of the important concepts that comprise the framework of governmental accounting and financial reporting. Specifically, this chapter will discuss the following:

- What are generally accepted accounting principles?
- Who sets generally accepted accounting principles?
- Do governments need to comply with generally accepted accounting principles?
- Why is governmental accounting and financial reporting different from commercial and not-for-profit accounting and financial reporting?
- To what entities do governmental generally accepted accounting principles apply?

Understanding these broad concepts will help put in context the more specific discussions and explanations of financial statements and accounting rules described in later chapters of this book.

WHAT ARE GENERALLY ACCEPTED
ACCOUNTING PRINCIPLES?

Generally accepted accounting principles (commonly referred to as GAAP) are basically the accounting rules and conventions that

1

are used to prepare financial statements. They provide guidance to financial statement preparers to tell them how to account for various types of transactions, how various types of transactions (as well as assets and liabilities) are to be reflected in the financial statements, and what disclosures are required to be included in the financial statements. The next section describes who determines what accounting principles are GAAP. However, it is important for the reader to know that the accounting principles that comprise GAAP come from a variety of sources. In some cases GAAP may result simply from common practices that have been used by financial statement preparers over a long period of time. These rules are said to have *general acceptance* meaning that you cannot go to an authoritative accounting rule book and find an accounting rule that results in that specific accounting principle. On the opposite side of the spectrum, accounting rule makers (discussed in the next section) issue accounting standards that specify accounting treatments for specific types of transactions. In between these two extremes are various authoritative accounting resources that provide interpretations and analyses of existing accounting rules to assist financial statement preparers in applying these rules to various types of transactions.

More often than not, GAAP consists of accounting *principles* rather than specific rules for accounting for specific types of transactions. Recent accounting scandals that have grabbed national attention have generated a debate as to whether GAAP needs to be even more principle-based and less rule-based. The reason supporting more principle-based GAAP is that, in some instances, the accounting scandals involved transactions that were accounted for technically within the letter of the law known as GAAP. In other words, transactions were structured in ways that met the technical requirements of GAAP, but were accounted for in misleading ways—they violated the spirit or intention of the GAAP requirements. Shifting to an even more principle-based approach reduces the risk that clever accountants will find ways to circumvent GAAP rules that violate GAAP principles. Others in the debate would argue that to avoid financial statement preparers circumventing accounting rules, what is needed are better and tougher rules, rather than increased flexibility afforded by a principles-based approach.

Why should the reader of this book care whether GAAP is principle-based or rule-based? There are two primary reasons. First, the reader should understand in learning about GAAP used by governments that GAAP usually does not specifically address every accounting situation that a financial statement preparer encounters. Often GAAP has to be interpreted using guidance provided for other similar transactions to determine the appropriate accounting treatment for a specific transaction entered into by a government. The variety and nuances of specific transactions are too many to expect to find a specific accounting answer in GAAP to every accounting question. Interpretation is often required. Second, the reader should understand that technical compliance with a GAAP requirement does not always result in the best accounting for a specific transaction, all other factors being considered. Governments do structure transactions in specific ways for the express purpose of enabling a desired accounting treatment in conformity with GAAP. This is not necessarily a bad thing. The reader just needs to be aware that it happens.

Another feature of GAAP that needs to be understood is that in a number of instances there is more than one acceptable way to account for a specific type of transaction. For example, later chapters will describe the accounting for capital assets that are depreciated by governments. Depreciation expense can be calculated using any of several accepted methods. One method charges depreciation expense in equal amounts each year over the life of the asset—this is called straight-line depreciation. Another method charges more depreciation expense in the early years of a capital asset's life and less depreciation expense each year in the later years of a capital asset's life—this is called accelerated depreciation. Both of these methods are acceptable under GAAP. As accounting rule makers address more and more accounting issues, the existence of more than one acceptable method of accounting for the same transaction is gradually, but steadily, declining. Often accounting rule makers select accounting areas to address because there is a diversity of accounting treatments for the same type of transaction. In other words, their purpose in these cases would be to eliminate the diversity of accounting treatments for similar transactions. Accordingly, once an accounting area is addressed by an accounting rule maker, usually only one acceptable method of accounting for this area results.

However, the reader should not be surprised by the remaining flexibility in some accounting treatments when trying to understand and compare the accounting for the same transaction by two different governments. It is also interesting to try to understand why a government selected a particular accounting method to use when there are several alternative acceptable methods.

One final note on GAAP is that these accounting principles apply only to *material* items. If an accounting transaction is not material to the financial statements, the financial statements need not follow GAAP in recording and presenting that transaction in the financial statements. Before jumping to conclusions that this concept will permit a tremendous amount of flexibility in recording relatively small transactions, an understanding of what is meant by being material to the financial statements is necessary.

Materiality is a concept that accountants have long struggled to define. The broad concept is that an item is material to the financial statements if its improper recording would have an impact on an informed reader of the financial statements. Applying this concept to individual circumstances in practice clearly results in the need for a good deal of judgment. It is not easy to try to anticipate what an "informed reader" of the financial statements will be affected by in reading the financial statements.

Accountants and independent auditors have attempted to provide quantitative measurements to determine when a misstatement of the financial statements would be considered material to those statements. For example, a common measure for determining whether a misstatement was material to the statement of financial position was to determine whether the amount of the misstatement was more than ten percent of total assets. Similarly, a common measure for determining whether a misstatement was material to the statement of activities (operations) was to determine whether the amount of the misstatement was more than five percent of the net increase or decrease in net assets (similar to what is often referred to as "net income" outside of the governmental accounting world.

Accountants have come to recognize, however, that materiality also has qualitative aspects. In other words, misstatements that do not meet quantitative measures, such as the five and ten percent measures described above, may still be considered material because of one or more qualitative aspects. For example, say that a city's general fund has just barely underspent its budgeted expenditures for a fiscal year. (Later chapters will provide much more information about funds, but the reader should not need this information to understand this example.) As part of "closing its books" for the year, the accountants discover an expenditure that should have been recorded in the general fund, but was not. This expenditure is clearly not material from any quantitative measure to the city's financial statements. However, if this expenditure was properly recorded in the general fund, the general fund would go from slightly underspending its budget to slightly overspending its budget. Depending on the specific circumstances of the government, this may be important or it may not be important. The point is that a strict quantitative approach to materiality will not always provide enough information to make intelligent decisions about what is material to a government's financial statements.

WHO SETS GENERALLY ACCEPTED ACCOUNTING PRINCIPLES FOR GOVERNMENTS?

Generally accepted accounting principles for governments are basically set by the Governmental Accounting Standards Board, or as it is commonly called, the GASB. The GASB is a private organization that is financially controlled by the Financial Accounting Foundation (FAF), which is a not-for-profit organization. Readers with some familiarity with commercial accounting or not-for-profit accounting might be somewhat familiar with the Financial Accounting Standards Board, or as it is commonly called, the FASB. The GASB does for governments what the FASB does for commercial and not-for-profit organizations. The GASB was created in 1984 and is currently located in Norwalk, Connecticut. The GASB is composed of seven board members. The Chair of the GASB is a full-time board member, while the other six members serve on a part-time basis. The GASB has full-time technical staff, which reports to its Director of Research.

Note The reader might be wondering whether the GASB and the FASB are identical in terms of their standard-setting roles. The

GASB and the FASB perform similar functions in terms of establishing GAAP, but structurally and economically there is a divergence between these two boards. The reason is that the FASB sets the accounting principles that are used by publicly traded companies. Legally, this responsibility is that of the United States Securities and Exchange Commission (SEC), which delegated this responsibility to the FASB. The accounting scandals that occurred which resulted in the passage of the Sarbanes-Oxley Act of 2002, created the Public Company Accounting Oversight Board (PCAOB), which, as an arm of the SEC, is charged with setting auditing standards for public companies. The SEC continues to delegate accounting standards setting to the FASB. However, under the Sarbanes-Oxley Act of 2002, the FASB no longer receives its funding from the FAF, but rather is funded by a charge or fee levied on publicly traded companies. The GASB has no such "legal" type standing for its accounting principles, nor is it funded from these fees charged to publicly traded companies.

The reader might encounter the names of several other organizations that might lend some confusion as to what organization sets the accounting rules for governments and governmental entities. The National Council on Governmental Accounting (NCGA) was the name of the organization that set accounting principles for governments prior to the creation of the GASB. Some of its accounting principles resulting from its "municipal accounting standards" and other standards are still in use today. The NCGA, which no longer exists, was sponsored by the Government Finance Officers Association (GFOA). The GFOA is still in existence today and periodically issues a new version of its book, *Governmental Accounting, Auditing and Financial Reporting* (commonly referred to as the GAAFR). Prior to the establishment of the GASB, the GAAFR was an authoritative source of accounting principles. Today, the GAAFR is used by the GFOA to establish the rules for its Certificate of Achievement for Excellence in Financial Reporting. This is a voluntary program for governments that prepare Comprehensive Annual Financial Reports (described later in this book) and that desire to

obtain this award from GFOA to demonstrate their ability to prepare and issue excellent financial reports.

While the quick answer to the question of who sets accounting principles for governments is "the GASB," the GASB sets
these accounting principles and provides interpretations and implementation guidance through several different mechanisms.
This is done by several different types of documents and
mechanisms that together comprise what is termed the "GAAP
hierarchy" for governments. Not all of the documents and
mechanisms used by the GASB to set accounting principles and
standards have the same weight and importance, hence the term
hierarchy which implies that some are going to be more important than others.

The GASB recently issued Statement No. 55, "The Hierarchy
of Generally Accepted Accounting Principles for State and Local
Governments" (GASBS 55) which formally brings the hierarchy
of those pronouncements and documents comprising generally
accepted accounting principles into the GASB's purview.
Previously, the hierarchy was set by the auditing standards used
by independent auditors performing audits of financial
statements. The hierarchy remains essentially the same as used
in the past and is lettered A through D (with A being the highest
level of authority) and consists of the following documents:

Level A

- GASB Statements (currently numbered 1 through 56)
- GASB Interpretations (issued by the GASB to provide an
  interpretation of accounting guidance for an accounting
  standard that already exists)

Level B

- GASB Technical Bulletins (These are prepared by the
  GASB staff to provide guidance on applying an existing accounting principle. Technical Bulletins are reviewed by the
  GASB board and a majority of the board members must not
  object to their issuance.)

- AICPA Audit Guides and Statements of Position that are made specifically applicable to governmental entities by the AICPA and that have been cleared for issuance by the GASB (The AICPA Audit and Accounting Guide "Audits of Statement and Local Governments" is an example of this type of document.)

Level C

- AICPA Practice Bulletins if specifically made applicable to governmental entities and that have been cleared by the GASB

Level D

- Implementation Guides that have been published by the GASB staff (These are typically in a question-and-answer format and are issued more frequently in recent years than in the past.)
- Practices that are widely recognized and prevalent in state and local governments (This category includes those accounting practices that are generally used by governments, but are not the result of a specific accounting standard issued by the GASB or its predecessors.)

In the absence of a pronouncement or another source of accounting literature, the financial statement preparer may consider what is termed *other accounting literature*. Other accounting literature includes a variety of different sources ranging from GASB Concepts Statements (which are GASB documents that describe the conceptual framework from which GASB Statements arise) on the more authoritative side to accounting textbooks and articles on the less authoritative side. In between these extremes, other accounting literature includes such items as FASB pronouncements not made applicable to governments, various AICPA Issue Papers and Practice Aids, and International Public Sector Accounting Standards, among many others.

The message that the nonaccountant should take away from the above discussion about the sources of generally accepted accounting principles for governments is that in many cases, analysis of an accounting issue is not an exact science and the selection of the most appropriate accounting treatment for a particular transaction is often based on a broad range of accounting principles that do not precisely fit the transaction at hand.

DO GOVERNMENTS NEED TO COMPLY WITH GENERALLY ACCEPTED ACCOUNTING PRINCIPLES?

There are both legal and practical answers to this question. There is virtually no way that it can be answered on a global basis for all governments and governmental entities in the United States because there is no national requirement for state, local, and other governmental entities to issue financial statements in accordance with generally accepted accounting principles. Unlike publicly traded corporations that are subject to SEC requirements that require audited, GAAP financial statements on an annual basis, there is no such requirement for governments. The SEC, because of states' rights issues that are well beyond the scope of this book, does not have the same ability to dictate accounting requirements for governments. This is so even though governments sell their debt securities to the public. As such, there is no national, legal requirement for governments to prepare GAAP-based financial statements.

At the state or local government levels, however, many governments' charters, constitutions, enabling legislation, and so on do require the issuance of GAAP-based financial statements. These governments would have a legal requirement to issue financial statements prepared in accordance with GAAP. In addition, there may be instances where states or state comptrollers prescribe the accounting requirements for municipalities and other types of local governments within a state. In these cases, these municipalities and local governments would also be required to prepare GAAP financial statements.

In the absence of legal requirements to prepare GAAP financial statements, there may well be practical requirements that would cause governments to prepare GAAP financial statements. The best example would be the issuance of debt. Governments that sell debt to finance operations, capital projects, or other resource needs may find it necessary to issue GAAP financial statements in order to facilitate the sale and marketing of the debt. In some cases, debt covenants may require periodic reporting of financial statements in accordance with GAAP.

Beyond a specific example such as selling debt, a government may find that it must provide accountability for its collection and use of resources by issuing financial statements. GAAP-based financial statements provide the fullest picture of a government's financial position and the results of its activities, as well as in some instances, its compliance with certain financial requirements to which it may be subject. While not all government accountants agree with every aspect of GAAP for governments, by and large, GAAP financial statements are the most widely accepted means of conveying information about a government's financial position and the results of its activities. In other words, if a government is going to issue annual financial statements, it may simply make more sense to issue GAAP financial statements rather than justify why GAAP financial statements were not prepared.

Note that preparing GAAP-based financial statements does not mean that a government needs to prepare its budgets on a GAAP basis. As we will examine later in the book, a government's general fund and certain other funds that legally adopt a budget are required to present budget-to-actual financial information along with the GAAP-based financial statements. The budget-to-actual financial information is presented using whatever accounting basis is used to prepare the budget, meaning that there is no accounting requirement that this information be prepared in accordance with GAAP.

WHY IS GOVERNMENTAL ACCOUNTING AND FINANCIAL REPORTING DIFFERENT FROM COMMERCIAL AND NOT-FOR-PROFIT ACCOUNTING AND FINANCIAL REPORTING?

This is an important question for someone trying to understand the basic concepts that underlie the accounting used by governments and governmental entities. In fact, it was one of the earliest questions addressed by the GASB soon after its creation in 1984. The newly formed GASB undertook a project and issued a resulting Concepts Statement (GASB Concepts Statement No. 1, "Objectives of Financial Reporting," or GASBCS 1) in 1987 that addressed what the objectives of governmental accounting and financial reporting should be. In examining this, the GASB identified various characteristics of the environment in which governments and governmental entities operate and distinguished this environment from those of other types of organizations. The following paragraphs describe these distinguishing characteristics:

- *The primary characteristics of a government's structure and the services it provides.* Governments derive their authority from the citizenry and are commonly based on a separation of power from three branches (i.e., the executive, legislative and judiciary). There are also various layers of government and there are usually substantial amounts of resources that flow between the layers. For example, there are three basic layers of government that consist of the federal government, state governments, and local governments. Local governments may consist of further layers, such as cities, towns, or villages that are part of a county, which has its own government. Finally, there are distinguishing characteristics as to the relationship between a government's taxpayers and the government as well as the relationship with the services that they receive. GASBCS 1 highlights these differences:

  - Taxpayers are involuntary resource providers. They cannot choose whether to pay their taxes.
  - Taxes paid are generally based on factors such as property values or income, rather than the value of services received by individual taxpayers.
  - There is generally no exchange relationship between resources provided and services received. Most individuals do not pay for specific services.
  - The government generally has a monopoly on the services provided.
  - It is difficult to measure the optimal quality or quantity for many services provided by governments. Those re-

ceiving services generally cannot decide the quantity or quality of a particular service of a government.

- *Control characteristics resulting from a government's structure.* Governments usually prepare a budget for the "general" or main operating fund. This budget is an expression of public policy as well as a control mechanism for operating the government. Underspending the budget in a particular area might be considered a good thing, if the expected level of service was provided to constituents. However, underspending a budgeted amount for a particular area when service levels are below the expected levels might indicate that the "public policy" features of the budget were not adhered to. Another unique aspect of budgets in the government environment is that when a budget is recommended by a government's executive branch and adopted by the legislative branch, a legal authority for spending the government's resources is established. In this case, the government may legally spend only what is authorized in the budget. In the commercial environment, budgets are more often targets rather than legal spending authorizations.
- *Use of fund accounting for control purposes.* Users of governmental financial statements are accustomed to the government reporting information about its funds, particularly the major (or more important, larger) funds. As we will see later in this book, sometimes governments are legally required to set up separate funds for certain sets of transactions, whereas other times governments set up funds for their own control and financial reporting purposes. Regardless of the reason, reporting information by fund is now unique to the governmental environment. Readers familiar with not-for-profit accounting may recall that not-for-profit organizations were formerly required to present fund information in their financial statements. Financial reporting for not-for-profit organizations was changed a number of years ago to eliminate the need to report fund information, although some not-for-profit organizations continue to use fund accounting for internal control purposes.
- *Dissimilarities between similarly designated governments.* This aspect of governmental accounting highlights that

comparing the financial statements of two different governments at the same level—such as the financial statements of two counties—may be the equivalent of comparing apples to oranges. The range of services provided to constituents as well as the sources of revenues from which those resources are obtained may vary greatly between two entities that are both called "counties."

- *Significant investment in non-revenue-producing capital assets.* Capital assets of a government usually include its buildings, equipment, vehicles, and so on. Capital assets also include infrastructure, such as roads, bridges, parks, piers, and so on. Governments do not purchase or construct capital assets because they expect a direct monetary return on their investment. Building a new school building will not directly generate revenue from its use. Rebuilding Main Street will not generate revenue from its use (unless, of course, it is a toll road). Commercial enterprises invest in many of their capital assets because they generate a rate of return, such as a new factory or a new retail store. While the new school and rebuilt Main Street may make a jurisdiction a more attractive place to live and work, resulting at some point in higher tax revenues, the resulting revenues are not directly related to these investments in capital assets made by this hypothetical government.

- *Nature of the political process.* There is an inherent conflict in governments between the citizens' demand for services and the citizens' willingness to pay for those services. There is a concept in the government accounting world called *interperiod equity*. This concept means that the current citizens should be paying for the services they are currently receiving. Governments can sometimes not live up to this principle, many times by borrowing money (which will be repaid by future citizens) to pay for the current operating expenses (whose benefit the current citizens are enjoying). GASBCS 1 concludes that to help fulfill a government's duty to be accountable, government financial reporting should enable the financial statement user to assess the extent to which operations were funded by nonrecurring revenues or long-term liabilities were incurred to satisfy current operating needs.

- *Users of financial reporting.* The users of governmental financial reporting and financial statements are different from those of commercial enterprises. GASBCS 1 identifies three primary groups as the users of governmental financial reports.

  - The citizenry (taxpayers, voters, and service recipients), the media, advocate groups, and public finance researchers
  - Legislative and oversight officials, such as members of state legislatures, county commissions, city councils, boards of trustees, school boards, and executive branch officials
  - Investors and creditors, including individual and institutional investors, municipal security underwriters, bond rating agencies, bond insurers, and financial institutions

- *Uses of financial reporting.* As governments have different users of financial reporting, it is logical to expect that there will be differences in the uses of their financial reports. In addition to assessing the accountability of the government, governmental financial reports are used for economic, political, and social decisions. These uses can be viewed as falling into the following broad categories:

  - Comparing actual financial results with legally adopted budgets
  - Assessing financial condition and the results of operations
  - Assisting in determining compliance with finance-related laws, rules, and regulations
  - Assisting in evaluating the efficiency and effectiveness of the government. (This last category is sometimes referred to as service efforts and accomplishments [or performance] reporting, which uses financial and nonfinancial information to assess whether the government's "service efforts" actually result in "accomplishments." This is currently a controversial area in government accounting. Not all interested parties believe that this is an area that should be part of the financial reporting required by the GASB under generally accepted accounting principles or an area

for which the GASB should be providing guidance for voluntary reporting.)

When all of the differences and nuances of governmental financial reporting are examined, the GASB concludes in GASBCS 1 that the cornerstone of financial reporting by governments is accountability. Accountability requires that governments answer to the citizenry in order to justify the raising of public resources and the purposes for those resources. Accountability is based on the general belief that the citizenry has a right to know financial information and has a right to receive openly declared facts that may lead to a public debate by the citizens and their elected representatives.

GASBCS 1 highlights the concept of interperiod equity (discussed earlier) as a significant part of accountability and notes that it is fundamental to public administration. Accordingly, as encouraged by GASBCS 1, the concept of interperiod equity is reflected in many of the accounting requirements established by the GASB since its creation.

TO WHAT ENTITIES DO GOVERNMENTAL GENERALLY ACCEPTED ACCOUNTING PRINCIPLES APPLY?

Throughout this chapter there have been a number of references to accounting principles followed by governments and governmental entities compared to accounting principles applied to commercial enterprises and not-for-profit organizations. The reader should have a clear understanding of what types of entities are considered to be governments or governmental entities in order to be clear as to which types of accounting and financial reporting requirements are to be applied by any particular entity.

The following is a listing of the entities that, in general, are covered by governmental generally accepted accounting principles:

- State governments
- Local governments such as cities, counties, towns, and villages

- Public authorities, such as housing finance, water and other utilities, economic development, and airport authorities
- Governmental colleges and universities
- School districts
- Public employee retirement systems
- Public hospitals and other health care providers

Throughout this book, when governmental entities or governments are mentioned, the reference is to these types of entities. Governments covered by governmental accounting principles are sometimes distinguished as general-purpose governments (which includes states, cities, towns, counties, and villages) and special-purpose governments. Special-purpose governments are those that are other than general-purpose governments. Both general-purpose and special-purpose governments are covered by the governmental generally accepted accounting principles that are the subject of this book.

A special word is needed about distinguishing governmental entities from not-for-profit organizations. As a rule, not-for-profit organizations are not covered by generally accepted accounting principles for governments. Not-for-profit organizations follow accounting principles prescribed by the FASB. For the most part, this distinction is fairly obvious. It does create some apparent discrepancies, such as a state university following governmental accounting principles while a private university follows accounting principles for not-for-profit organizations prescribed by the FASB. Even though the state university and the private university are basically in the same business, the state university follows GASB accounting rules and the private university follows FASB accounting rules.

In some cases, however, distinguishing between a government and a not-for-profit organization is not so simple. For example, a local government may set up an economic development corporation that has many characteristics of a not-for-profit organization, including federal tax-exempt status under section 501(3) of the Internal Revenue Code. However, these organizations are usually considered governmental not-for-profit organizations that should follow governmental generally accepted accounting principles. The AICPA Audit and Accounting Guide *Not-for-Profit Organizations* (the AICPA Guide) defines governmental organizations (i.e., ones that should follow accounting principles for governments) as "public corporations and bodies corporate and politic."

Public corporations are created for the administration of public affairs and include instrumentalities created by the state, formed and owned in the public interest, supported in whole or in part by public funds, and governed by managers deriving their authority from the state. Other organizations are governmental organizations under the Guide's definition if they have one or more of the following three characteristics:

- Popular election of officers or appointment (or approval) of a controlling majority of the members of the organization's governing body by officials in one or more state or local government
- The potential for unilateral dissolution by a government with net assets reverting to the government
- The power to enact or enforce a tax levy

Using the economic development corporation example mentioned earlier, in a common scenario, the mayor appoints the majority of the corporation's board of directors, meeting the first criterion described. Similarly, if the city decided to dissolve this economic development corporation and received all of the corporation's net assets upon dissolution, the second criterion would be met. Accordingly, the hypothetical economic development organization should follow GAAP for governments.

SUMMARY

The purpose of this chapter is to describe a broad framework and context about accounting principles used by governments so that more specific information about accounting principles can be understood. Governments are unique entities and the accounting principles applied by these entities need to be reflective of the environment and types of activities in which these organizations engage.

CHAPTER 2

Basic Governmental Accounting Concepts

This chapter focuses on some of the underlying accounting principles and concepts that underlie all governmental accounting and financial reporting. In order to understand governmental financial statements, the reader needs to understand these basic concepts. Specifically, this chapter addresses the following areas:

- Understanding the different bases of accounting
- Understanding what measurement focuses are used by governments
- Defining and understanding the nature of assets
- Defining and understanding the nature of liabilities
- Defining and understanding the nature of net assets

In reading this chapter, keep in mind that a government reports different types of financial information within different types of specific financial statements that are discussed later in this book. For example, a government's "fund" financial statements will report fund balances while its "government-wide" financial statements will report net assets. Both represent the difference between the assets and liabilities presented on each financial statement. The important point of this chapter is to obtain an overview of many concepts and then see how they get sorted out into various types of financial statements in later chapters.

UNDERSTANDING THE DIFFERENT BASES OF ACCOUNTING

Nonaccountants tend to think, understandably, that there is only one way that organizations record transactions. If a government buys something and then pays the bill, one would expect that all governments universally would record that transaction or event the same way, at the same time. Not so; in fact, the *same* government, within its *same* set of financial statements, may record that simple purchasing and bill-paying transaction in as many as *three* different ways. Please resist the temptation to close this book, and read on as to how this could possibly be the case.

The simplest way to understand the concept of "basis of accounting" is to view the basis of accounting as determining *when* a particular transaction will be recorded in the financial statements. In order to understand this concept, three different bases of accounting will be examined—the cash basis, the accrual basis, and the modified accrual basis. A fourth basis—the budgetary basis—may also be used by certain governments when they prepare budgets that do not use generally accepted accounting principles. Only the accrual basis and the modified accrual basis are actually used in preparing governmental financial statements that are in accordance with GAAP for governments. Generally accepted accounting principles for governments do require, in certain cases, that certain budget-to-actual comparison information accompany the financial statements, using whatever basis of accounting was used to prepare the government's budget (i.e., the budgetary basis). The cash basis of accounting is not acceptable for use in a government's financial statements prepared in accordance with GAAP, but learning about the cash basis of accounting will certainly help in understanding the accrual basis and modified accrual basis and perhaps even the budgetary basis.

Cash Basis of Accounting

As stated earlier, the cash basis of accounting is not an acceptable basis of accounting for preparing governmental financial statements in accordance with GAAP. So why look at the cash basis first? Because it is the easiest to understand and will help you to understand the other accounting bases.

Under the cash basis of accounting, revenues are recorded when cash is received. Expenses are recorded when cash is paid out. For example, a government purchases office supplies from a neighborhood office supply store, Clips. The supplies are ordered on January 1, received on January 15, and paid for on January 31. Under the cash basis of accounting, no accounting entries are recorded until January 31, when the office supplies are actually paid for. For an example on the revenue side, assume a town's real estate tax for the town's fiscal year, which begins July 1, is levied on June 10 (just before the end of the fiscal year) and is due on July 15. If a taxpayer pays his or her tax bill on July 13, then that is the date the real estate tax revenue is recorded under the cash basis of accounting. If the taxpayer pays his or her tax early, say June 20 in the prior fiscal year, the real estate tax revenue would be recorded in the prior fiscal year (the one that ends on June 30, ten days after the receipt of the real estate tax) under the cash basis of accounting.

Again, from an accounting perspective, recording transactions on the cash basis could not be simpler. *When* are transactions recorded? Transactions are recorded when cash is received and when cash is disbursed. If the cash basis were acceptable for preparing governmental financial statements in accordance with GAAP, this book would end here, because that would be about all you would need to know about governmental accounting. Since it is not, read on.

Accrual Basis of Accounting

As we will see in later chapters, the accrual basis of accounting is what is used in preparing the government-wide financial statements as well as the types of fund financial statements for what are termed *proprietary* funds, meaning that they closely resemble a business-type activity. Accordingly, understanding the accrual basis of accounting is important for understanding a government's financial statements prepared in accordance with GAAP.

Under the accrual basis of accounting, transactions are recorded when they occur, irrespective of when actual cash is received or paid. Revenues are recorded when earned or when the government has the right to receive the revenue. Expenses are recorded when incurred. Some examples will help clarify these concepts.

Continuing the examples started in the cash basis of accounting discussion, for the purchase of office supplies, the transaction actually occurs when the government receives the office supplies. That is when it has a legal obligation (i.e., a liability) to pay the supplier. So, under the accrual basis of accounting, the expense (and a corresponding liability) is recorded on January 15, the date that the supplies are received and the government owes the supplier the money for those supplies. For those readers who guessed that the transaction occurred on January 1, when the supplies were ordered, the distinction is that there is no real obligation on January 1 on the part of the government. The order might be canceled prior to delivery, the supplier may be out-of-stock of the items ordered, and so forth. (Later chapters will discuss a "budgetary" entry wherein the government might record an "encumbrance" on the date of the order to reserve the budgetary spending authority that it will ultimately use to pay for the supplies. This is not an accounting entry for purposes of recording an expense. An encumbrance is not the equivalent of an expense for accounting purposes.) Note that when the supplies are paid for, the financial statements of the government will reflect payment of cash (it will have less cash) and the payment of the liability (it will no longer have a liability to the supplier).

To continue the earlier examples for the accrual basis for revenues, the goal would be to match the real estate tax revenue with the year to which it relates. In other words, the real estate tax payment that was received in advance—on June 20—would not be recognized as revenue until the fiscal year that begins on the following July 1, since that is the year to which it relates.

Since applying the accrual basis of accounting to tax revenues is discussed in its own chapter on nonexchange revenues (Chapter 6), let us supplement this example with one that is not tax-based. If a governmental water utility bills its customers based on the actual water used (assume that all customers have water meters), revenue is recognized by the governmental water utility when the customer actually uses the water. Let us again assume a fiscal year that ends on June 30. A meter reader visits a customer on July 10 and reads the customer's meter to measure the water used by the customer from June 11 (the date of the last meter reading) to July 10. The water utility bills the customer on July 15 based on the July 10 meter reading. The customer pays the bill on July 31. When would the governmental water utility recognize the revenue from the water sales to this customer based on this meter reading on the accrual basis of accounting? The answer is that the revenue is split over two fiscal years. Revenue is recognized from June 11 through June 30 for the water sales that occurred during that period in the fiscal year that ended on June 30. Water sales that occurred from July 1 through July 10 will be recognized as revenue in the fiscal year that began on July 1. Since a meter reading was not available on June 30, this utility would likely use a simple method of prorating the total month's bill between the two fiscal years. It would allocate the total monthly revenue over the number of days in the previous fiscal year that ended June 30 (20 days) and the number of days in the next fiscal year (10 days). The date of the bill and the date that the customer pays the bill are not relevant in this example for purposes of determining when the revenue is recognized.

In comparing governmental accounting to nongovernmental entities, the reader should know that the accrual basis of accounting is the only accounting basis that is acceptable for commercial enterprises and not-for-profit organizations in preparing those organizations' financial statements in accordance with generally accepted accounting principles.

Modified Accrual Basis of Accounting

As we will see in later chapters, the modified accrual basis of accounting is used by funds that are considered "governmental funds" (these are the funds that are *not* considered proprietary, or business-type, funds which use the accrual basis of accounting described earlier) in the fund financial statements. The modified accrual basis of accounting is never used in the preparation of the government-wide financial statements.

The modified accrual basis of accounting can be thought of as falling somewhere between the cash basis of accounting and the accrual basis of accounting. In other words, transactions are generally recognized when they occur (similar to the accrual basis of accounting), *but* the timing of the ultimate cash receipt or cash disbursement *may* have an impact on *when* the transaction is recorded (similar to the cash basis of accounting.)

Many of the differences between the modified accrual basis of accounting and the accrual basis of accounting concern the timing of when revenue is recognized. Under the modified accrual basis of accounting, revenues are recognized (i.e., recorded in the financial statements as revenue) when they are susceptible to accrual. To be susceptible to accrual, revenues need to be both measurable and available. In determining whether revenues are *measurable*, the government does not have to know the exact amount of the revenue in order for it to be subject to accrual. As long as a reasonable estimate of the revenue can be made, this criterion will be met. The *available* criterion is a bit more complicated. Available means that the revenue is collectible within the current accounting period or soon enough thereafter to pay liabilities of the current period. This criterion results in the recording of only those revenues within a fiscal year that are received within a relatively short period of time after the close of the fiscal year.

For real estate taxes, the *susceptible to accrual* criterion, based on the availability of the funds, is defined in GAAP as being 60 days after the close of the fiscal year. Going back to the real estate tax example discussed previously, the modified accrual basis of accounting would result in the same amount of real estate tax being recognized as revenue as with the accrual basis of accounting. The June 20 payment would not be recognized until the subsequent fiscal year and the July 13 payment is recognized within the fiscal year that it was paid. Let us change the facts to assume that this July 13 payment is not received until September 13 of the following fiscal year. So, for the June 30, 20X1 fiscal year-end, the tax payment related to that year that was due on July 1, 20X0, is not received until September 13, 20X1. Under the accrual basis of accounting, the revenue would be recognized in the fiscal year ending on June 30, 20X1, irrespective of the fact that it was received more than 60 days after the end of the fiscal year when it was due. Under the modified accrual basis of accounting, the September 13, 20X1 tax payment does not meet the susceptible to accrual criterion—it is not considered available since it was received more than 60 days after the fiscal year-end of June 30, 20X1. Using the modified accrual basis of accounting, the September 13, 20X1 payment will not be recognized as revenue until the fiscal year that ends on June 30, 20X2. This is despite the fact that the real estate tax relates to the town's fiscal year that ended on June 30, 20X1.

Budgetary Basis of Accounting

The budgetary basis of accounting refers to the accounting principles that a government uses to prepare its budget for its main operating fund, the general fund, as well as certain other funds called special revenue funds. Sometimes governments use generally accepted accounting principles to prepare their budgets for these funds, in which case the budgetary basis of accounting would be the same as the basis of accounting required for fund financial reporting for these funds, which would be the modified accrual basis of accounting.

When the budgetary basis of accounting for budget preparation is not the same as the GAAP basis of accounting for these funds, a government has latitude, generally set by the local laws governing the government's budget process, as to what accounting principles it will use to prepare its budget. Sometimes the cash basis of accounting is adopted as the budgetary basis. Sometimes the cash basis of accounting, modified for certain specific ways certain types of transactions are accounted for, is adopted as the budgetary basis. Other times, governments may take the modified accrual basis of accounting and modify the accounting for certain types of transactions and adopt that basis of accounting as the budgetary basis. Since the budgetary basis is something specifically set by governments, there is no way that a book such as this can describe what the budgetary basis is for governments in general. In other words, if the budgetary basis adopts a GAAP basis of accounting, then the budgetary basis equals the GAAP basis. If the budgetary basis is other than GAAP, the accounting principles used to prepare a government's budget will vary from GAAP.

Why is the budgetary basis of accounting important? In later chapters, requirements within generally accepted accounting principles to present budget-to-actual comparison information on the budgetary basis of accounting as required supplemental information to the financial statements will be discussed. This can be viewed as a bit of an anomaly because generally accepted accounting principles are requiring budget-to-actual comparison information to be presented when the accounting principles used to prepare these budget and actual numbers are not in accordance with GAAP. More information on the requirements for these comparisons and related required disclosures will be discussed later in this book.

UNDERSTANDING WHAT MEASUREMENT FOCUSES ARE USED BY GOVERNMENTS

If the basis of accounting describes *when* transactions are recorded, the measurement focus can be viewed as defining *what* transactions are recorded. There are two different measurement focuses that are used in the preparation of financial statements for governments. They are the economic resources measurement focus and the current financial resources measurement focus. The economic resources measurement focus is used in the preparation of the government-wide financial statements and in the fund financial statements by funds that undertake business-type activities. These types of funds are called proprietary funds. The current financial resources measurement focus is used in the fund financial statements by funds that are called governmental funds. For simplicity, think of the governmental funds (general fund, special revenue, capital projects, and debt service are examples) as those funds other than the proprietary funds.

Economic Resources Measurement Focus

The economic resources measurement focus is based on whether an entity is economically better off or worse off as a result of the events and transactions that occurred during the fiscal period being reported. This measurement focus results in a broader range of transactions being recorded than does the current financial resources measurement focus. Think of it this way: Does a transaction or event affect the economic condition of an entity? If it does, record it, irrespective of whether the current or noncurrent, financial or nonfinancial resources of an entity are affected. The economic resources measurement focus described here is essentially the same measurement focus used by commercial organizations and not-for-profit organizations.

Transactions and events that improve the economic position of an entity are reported as revenues or gains. Transactions and events that diminish the economic position of an entity are reported as expenses or losses. Because the economic resources measurement focus reflects transactions regardless of whether they affect current financial resources, both long-term assets (such as capital assets) and long-term liabilities (such as the liability for long-term bonds) are reflected on the statement of financial position under the economic resource measurement focus. Accordingly, the government-wide financial statements and the fund financial statements for proprietary funds report long-term assets and long-term liabilities because they are prepared using the economic resources measurement focus.

Current Financial Resources Measurement Focus

The current financial resources measurement focus is used only in the fund financials by funds that are governmental funds, which basically are the funds that are not proprietary funds. (For simplicity, a group of funds called fiduciary funds are being left out of this discussion. Accounting for these funds is discussed in later chapters.)

Financial statements prepared using the current financial resources measurement focus, as its name implies, reflect changes in the financial resources available in the near future as a result of transactions and events of the fiscal period being reported. Increases in spendable resources are reported as revenues or other financing sources and decreases in spendable resources are reported as expenditures or other financing uses.

Since the current financial resources measurement focus is on the financial resources available in the near future, the operating statements and balance sheets of governmental funds in the fund financial statements reflect transactions and events that involved current financial resources: for instance, those assets that will be turned into cash and spent and those liabilities that will be satisfied with those current financial resources. In other words, long-term assets and those assets that will not be turned into cash to satisfy current liabilities are not reflected on the balance sheets of governmental funds in the fund financial statements. At the same time, long-term liabilities (those that do not require the use of current financial resources to pay them) will not be recorded on the balance sheets of governmental funds.

Practical Example Say that a government purchases a new computer (a capital asset) for $10,000 that is expected to last five years. After the five years, the computer will be discarded and not sold as scrap. Under the economic resources measurement focus, the computer would be recorded as an asset on the statement of financial position (synonymous with balance sheet) at $10,000. Each year the computer will be depreciated, reducing the asset recorded by $2,000 ($10,000 divided by the five-year estimated useful life) and depreciation expense of $2,000 is recorded. On the date of purchase, there is no economic change in the organization. It traded $10,000 in cash for a $10,000 computer. There is no effect on the statement of activities (think of this as the income statement) because there is no change in the economic condition of the organization. It gave up cash and received a computer in return. In subsequent years, the economic condition of the organization is worse off because the computer has fewer years of useful life remaining. Accordingly, the statement of activities reflects an expense each year equal to $2,000 of depreciation expense.

Now look at this transaction under the current financial resources measurement focus. On the date of purchase, the governmental fund has $10,000 less in current financial resources because it gave up $10,000 in cash (a current financial resource) and traded it for a computer, which is not a current financial resource because it is not expected to be turned into cash to pay this fund's bills. The operating statement (think of this as the income statement) of the governmental fund will show an expenditure of $10,000 to reflect that, in terms of current financial resources, the governmental fund is $10,000 worse off than it was before the computer purchase. It gave up $10,000 of its cash and did not receive a current financial resource in return. Since there are no other impacts on current financial resources relating to this computer, the governmental fund's financial statements would not reflect any other transactions in subsequent years relating to this computer.

The remaining sections of this chapter discuss the nature of various asset, liability, and net asset amounts typically found in governmental financial statements. If the previous sections were understood, the reader will understand that different assets and liabilities are recorded on the government-wide financial statements than on the fund financial statements when there are governmental funds being reported. The following discussion pertains to amounts recorded on the government-wide financial statements—that is, assuming the accrual basis of accounting and the economic resource measurement focus are being used. This discussion will also pertain, in general, to the financial statements of proprietary funds. Where differences in accounting exist between these statements and the governmental fund financial statements, those differences will be discussed in the later chapters that describe the accounting for the various types of governmental funds.

DEFINING AND UNDERSTANDING THE NATURE OF ASSETS

Let us start by looking at the GAAP definition of an asset. The GASB provides a useful definition of assets (and other financial statement elements) that will be examined below.

GASB Concepts Statement No. 4, "Elements of Financial Statements" (GASBCS 4), defines assets in the following way: "Assets are resources with present service capacity that the government presently controls." And all this time you thought that assets were stuff that you owned! The fact is, the GASB definition is meant to provide a broader context to assets, rather than a narrower definition that only implies ownership. For example, if a government prepays its liability for an insurance premium for the following year, it really does not *own* anything as a result of that prepayment. However, the prepayment is a resource of the government which will be insured during the following year without having to pay an insurance premium in that year. Thinking of assets as including things that the organization owns as well as other types of resources that it is entitled to will help the reader understand what types of items are considered assets.

Note also that assets are measured in financial statements as of a point in time, that is, as of the date of the statement of net assets, which is sometimes referred to as the balance sheet. For example, if the government's fiscal year-end is June 30, its statement of net assets will report its assets as of that date. Assets are also presented in the statement of net assets in their order of liquidity, which means the assets that can be converted the most readily into cash are reported first. More information on this concept will be presented in Chapter 4.

Some of the types of assets often found on a government's statement of financial position are

- Cash
- Cash equivalents
- Investments
- Taxes receivable
- Accounts receivable
- Grants and other receivables
- Inventories
- Capital assets
- Prepaid expenses

Cash

Cash is a fairly obvious asset. It represents the funds in the government's bank accounts. The presentation of cash represents the book balances of the bank accounts, not the amounts reported on the bank statements. The book balances are similar to what individuals keep as balances in their own checkbooks, that is, checks that have been written and deducted from the balance but that have not yet cleared the bank. Similarly, deposits that have been received but have not yet cleared the bank are also included in the balance.

The cash amount reported on the statement of financial position should include

- *All demand bank accounts that the government has, including those for general disbursements, payroll imprest accounts, separate accounts for wire transfers, and so forth.* (One cash balance is reported on the financial statements representing the aggregation of all of these accounts.)
- *All petty cash accounts that are maintained by the government*

The "cash" caption on the statement of net assets should *not* include the following, which should be disclosed as separate lines on the statement of net assets:

- *Cash that is restricted by some legally enforceable instrument.* Generally, this would include cash maintained in debt service reserve accounts required to be maintained by the related debt instruments. Restricted cash is usually shown as a separate line item in the statement of net assets to make it clear to the reader that it is not available to pay the government's current bills.
- *Cash that is received and held as a security deposit that will be returned to the provider at the end of some agreement.* For example, if a government rents a part of its office space to another organization and holds a $1,000 security deposit that it collects from the renter, that security deposit cash should not be included in the cash balance of the government on the statement of net assets.

Cash Equivalents

The term cash equivalents refer to investments that are so close to being realized as cash that they are viewed essentially as the equivalent of cash. The definition of what is considered a cash equivalent originated in the rules for preparing statements of cash flows (which will be discussed in Chapters 4 and 6). These rules for determining what can be considered a cash equivalent were promulgated by GASB Statement No. 9, "Reporting Cash Flows of Proprietary and Nonexpendable Trust Funds and Governmental Entities That Use Proprietary Accounting" (GASBS 9). These requirements define cash equivalents as short-term, highly liquid investments that are both readily convertible to known amounts of cash and so near their maturity that they present an insignificant risk of changes in value because of changes in interest rates. This is interpreted by GASBS 9 to mean that for an investment to be considered a cash equivalent, it must mature within three months of being bought by the organization. This means that a one-year treasury note that is purchased by a government two months before it matures can be considered a cash equivalent. However, if the government purchased the one-year Treasury note when it was first issued (so that it matured in one year), it would not be considered a cash equivalent. Also, this investment would not be considered a cash equivalent if it was held by the organization and then reached a point where it only had three months left to maturity. Classification as a cash equivalent occurs when the investment is acquired by the organization. Examples of cash equivalents include Treasury bills, money market funds, and commercial paper. Note again that the term original maturity refers to the length of time to maturity at the time that the security is purchased by the government, *not* to the security's original duration before maturity.

Investments

Chapter 9 discusses the accounting for investments by governments, so not much space will be spent here discussing investments. Suffice it to say that most investments (most stocks, bonds, and other debt instruments) are reported in the statement of net assets at their fair value (fair market value is an older term for what is now referred to as fair value). Changes in the fair value of investments from year to year are reported in the government's statement of activities as part of overall investment earnings (or losses).

Taxes Receivable

Taxes are one type of "nonexchange" transaction that will be described in Chapter 6. Earlier in this chapter, some information about recording receivables for real estate taxes, one of the more common taxes received by governments, was provided. For now, it is important simply to be aware that taxes that are owed to a government—be it real estate taxes, personal or corporate income taxes, sales taxes, or personal property taxes—that are due to a government on the date of its statement of net assets but that have not been paid, are reported on the statement of net assets as a receivable. In some cases the receivable recorded by a government for taxes reflects an estimate of the amounts owed to it.

Accounts Receivable

The other significant category of receivables, accounts receivable, is often referred to as trade accounts receivable. These receivables represent funds that are owed to the government from individuals or other organizations because of services provided or goods sold to these other entities. Some common scenarios where these types of receivables may be present on a government's financial statements are

- A governmental college may be owed tuition and fees from students that are past their due date, but have not as yet been paid.
- A government water utility may bill its customers for water that has been provided to the customers and the bill is due but has not as yet been paid.

These types of receivables occur from exchange transactions—the government is not just collecting a tax or a grant, it is providing specific services in exchange for money.

There are two basic considerations that the nonaccountant should understand about accounts receivable. First, a receivable (and the related revenue) should not be recorded until the organization actually *earns* the revenue and the right to receive the money from the entity to whom they are selling services. Second, not all receivables are ultimately collected.

In terms of revenue recognition, the general rule is that the government would earn the revenue when it provides the services and has a right to collect the revenue. In the case of the governmental college, revenue from tuition would be recorded at the end of the semester to which the tuition related. The revenue is matched to the period in which the college incurred expenses to earn that revenue, which is during the semester to which the tuition relates (assume that the fiscal year-end does not occur during the semester, which would require more complex calculations). As with the governmental water utility example, the utility earns revenue (and records a receivable) when services are provided to its customers. A receivable is recorded at the date of the statement of net assets for water services provided. Some of these services already will have been actually billed and some of these services may not have been billed because of waiting for meter readings or bill processing. An estimate of the unbilled amounts due the water utility would also be recorded as a receivable.

These are two very simplistic examples that are meant to demonstrate a concept. In practice, particularly for commercial enterprises, revenue (and receivable) recognition issues can be quite complex and have been the cause of more than one accounting scandal in recent years.

Another key point to understand about the accounting for these types of accounts receivable is that not all receivables are necessarily collected. This is particularly true of the types of non-tax-related receivables where the government does not have the ability to place a lien on a property to ultimately collect its receivable. Generally accepted accounting principles require that an estimate of receivables that will not be collected be made and that an "allowance for uncollectible receivables" be established. This account reduces the overall receivable balance (and charges bad debt expense) so that the net of the gross receivable balance and the allowance represents the best estimate of how much of the receivable balance actually will be collected. Receivables are therefore reported at the net realizable value, which is in accordance with GAAP. Note that the government does not really know which specific receivables (i.e., which students will not pay their tuition bills), but will use historical trends and an aging of receivables (which categorizes how long receivables have been outstanding) to estimate this amount. If the government knows that a particular receivable will not be collected, that particular receivable should be reduced from the gross receivable balance, which is another way of saying that the particular receivable should be written off.

Grants and Other Receivables

Governments often have other receivables reported on their statement of net assets representing money owed to them for reasons other than the main revenue categories mentioned earlier. The same principles generally apply to these other types of receivables, although grant revenue receivable and revenue recognition can be more complex. Grants are also "nonexchange" transactions which are more fully described in Chapter 6. Grants may be from the federal government, a different level of government (such as a state providing a grant to a city), or from private (i.e., nongovernmental) sources.

Some of these other common receivables, in addition to grants, are

- Fines and penalties, such as parking violation and other motor vehicle fines
- Expense reimbursements that are expected to be received by the government from individuals, donors, or others
- Reimbursement of expenses paid on behalf of another government. For example, a government might jointly share an expense with another government and bill that government for its allocated share of the expense.

If any of the receivables discussed in this "other" category are significant, they may warrant using a separate line item for them on the statement of net assets. The GASB also has some disclosure requirements concerning the *disaggregation* of receivables, meaning that information about the various types of receivables that a government has may need to be disclosed in the notes to the financial statements if the information is not readily apparent from the face of the statement of net assets.

Inventories

Inventories are most often associated with manufacturing and retail operations, rather than with governments or governmental entities. Many, if not most governments, however, do maintain inventories, because the definition of what is considered *inventory* is somewhat broader in the governmental environment. Most inventory amounts reported by governments, however, are not significant in relation to their overall financial statements and this section is not trying to overstate the importance of this item to these financial statements. However, it is useful to understand what the inventory caption means because although not generally large, it is seen frequently.

Traditionally, inventory is considered merchandise or goods that are being offered for sale. Governments, and particularly those with business-type activities, often have items that they sell. A governmental college bookstore would have an inventory of books that it sells. A governmental healthcare organization may have an inventory of medications and other medical supplies that are charged or "sold" to patients as they are being used. In the government accounting environment the financial statement caption called "inventory" often consists of various materials and supplies that are used by the government itself. This may consist of the usual variety of office and general supplies. A government's motor pool may keep a supply of commonly used automobile and truck parts. Other governmental entities, such as transit authorities, may have a large inventory of spare parts for buses, trains, and so forth.

The accounting for inventories can be fairly complicated and the details are beyond the scope of this book. However, a basic understanding of inventory accounting will go a long way in understanding inventories reported on the statement of net assets of a government.

Inventories are reported on the statement of net assets either at cost or at market value, whichever is lower. One important matter in accounting for inventories is referred to as the flow assumption. The flow assumption determines which items from inventory are considered to be sold or used first. The first-in, first-out (FIFO) flow assumption sounds complicated, but simply means that the oldest items from inventory (that is, the first items "in") are the first items to be sold or used. This is the most common flow assumption used by governments. Assuming that there is consistent inflation at some level, these older inventory items will have a lower cost assigned to them, because they were theoretically purchased at a lower cost. This means that when these items are sold, the profit realized by the government will be higher than when the last items brought into inventory are sold.

If the items are used by a government, there is no profit earned per se, but a lower cost will be charged to expense when the older item is assumed to be used first. The alternative flow assumption, last-in, first-out (LIFO), assumes that the last items brought into inventory (that is, assuming inflation, the ones with a higher cost) are the first ones sold or used. This means that when these items are sold, the net profit to the government is lower than it would be using the FIFO flow assumption (or if used, the expense will be higher). While the LIFO method has clear tax advantages to commercial organizations because reported profits are lower, its use by governments is less popular, because tax considerations are generally not of importance. A hybrid method, known as the average cost method, is sometimes used instead of a pure "flow assumption" method. Inventory is simply valued at the average of the costs to the government for the inventory items on hand. This would usually result in inventory recorded on the statement of net assets at amounts somewhere between FIFO and LIFO.

The second important consideration for inventory valuation in the statement of net assets is that the amount reported as the cost of inventories on the statement should not be more than the amount that the inventory can be sold for. The commonly used phrase that inventory is reported at the "lower of cost or market" means just that, with the term market referring to how much the item could be sold for, rather than what it would cost the government to replace the inventory item.

Tip There are many other inventory methods with intimidating names that are variations on these two basic concepts, such as the *dollar value retail LIFO method.* While the calculations may grow in complexity, the basic concepts remain as described above.

Capital Assets

Sometimes referred to as fixed assets or property, plant, and equipment, the capital assets of a government represent its long-lived assets used in the conduct of the organization's business. These would include land, buildings, equipment, office furnishings, computers, vehicles, and other similar assets. GASBS 34 created a significant change for governments, requiring that infrastructure assets (such as roads, bridges, tunnels, sidewalks, etc.) also be recorded as part of a government's capital assets.

The specific assets that are recorded as capital assets is generally determined by a government's capitalization policy. This policy determines what purchases are recorded as assets and what purchases are recorded as expenses. If a purchase of one of these types of assets meets the capitalization policy's criteria, it is recorded as an asset. The capitalization policy is usually based on the useful life of the item. Normally, a minimum useful life of three to five years is required before an item is recorded as an asset. The capitalization policy usually also sets a minimum dollar threshold in order for an item to be recorded as an asset. The threshold amount varies based on the size of the organization. A $500 threshold is reasonably popular among small organizations, although amounts as low as $100 and as high as $50,000 are not uncommon for very small and very large organizations, respectively.

Two other items should be included in fixed assets— leasehold improvements and capitalized leases. Leasehold improvements are purchases that meet the capitalization criteria of an organization, but are improvements to leased property rather than to property owned by the government itself.

Practical Example A government enters into a 20-year lease for office space. Prior to moving into the space, the government "builds out" the space by moving walls to create the desired office space, installing a reception area, carpeting, and so forth. These leasehold improvements would be considered part of the organization's fixed assets although the organization does not own the building to which these improvements are permanently attached.

Capitalized leases (which will be discussed in greater detail in Chapter 9) are an accounting creation that recognizes the substance of some lease transactions over their form. In other words, when a government enters into a lease for an item, which, in substance, is a purchase of the item, the item is recorded as a capital asset of the organization, even though the organization does not have title to the asset.

Practical Example A government leases a copier machine that has a useful life of 10 years. The term of the lease is 10 years. Since the government is using the asset for virtually its entire useful life, GAAP would require the government to record the copier as a capital asset, along with the liability for future lease payments. (These items will also be discussed in Chapter 7 of this book.)

Property, plant, and equipment is recorded on the statement of net assets at its cost to the government, reduced by accumulated depreciation (with two exceptions, which are discussed below). Accumulated depreciation represents the decline in value of capital assets as they are used in the operation of the government. Depreciation expense is the annual amount charged to expense in government's statement of activities, which represents an estimate of the amount of the asset that is "used up" in the organization's operations during the year. Accumulated depreciation sums up the annual amounts of depreciation expense for capital assets and represents a reduction in the recorded cost amount of the asset on the organization's statement of net assets.

Practical Example A government buys a PC for $2,200, which it estimates to have a five-year useful life. At the end of five years, the organization expects that it can sell the PC for salvage for $200. The amount to depreciate is $2,000 ($2,200 less the $200 salvage value). $2,000 divided by five years results in a depreciation expense of $400 per year. This table illustrates the calculations for the life of this asset.

Year	Depreciation expense	Accumulated depreciation	Remaining net book value
1	$400	$ 400	$1,800
2	400	800	1,400
3	400	1,200	1,000
4	400	1,600	600
5	400	2,000	200

At the end of Year 5, the remaining net book value of the asset ($2,200 original cost less $2,000 accumulated depreciation) equals the estimated salvage value of the asset, $200. No further depreciation would be taken and the asset would remain on the books until it was actually disposed of. If the organization managed to sell the asset for $300, it would remove $2,200 from the asset account and $2,000 from the accumulated depreciation account from the books and record a gain of $100 on the disposition of the asset. If the asset was sold for $100, the organization would remove $2,200 from the asset account and $2,000 from the accumulated depreciation account from the books and record a loss of $100 on the disposition of the asset.

Accumulated depreciation is a *contra account* to property, plant, and equipment, meaning that its balance (which is a credit) offsets the gross amount of capital assets that is recorded on the statement of net assets as an asset (debit). The accumulated depreciation account, as its name suggests, is the cumulative amount of depreciation that has been recorded on the assets that are included in property, plant, and equipment. Each year when the depreciation expense is recorded, the accumulated depreciation amount is increased for the amount of the annual depreciation expense. Conversely, when an asset is retired or sold, the amount of accumulated depreciation that is applicable to that particular asset is removed from accumulated depreciation, meaning that the accumulated depreciation account is reduced for this amount.

It was mentioned earlier that there are two exceptions to calculating and recording depreciation on capital assets. The first involves specific accounts that are not depreciation—land and construction work-in-progress. Land is not depreciated because it is not "used up" by the government—it retains its value and use-fulness even though things added to the land, such as a building, do decline in value and are depreciated. Construction work-in-progress represents a capital asset that is being built by a government over a period of time that extends over more than one fiscal year. As costs are incurred, they are recorded as an asset called construction work-in-progress, or something similar. Whatever is being built would not be depreciated until the construction is completed and the capital asset is placed in use.

The second large exception to depreciating capital assets involves infrastructure assets. GASBS 34 gave governments the option to depreciate infrastructure assets as they would their other capital assets, or to adopt something called the *modified approach* and not depreciate the assets. The modified approach attempts to reflect the notion that infrastructure assets do not decline in usefulness or value. Rather, the government is likely to maintain these assets by incurring additional repair and maintenance costs over the life of the asset, resulting in an almost indefinite life for some assets. As long as the government spends the money (and accounts for these costs as expenses) to maintain the infrastructure asset at a level established by the government, depreciation is not required on these infrastructure assets. The modified approach is one of the specific capital asset topics that is addressed in Chapter 7.

One other accounting term related to capital assets is *asset impairment*. This concept reflects the fact that sometimes events happen or circumstances change in a way that negatively affects the value or usefulness of a capital asset to a government. If an asset is impaired, even with the accumulated depreciation that may have already been recorded on that asset, the net book value of the asset on the statement of net assets is overstated. The GASB issued Statement No. 42, "Accounting and Financial Reporting for Impairment of Capital Assets and for Insurance Recoveries," which sets the rules for when and how governments should record impairments of capital assets. Capital asset impairment is another specialized area relating to capital assets that is discussed in Chapter 7.

Intangible Assets

A type of asset that is a bit more difficult to understand is called an "intangible asset." As its name implies, these are assets that you can't see or touch, but they are resources of the government that are recorded as assets. Intangible assets include patents, trademarks, easements, water rights, timber rights, and computer software.

The GASB issued Statement No. 51, "Accounting and Financial Reporting for Intangible Assets" (GASBS 51), which provides accounting guidance to governments on how and when to record intangible assets. Basically, intangible assets are considered capital assets, and the accounting rules discussed above related to capital assets would apply.

In order for an intangible asset to be recorded, it needs to meet certain criteria, namely that the asset is "identifiable." GASBS 51 defines "identifiable" as being capable of being separated from the reporting government (in other words, it can be sold, transferred, licensed, rented, or exchanged) or if the asset arises from contractual or other legal rights (these don't have to be separable from the government).

GASBS 51 also has special rules for when intangible assets are created or produced by the government (referred to as "internally generated"). Even more specific rules govern when governments can record an intangible asset for internally generated computer software.

While all of these details are beyond the scope of this book, what is important to know is the governments don't have carte blanche in terms of what assets they can record as intangible assets. The author believes that one of the intents of GASBS 51 is to make sure that governments are not able to record too many costs as assets when those costs really should be charged to expense.

Prepaid Expenses

Prepaid expenses are assets that arise because an organization has paid for services that it will receive in the future, with the future being defined as a time past the fiscal year-end. While GASB Concepts Statement No. 4 would define prepaid expenses as a special type of asset that is reported, called a "deferred outflow of resources." The most common example of a prepaid expense is an insurance premium. Let us say that a government has a June 30 fiscal year-end. It pays its general liability insurance premium (assume it is $1,000) on January 1, for the next full calendar year. By June 30, it has used up six months of insurance, but still has another six months of insurance to which it is entitled. The organization would allocate the $1,000 of insurance premium over the 12-month calendar year period. On June 30, it would record a reduction of its insurance expense and record a prepaid insurance expense asset of $500 ($1,000 times 6/12). Note that this organization uses up this prepaid asset during the period from July 1 through December 31. If the organization issued its 6-month financial statements on December 31, it would reduce the entire prepaid asset to zero and record the corresponding $500 as insurance expense, which makes sense because, since the insurance works on a calendar year basis, on December 31, the organization has not prepaid any of its insurance. Assuming in this example that the insurance premiums stay the same every year, the government would have recorded $1,000 of insurance expense in its fiscal year ($500 recognized as a result of the premium payment and $500 recognized when the prepaid expense asset is used up).

While prepaid insurance is the most common and easily understood example of a prepaid expense, there can be many others. Rental payments on facilities or equipment are another example. Some judgment should be used by governments in determining what should be recorded as prepaid expenses. For example, a motor vehicle registration fee is usually paid annually in advance. If the government only owns a few motor vehicles, it is probably not worth the administrative effort to calculate and record this type of prepaid expense, particularly when registrations expire throughout the year.

DEFINING AND UNDERSTANDING THE NATURE OF LIABILITIES

GASB Concepts Statement No. 4 provides this definition of liabilities: "Liabilities are present obligations to sacrifice resources that the government has little or no discretion to avoid." While this definition seems quite simple, applying it is more complicated. Nonaccountants generally think of liabilities as simply "money that you owe." While this is not too far off from a GAAP perspective, there are several ideas in Statement No. 4's definition that will make the simple definition more accurate.

First, liabilities are measured at a point in time, which means, for financial statement purposes, as of the end of the government's fiscal year. To be a present obligation means that the obligation has actually been incurred as of the year-end to be reported on the statement of net assets as a liability, meaning it is the result of past transactions or events. Second, the obligations are not simply those that must be satisfied by the payment of cash. Liabilities also consist of obligations of the organization to perform or transfer assets other than cash to the party to which the organization is obligated.

Some of the more common liabilities found recorded on the statement of net assets of governments are

- Accounts payable and accrued expenses
- Debt
- Deferred income

Accounts Payable and Accrued Expenses

Sometimes governments report both accounts payable and accrued expenses on one line on the statement of net assets. Other times, separate amounts are reported for each. For the purpose of explaining what these liabilities represent, it is helpful to discuss accounts payable and accrued expenses together.

Accounts payable essentially represent the unpaid bills of a government. These are bills for goods or services that have been received by the organization prior to the end of its fiscal year.

Practical Example The government receives an invoice in the amount of $1,000 for stationery that it ordered with the new mayor's name. The stationery was received on June 15. The fiscal year-end of the organization is June 30, and a check for $1,000 was issued to the stationery supply store on July 7. As of

June 30, the government records a $1,000 accounts payable (representing the unpaid invoice) along with a $1,000 supplies expense. (Note that accounts payable also arise when an organization buys assets or incurs expenses.)

There are two other situations that might also give cause to record amounts as accounts payable, and both of these situations involve issuance of checks. Let us say that a government with a June 30 year-end writes checks for all of its outstanding bills on June 29, even though it realizes that it will not have available funds in its bank account to clear the checks until the second week of July. The government holds all of the checks written on June 29 and first mails them on July 12. When the checks are written, most automated (and manual) accounting systems would record a decrease in cash and a decrease in accounts payable. However, in this example the government has neither expended cash nor reduced its accounts payable on June 30—all it really did was write checks. Accordingly, the total amount of the checks held by the government until past year-end would be added back to cash and to accounts payable.

A second similar situation arises when the government writes checks prior to its year-end and reduces the book balance of its cash below zero. It can do this because it knows that all of the written checks will take some time to clear the bank, at which time the government expects that the actual balance in its bank account—its bank balance—will be sufficient to clear the checks. The difference between this case and the first situation is that, in this case the government does not physically hold onto the checks. It mails them. In this case, the government would not report a negative balance for cash on its statement of net assets. Rather, it would bring the book balance of the account up to zero and would add the same amount to its accounts payable balance. Effectively, this reclassifies the negative book balance of cash to accounts payable. This makes logical sense because, in effect, the government "owes" the amount of the negative cash amount to the bank, rather than individual vendors.

Accrued expenses represent liabilities for goods and services received by a government for which either an invoice has not been received or the entire invoice does not apply to the fiscal year-end being reported. A simple example should make this clear.

Practical Example Referring to the $1,000 stationery purchase example used above, let us say that the government did *not* receive the invoice for the stationery until July 7. Assuming that the physical delivery of the stationery still occurred on or before June 30, the organization would record an accrued expense for this purchase. Basically, a liability is recorded for the accrued expenses and, at the same time, stationery expense is charged. Also keep in mind that amounts might have to be estimated for shipping or similar charges in establishing the accrued expense. Conversely, the government may take into consideration discounts for prompt payment that it intends to take, if it is the organization's normal practice to take advantage of such discounts.

Accrued expenses also arise because invoice amounts or service periods span the end of the fiscal year of an organization. For example, if a monthly telephone bill covers a period that ends on the 15th of each month, the government should accrue a telephone expense for that portion of the July 15 telephone bill that applies to the fiscal year ending on June 30, which would be for the period from June 16 (first day of the bill period) through June 30.

A similar accrued expense concept applies to salary expenses where the pay period does not coincide with the end of a fiscal year. Only the portion of the weekly or biweekly salary expense (including related fringe benefit expenses) that is earned by employees up to and including the date of the fiscal year-end should be accrued as salary (and fringe benefit) expense through the end of the government's fiscal year-end.

Debt

In addition to the accounts payable and accrued expense liabilities described above, governments almost always have a liability for some form of debt that they have issued. Debt is known by several different names, usually based on how long the debt has before it becomes due, or matures. For example, a short-term loan is generally evidenced by some type of legal instrument, commonly referred to as a note. These types of loans are usually recorded in the financial statements as notes payable, and generally mature in five years or less. There are a wide variety of transactions that may give rise to notes payable, some of which are very common.

Several types of notes are unique to governments. These notes are call bond anticipation notes and revenue (or tax) anticipation notes. A bond anticipation note is issued to provide short-term financing that will be repaid with the proceeds of a long-term bond that will be issued. Hence the note "anticipates" the bond to be issued in the future. Another type of note anticipates a future revenue that will be used to repay the note. The future revenue may be in the form of a tax or it may be another type such as a grant that will be received from another level of government.

Most debt issued by governments, however, is in the form of long-term bonds. Governments are often restricted by state and/or local requirements as to the amount of debt that they can issue and the purposes for which debt can be used. While some governments issue debt to fund operating deficits, more often debt is issued to finance construction or purchase of significant facilities. The specific mechanics of these types of transactions are beyond the scope of this book. Suffice it to say that the unpaid principal of the debt, usually in the form of bonds, will be recorded as a liability on the statement of net assets of the government. Since bonds can be sold at either a discount (e.g., a $1,000 face value bond can only be initially sold for $980) or a premium (e.g., a $1,000 face value bond is initially sold for $1,020), the liability recorded on the financial statements would represent the face amount of the bonds (also called their par value), decreased by discounts and increased on premiums on the initial sales of the bonds. Note that the total of the discounts or premiums is amortized (reduced) over the life of the bond. This amortization results in either a decrease in interest expense (in the case of a discount) or an increase in interest expense (in the case of a premium).

All types of debt incurred by governments will give rise to interest expense. Interest expense follows similar concepts for accruing other types of expenses. (The fund accounting discussion in Chapter 3 will point to some important differences as to how principal and interest are accounted for in governmental funds.) Interest expense is recognized as an expense when it is earned by the holder of the government's debt, regardless of when the interest is actually paid, as explained in this example.

Practical Example A governmental entity with a September 30 year-end makes semiannual interest payments—on January 1 and July 1 each year—on bonds that it has sold. Interest is paid in arrears, which means that it is paid after it has been earned by the bondholder. In other words, the January 1 interest payment is for interest earned by the bond holder from July 1 to December 31. Accordingly, the January 1 interest payment includes interest relating to the period of July 1 through September 30. Interest related to this period must be accrued in the September 30 government-wide financial statements. Accruing interest results in the recording of an accrued interest liability (another type of accrued expense liability as previously discussed), with a corresponding amount recorded as interest expense. When the actual payment is made on January 1, the accrued interest liability is reduced to zero, with the balance of the interest payment recognized as interest expense in the year that the payment is made.

Deferred Income

The liabilities discussed in the preceding pages are relatively easy to understand. However, liability for deferred income requires a little more conceptual thinking to understand. In fact, GASB Concepts Statement No. 4 refers to this special type of liability as a "deferred inflow of resources." The idea of recording deferred income is matching the recording of income with the period in which the revenue is earned, which in some cases also matches the revenue to the costs incurred to generate that revenue. When cash is received by a government prior to its either having earned the income or the right to keep the income, it records the cash along with a liability-type account called deferred income.

One of the more common types of deferred income recorded by governments is for funds received in advance for a grant. Many grants are structured so that the government is entitled to the grant revenue only after it spends the money for the grant program. In other words, it is reimbursed for the expenses of the program. In the not-so-old days, these were called "expenditure-driven revenue" grants because the level of expenditures drove the amount of revenue to be recorded, up to the maximum amount permitted by the grant. In the current terminology of "nonexchange" transactions (which are discussed in Chapter 6) this means that "all of the eligibility requirements" have been met (i.e., you have to spend the money to be entitled to the reimbursement revenue). If a government receives cash as an advance under a grant such as this, the cash advance is recorded as deferred revenue, which appears just like a liability (that is, a credit) on the statement of net assets. Note that this is really a different kind of liability in that the government is not expecting to write a check to pay off the liability. Rather the government has an obligation to spend the money that has been advanced. If the money is never spent on the grant program, then the government would have an obligation to return the advanced funds to whomever it received them from.

DEFINING AND UNDERSTANDING THE NATURE OF NET ASSETS

Net assets are easy to understand in that they represent the difference between a government's total assets and its total liabilities. Looking at it a different way, if you add a government's net assets to its liabilities, the amount will equal the government's total assets.

The discussion of government funds later in this book will also address "fund balance" which is essentially the difference between a governmental fund's assets and liabilities. What makes the concept of net assets a little more difficult to understand for a government's financial statements is that GASBS 34 requires that net assets be divided into three categories, assuming that they all apply to a particular government.

1. *Invested in capital assets, net of related debt.* This amount represents the difference between two amounts: the government's capital assets reduced by any accumulated depreciation (this is the first amount) and the outstanding balance of any debt that was used to purchase or construct those capital assets (this is the second amount). Conceptually, this is not too difficult to understand. For governments trying to calculate this number, however, it can be a nightmare. The complications, which thankfully are beyond the scope of this book, result from trying to properly reflect bond premiums, discounts and issuance costs (which are complicated by amortization and by bonds that have been refunded), and unspent bond proceeds restricted for capital asset purposes, not to mention simply trying to determine which capital assets were purchased or constructed using debt. For the nonaccountant's view, understanding what the caption is trying to represent should be adequate.

2. *Restricted net assets.* This amount of net assets reflects the net assets that the government has that have some strings attached to them. The attached strings are constraints that are either

   • Externally imposed by creditors (such as those imposed by debt covenants), grantors, or contributors, or through laws and regulations of other governments, or
   • Imposed by law through constitutional provisions or enabling legislation.

   A common example of restricted assets for governments is that of debt service reserve funds. Many times in a debt issuance, the government agrees to put a certain amount (sometimes equal to one year's debt service) in a special account that it cannot use for any purpose other than paying debt service if it happens to default on the debt, which means this money basically cannot be touched. Displaying these types of assets subject to these types of restrictions as "restricted" net assets alerts the financial statement reader that these net assets cannot be freely used by the government.

One other important point regarding restricted net assets is that the government may, or may not, be able to impose restrictions on itself. Let's say that a government decides it would like to accumulate $100,000 each year for the next three years so that in year four it can build some capital project. This would generally not constitute a restriction for reporting purposes. It would not classify these resources as restricted. The government could unilaterally change its mind and decide to not keep the assets for the capital project and use them for something else—meaning that there is no real restriction on the assets in this example.

One of the ways that net assets can be restricted mentioned above is through "enabling legislation." In this case, the government isn't simply setting aside some budgetary funds for some future purpose—it is actually passing legislation that is mandating how certain net assets can be used. Can the government impose restrictions on itself through legislation? Are these restrictions legally enforceable? Could future legislation simply eliminate the requirement? After the issuance of GASBS 34, diversity in practice developed, which caused the GASB to issue Statement No. 46, "Net Assets Restricted by Enabling Legislation" (GASBS 46), to provide additional guidance.

GASBS 46 "clarifies" that a legally enforceable enabling legislation restriction is one that a party outside the government—such as citizens, public interest groups, or the judiciary—could compel the government to honor. Since it is unlikely that the legal enforceability of a restriction would actually be tested in the courts, there is still a significant amount of judgment required to determine whether the affected net assets should be reported as restricted or not. GASBS 46 does require that the amount of net assets restricted by enabling legislation be disclosed in the financial statements.

3. *Unrestricted net assets.* Any net assets that do not belong in the above two categories are called unrestricted net assets.

One final note in discussing net assets is that these categories may have negative amounts on the financial statements. While it should be rare that restricted net assets would be negative, the invested in capital assets net of related debt, and as well as unrestricted net assets can be negative. For example, if a government depreciates capital assets faster than it pays off the related debt, the invested in capital assets net of related debt may be negative. Unrestricted net assets may be negative as a result of accumulated deficits incurred by a government. In other cases, governments may issue debt to provide funds to other governments or other organizations. In these cases, the government has the debt on its statement of net assets, without a corresponding asset, which could cause the unrestricted net asset amount to be negative. Finally, certain long-term liabilities that will be discussed later in this book for landfills, judgments and claims, and compensated absences are usually not currently funded by governments, meaning that these long-term liabilities will impact the net asset amount negatively.

SUMMARY

The goal of this chapter is to give the reader a flavor of some of the accounting concepts that can be expected to be found in reading the financial statements of governments. These concepts will be needed in understanding some of the specific topics discussed in later parts of this book. The important point to re-emphasize is that all of the above asset, liability, and net asset examples pertain to the government-wide financial statements and proprietary funds. Governmental funds, discussed in the next chapter, use different accounting principles in the fund financial statements that result in accounting treatments different from many of the items discussed in this chapter. When the governmental fund financial results are converted from the separate fund financial statements to be included in the government-wide financial statements, the financial results are "converted" to the accounting principles used in this chapter. This will all come together in Chapter 4, where the entire financial reporting model is discussed.

CHAPTER 3

Understanding Fund Accounting

If you have read the first two chapters of this book, you may be asking yourself why more time has not been spent on fund accounting. Under the financial reporting model for governments brought about by GASBS 34, fund accounting, or more correctly fund financial statements, are not the primary reporting tool for governments. Rather, fund financial statements are one of the two methods used by GASBS 34 to present a government's financial position and results of operations. The first method is the government-wide financial statements. These use the accrual basis of accounting and use the accounting concepts as the foundation for reporting the various types of assets and liabilities that were discussed in Chapter 2. The second method is the fund financial statements. These financial statements use both the modified accrual basis of accounting (for funds that are considered "governmental" funds) and the accrual basis of accounting (for funds that are considered "proprietary" funds). Just to complicate things a bit more, a third type of funds, "fiduciary" funds, may use either modified accrual or accrual, depending on which sub-type of fiduciary fund they are.

In order to complete our foundation of accounting concepts, this chapter discusses fund accounting concepts. Here is what will be covered:

- Fund fundamentals
- Governmental funds (general fund, special revenue funds, capital projects funds, debt service funds, and permanent funds)

- Proprietary funds (enterprise funds and internal service funds)
- Fiduciary funds (pension and other employee benefit trust funds, investment trust funds, private-purpose trust funds, and agency funds)

The discussion of the governmental funds also considers how the accounting for various types of transactions differs using the modified accrual basis of accounting for the fund financial statements versus using the accrual basis of accounting for the government-wide financial statements. Be forewarned that some of the accounting for governmental funds in the fund financial statements will be different from accounting for the same transaction in the government-wide financial statements. The GASB used to call this the "dual perspective" in governmental financial reporting, although they have since backed away from using this term. Some cynical commentators on GASBS 34 called this "two sets of books." Whatever; suffice to say that there are *supposed to be* differences in the accounting between the two sets of financial statements and this chapter will do its best to describe the fund perspective.

FUND FUNDAMENTALS

Before looking at the details, it is important to understand just what a fund actually is. *Fund* was defined by Statement 1 of the National Council on Governmental Accounting (NCGAS 1), entitled "Governmental Accounting and Financial Reporting Principles," as follows:

> A fund is defined as a fiscal and accounting entity with a self-balancing set of accounts recording cash and other financial resources, together with all related liabilities and residual equities or balances, and changes therein, which are segregated for the purpose of carrying on specific activities or attaining certain objectives in accordance with special regulations, restrictions, or limitations.

A fund is a separate accounting and financial reporting entity. It is what is called a "self-balancing" set of accounts. This means that a fund's assets will equal the total of its liabilities and its fund balance (or net assets), similar to the way financial statements for a legal entity work, although funds are usually not separate legal entities. Fund accounting for governments was developed in response to the need for governments to be fully accountable for their collection and use of public resources. The use of funds is an important tool for governments to demonstrate their legal compliance with the lawfully permitted use of resources. One thing to keep in mind is what a fund is not—it is not the equivalent of a bank account. The fund will have various assets and liabilities recorded, the difference between the assets and liabilities being called *fund balance*. That fund balance does not represent "cash" that can be readily spent. Not all of the assets will be in the form of cash, so it cannot be expected that the fund balance is the equivalent of the balance of cash in a bank account. This is a common mistake that nonaccountants sometimes make when reviewing fund financial statements.

Fund accounting remains an important aspect of financial reporting for governments: GASBS 34 includes within its financial reporting model fund financial statements. Fund financial statements enable governments to continue to demonstrate legal compliance, as described above. Since the overwhelming number of governments have legally adopted budgets at the fund level, demonstration of compliance with budgets is an important component of fund reporting under the GASBS 34 reporting model.

One additional aspect to consider is that while governments use fund accounting, most "governmental entities" that are not like general-purpose governments do not use fund accounting. The governmental entities that do not use fund accounting are often those separate legal entities whose activities are accounted for as proprietary activities. These are typically the public authorities (utilities, hospitals, etc.), whose activities use proprietary accounting as described in Chapter 2. These entities usually do not use fund accounting as would a government, such as a city or county.

Number of Funds to Be Established

The number of separate funds that a government establishes is based on both legal requirements and management's judgment as to how many funds it needs to enable sound administration of the financial affairs of the government. In other words, where statute or law requires the establishment of particular funds, certainly the government is going to establish those funds. Similarly, contracts, such as debt indentures, may also require the establishment of certain funds and certainly the government will establish the funds required by contract. Beyond these legal and contractual requirements, the government's management should determine how many funds should be established to separate the activities involved in carrying on specific programs or attaining certain objectives relating to special regulations, restrictions, or limitations.

There is a wide disparity among governments as to the number of funds established. Some moderate-size governments have literally hundreds of funds. Other, larger governments might have no more than a few funds to manage their affairs. It seems that the historical practices of governments, as determined by their executive and legislative branches, have a lot to do with how many funds are established. If new revenue is obtained that must be used for a particular purpose, some governments automatically set up a new "special revenue" fund. Over time, this practice can result in numerous funds. Other governments may simply record this revenue in the general fund and set up general ledger accounts within the general fund to track revenues and expenditures. There is no real "right" answer as to the number of funds that a government should have beyond those required by law or contract. The government must balance the benefits of using separate funds with the costs in terms of accounting and financial reporting complexity that comes with having numerous funds.

GOVERNMENTAL FUNDS

This section will discuss the various types of governmental funds. The governmental funds basically account for the activities of the government that are not considered proprietary (business-type) or fiduciary. These activities are sometimes referred to as the general governmental activities, although the best way to understand what are considered activities to be accounted for in governmental funds is to examine the specific types of funds themselves. Remember from Chapter 2 that governmental funds use the modified accrual basis of accounting and the current financial resources measurement focus.

General Fund

The general fund is the chief operating fund of a government. Generally accepted accounting principles permit a government to have only one general fund. The general fund is a catchall fund. It accounts for all current financial resources of a government except for those current financial resources that are accounted for in another fund. Often when governments talk about "balancing their budget," what they really mean is that they are balancing the budget of their general fund. Many times when it is said that a government is over budget or has a deficit, the meaning is not for the government as a whole, but for the government's general fund, since this is usually considered the main operating fund of a government.

The balance sheet of the general fund will include those current financial resources related to transactions that will be accounted for in the general fund. Usually the asset side of the balance sheet consists of cash, investments, receivables, and inventories. Cash and investments are a subject of Chapter 9 and receivables will be discussed as part of Chapter 6 on nonexchange transactions.

A few words are needed on the accounting for inventories in the general fund. These accounting rules would also apply to other governmental funds discussed in this section of the chapter, but inventories are most often found in the general fund.

There are two acceptable accounting methods for inventories in the general fund and other governmental funds. The first is called the *purchase* method. This method simply records an expenditure for materials and supplies when they are purchased. The second method is called the *consumption* method. This method records an expenditure for inventories when they are consumed. Under this method, when inventories are purchased, they are recorded on the balance sheet as an asset. As they are used during the year, the asset account is reduced and an expenditure is recorded. At the fiscal year-end, the amount recorded as "inventory" on the balance sheet represents the cost of the inventory that the government still has on hand, which are those that it has not consumed during the year. While GAAP does permit either the purchase method or the consumption method to be used, it should be noted that GAAP also requires that when a government has significant amounts of inventory at year-end, those inventories should be recorded on the balance sheet. This would point to the use of the consumption method in order to accomplish this.

In reading a government's fund financial statements, the fund balance of the general fund usually has an amount as one of its components called "reserved for inventories" that is equal to the amount of inventories recorded as an asset on the same balance sheet. The reason this is done is to alert the financial statement reader that the balance sheet contains an asset, inventories, that is technically not a current "financial" resource that is available to be spent or to pay the fund's current liabilities. Note that in the near future this term will change from "reserved" to "nonspendable" for these types of assets that are not in spendable form.

The typical liabilities found in the general fund are those for accounts payable and accrued expenditures, deferred revenues, and revenue or tax anticipation notes. Deferred revenues are discussed in Chapter 6 on nonexchange transactions.

The general fund accounts for accounts payable and accrued expenditures in conjunction with its accounting for expenditures. The expenditure is generally recorded in the fund when a liability is incurred. In the simplest example, goods and services received prior to the end of the fiscal year should be accrued as expenditures (i.e., an account payable or an accrued expense is recorded) because the liability for the goods or services has been incurred. In other words, since the government received the goods or services it is obligated to pay for them. If a bill has been received for the goods and services by the fiscal year-end, the liability is called an "account payable." If a bill has not been received for the goods and services by the fiscal year-end, the liability is called an "accrued expense." This distinction is often not important to the financial statement reader, since accounts payable and accrued expenses are often presented on the same line on the balance sheet.

As usual, there are exceptions to every rule. The special nature of the current financial resource measurement focus used by the general fund and other governmental funds results in eight different types of expenditures that are not to be recognized when a liability is incurred. These types of expenditures are those for

- Compensated absences
- Judgments and claims
- Unfunded pension and other postemployment benefit contributions
- Special termination benefits
- Landfill closure and postclosure costs
- Debt service
- Inventories (discussed above)
- Operating leases with scheduled rent increases

These exceptions are discussed in the related chapters of this book dealing with these types of issues (either in Chapter 9, or the debt service fund discussion below, leases, etc.). These exceptions arise because governmental funds, such as the general fund, record expenditures when a liability is incurred, but only record the liability for the fund when the liability will be liquidated with expendable available financial resources. As a quick example, most governments have large liabilities that they will owe to employees on termination or retirement for unused vacation and sick leave time (compensated absences). This liability will not be paid with current financial resources. Only some employees leave or retire during the year and are paid for unused vacation and/or sick leave balances. The general fund will not record a liability for all of the compensated absences that will ultimately be expected to be paid by the government because it will not be paid with current resources. In fact, many governments do not record the portion of the liability that can be expected to be paid during the year in the general fund, which is acceptable. What the general fund would be required to record is a liability for any employees that left employment or retired prior to the fiscal year-end, but have not been paid by the end of the fiscal year.

Another liability sometimes found recorded on the general fund's balance sheet is that for revenue or tax anticipation notes. These are short-term borrowings that governments sometimes use to smooth fluctuations in a government's cash flow during the year. For example, suppose a town collects real estate tax revenues on a semiannual basis, say July 1 and January 1. Let us also say the town has very heavy cash needs during the period from September through December. This town may decide to issue tax anticipation notes in which it receives the proceeds from the note in September and pledges the tax revenues that it "anticipates" to receive in January to pay off the note. Since these types of liabilities will be liquidated using current financial resources, this liability is recorded on the balance sheet of the general fund, assuming that this is the fund that will receive the note proceeds and the fund that will repay the note.

Special Revenue Funds

Special revenue funds are used to account for the proceeds of specific revenue sources that are restricted or committed to be expended for specific purposes other than capital projects and debt service. The creation and use of special revenue funds is optional unless there is a legal requirement of the government that a special revenue fund be created. In other words, simply restricting the use of the revenue does not automatically mean that this revenue and the related expenditures must be accounted for in a special revenue fund. In the absence of a legal requirement to create one or more special revenue funds, governments consider whether the creation of a special revenue fund is really necessary. Simply because a certain revenue must be used for a specific purpose does not mean that this revenue and the related expenditure cannot be accounted for in the government's general fund. Generally accepted accounting principles for governments prescribe that a minimum number of funds be used. However, a government may feel that a special revenue fund improves accountability over compliance with a special revenue source's requirements. In these cases, the government will set up one or more special revenue funds to account for these types of resources.

There are two common examples of revenues that are accounted for in special revenue funds. The first are for grants received from other levels of government, such as a federal or state grant, or from individuals or foundations that restrict the use of the funds for specific purposes. For example, a city receives a state grant to build a new recycling center. A special revenue fund may be established to account for the revenue received from the state and the expenditures related to building the recycling center.

The second common example where special revenue funds are used is instances where the proceeds from specific taxes are restricted for certain purposes. For example, a state may impose a gasoline tax, the proceeds from which are required to be used for the construction and maintenance of state highways. A special revenue fund may be established to account for the gasoline tax revenues and the expenditures related to state highways.

Note that in the first example, the special revenue fund has a limited purpose and duration. After the recycling center is built and all bills have been paid and state revenues received, the special revenue fund that was created should be closed. In the second example, the special revenue fund would be expected to continue in perpetuity as long as the gasoline tax was still being levied and as long as the proceeds continued to be restricted to state highway expenditures.

One caveat to the use of special revenue funds is that if the special revenue is a grant or other source that requires that the resources be used for a capital project, a special revenue fund should not be used. This revenue and the related expenditures should be accounted for in a capital projects fund, which is discussed in the following section.

Capital Projects Funds

Governments often use capital projects funds to account for and report resources that are restricted, committed, or assigned for expenditure for capital outlays, including the acquisition or construction of capital facilities and other capital assets. The capital projects fund does not account for the capital activities of proprietary funds or for assets that will be held in trust for others— those activities are accounted for within the proprietary funds or trust fund, where appropriate. The capital projects funds would account only for the capital activities of those projects that are considered to be governmental, rather than proprietary.

Most governments use one or more capital projects funds to account for the acquisition and/or construction of capital assets. As will be seen in the following discussion, the significance of the dollar amounts that flow through the capital projects fund might well result in an overshadowing of the general governmental activities reported in the general fund. Capital projects funds are also used to account for special revenues that relate to capital projects as well as capital improvements financed by special assessments, which will be discussed later. The only instance where GAAP requires that a government use a capital projects fund is where capital grants or shared revenues are restricted for capital acquisition or construction.

Once a government determines that it desires to establish a capital projects fund (or is required by GAAP to establish one), the government then needs to decide how many capital projects funds will be established. A government may determine that it can adequately account for and manage its capital projects with one capital projects fund. However, a government may decide that establishing a number of capital projects funds will better serve its accountability and financial management needs.

The number of categories and types of revenues and "other financing sources" that are typically found in capital projects funds are usually fewer that those found in the general and special revenue funds. Since governments typically finance the acquisition and construction of capital assets through the use of long-term debt, the issuance of long-term debt is typically the most important source of resources for capital projects funds. Proceeds from long-term debt are reported as an "other financing source" of resources. This term refers to those sources of resources that are not considered "revenue" but nevertheless need to be reported on the operating statement of the fund. In addition, capital projects funds may account for receipt of resources in the form of nonexchange transactions from federal, state, or other aid programs, transfers from other funds, and capital leases.

Remember from Chapter 2 that the capital projects fund, as a governmental fund, uses the modified accrual accounting basis and the current financial resources measurement focus. This means, among other things, that long-term assets and long-term liabilities are not recorded in this fund. Therefore, do not expect to find that the capital assets that are purchased or constructed with money from the capital projects fund are recorded as assets of the capital projects fund. You will find the capital assets purchased or constructed through the capital projects fund recorded only on the government-wide statement of net assets. When the capital projects fund spends resources to purchase or construct an asset it charges an expenditure on its operating statement. There is no asset recorded on the balance sheet of the fund. Similarly, do not expect to find a liability on the balance sheet of the capital projects fund for the long-term debt issued to provide funds to purchase or construct the capital assets. You will find the long-term liability for the debt only on the government-wide statement of net assets. When proceeds from long-term debt are received by the capital projects fund, the operating statement records an "other financing source" of funds, which, although titled differently, works just like a revenue in the operating statement.

The astute reader may notice that *long-term* is used in the above discussion about whether the debt is recorded in the capital projects fund. Keep the following in mind about debt being recorded in the capital projects fund. First, if short-term debt was issued and the proceeds recorded in the capital projects fund, this short-term liability would be paid with current financial resources and would be recorded as a liability of the fund. Second, there are two types of financing vehicles, bond anticipation notes and demand bonds, that, if certain conditions are met (really if certain conditions are *not* met), can result in these liabilities being recorded as a liability of the capital projects fund. The following sections explain these types of financings.

Bond Anticipation Notes

Bond anticipation notes are short-term notes that are expected to be repaid with the proceeds of long-term debt issued after the bond anticipation notes are issued. The accounting question arises as to whether (1) the bond anticipation notes should be considered a short-term liability and recorded in the fund that receives the proceeds from these notes (usually the capital projects fund) or, (2) since they are expected to be repaid using the proceeds from a long-term debt issuance, they should be treated as a long-term liability. Treating them as a long-term liability means that they would not be recorded in the fund, but would be recorded only on the government-wide statement of net assets. The answer is—*it depends*. It depends on whether there is strong evidence that the government has the ability to issue the long-term debt to repay the bond anticipation notes. If the government issues long-term debt and repays the bond anticipation notes with the bond proceeds after the end of the fiscal year, but before the financial statements are issued, the bond anticipation notes would be treated as long-term debt at the fiscal year-end and not recorded as a liability of the fund. There is clear evidence that the government has the ability to repay these notes because it actually did so shortly after the fiscal year-end. Another way that allows a government to treat these bond anticipation notes as a long-term liability is if there is a financing agreement in place before the financial statements are issued that meets certain criteria that demonstrate that the government can issue long-term debt that will be used to repay the bond anticipation notes. All of the specific criteria of the financing agreement are beyond the scope of this book. Suffice to say that the financing agreement must clearly be one that is solid enough to provide assurance that the government will be able to issue long-term debt to repay the bond anticipation notes.

Demand Bonds

The second type of financing that may or may not be recorded as a liability of a governmental fund, usually the capital projects fund, depending on whether certain conditions are met, are demand bonds. Demand bonds are financial instruments that create a potential *call* on a government's current financial resources. Demand bonds are a type of debt that has demand provisions (sometimes called put provisions) as one of the features that give the bondholder the right to require the government issuer to redeem the bond within a certain period. Usually there is some contractually agreed-on term that requires the bondholder to give the government some notice prior to requiring payment, such as a 30-day period. In some cases, the demand provisions can be exercised by the bondholder immediately after the bonds have been issued by the government. In other cases, there is a waiting period, for example, five years, until the put or demand provisions of the bond may be exercised by the bondholder. These provisions mean that the bondholder is less subject to risks caused by rising interest rates. Because the bondholder is assured that he or she can receive the par value of the bond at some future date, a demand bond has some features and advantages of a short-term investment for the bondholder in addition to being a potential long-term investment. Accordingly, depending on the current market conditions, governments can generally issue demand bonds at lower interest rates than would be possible with bonds that did not have the demand bond's put provisions.

Because the issuance of demand bonds can result in signifi- cant potential cash outlays by governments if their demand fea- tures are exercised by the bondholders, steps are usually taken to protect the government from having to fund, from its own cash reserves, demand bonds redeemed by bondholders. Governments usually appoint remarketing agents whose function is to resell bonds that have been put to the government by the bondholder. In addition, governments usually obtain letters of credit or other ar- rangements that would make funds available to cover demand bonds for which payment has been demanded.

To provide for long-term financing in the event that the re- marketing agents are unable to sell the redeemed bonds within a specified period, the government issuing demand bonds generally enters into an agreement with a financial institution to convert the bonds to an installment loan that is repayable over a specified pe- riod. This type of arrangement is known as a takeout agreement and may be part of the letter of credit or may be a separate agreement.

The question as to the accounting for demand bonds centers around whether a demand bond that matures in ten years but may be redeemed by the bondholder at any time with thirty days' no- tice is a long-term liability or a short-term liability. The account- ing for demand bonds was established by GASB Interpretation No. 1, "Demand Bonds Issued by State and Local Governments" (GASBI 1). It addresses the accounting for demand bonds that have demand provisions that are exercisable at the balance sheet date or within one year from the date of the balance sheet. Inter- pretation No. 1 requires that these bonds be reported as a liability of the fund (usually the capital projects fund) unless all of the following conditions are met:

- The government bond issuer has entered into a financing (takeout) agreement to convert the bonds into some other form of long-term obligation. (Also, this takeout agreement must be with an unrelated third party.)

- The takeout agreement does not expire within one year from the date of the government's balance sheet.
- The takeout agreement is not cancelable by the lender or the prospective lender during that year, and obligations incurred under the takeout agreement are not callable during the year.
- The other party to the takeout agreement is expected to be financially capable of honoring the takeout agreement. During recent turmoil in the financial markets, this became a condition that required more extensive considerations than in the past.

So what does all this mean in English? If a government has a fairly ironclad ability to avoid paying demand bonds out of current financial resources by using a takeout agreement, the liability does not have to be recorded in the governmental fund and would appear only on the government-wide statement of net assets since it would be considered a long-term liability. However, if there is no takeout agreement, or if the takeout agreement has some loopholes, the assumption is that current financial resources may have to be used to pay the demand bonds, and the liability for the demand bonds would be recorded as a liability on the balance sheet of the governmental fund as well as on the government-wide statement of net assets.

Special Assessment Debt

Special assessment debt is another type of debt that might be recorded in the capital projects fund. The reader may be wondering why the capital projects fund section is discussing mostly debt-related matters. To reiterate, governments generally finance capital projects with debt and there are a number of accounting issues that address when that debt is actually recorded as a liability of the capital projects fund.

The capital projects fund typically accounts for capital projects financed with the proceeds of special assessment debt. More often than not, special assessment projects are capital in nature and are designed to enhance the utility, accessibility, or aesthetic value of the affected properties. The projects may also provide improvements or additions to a government's capital assets, including infrastructure. Some of the more common types of capital special assessments include streets, sidewalks, parking facilities, and curbs and gutters. For example, the government will build sidewalks in a neighborhood that previously had no sidewalks and charge the homeowners a special assessment for the portion of the sidewalk that is on their property.

The costs of a capital improvement special assessment project are usually greater than the amount the affected property owners can or are willing to pay in one year. To finance the project, the affected property owners effectively mortgage their property by allowing the government to attach a lien on their property so that the property owners can pay their pro rata share of the improvement costs in installments. To actually obtain funds for the project, the government usually issues long-term debt. Ordinarily, the assessed property owners pay the assessments in installments, which are timed to be due based on the principal and interest payments that must be made for the debt. The assessed property owners may also elect to pay for the assessment immediately, or at any time thereafter, but prior to the installment due dates. When the assessed property owners satisfy their obligations, the government removes the liens from the respective properties.

There is a specific GASB Statement (No. 6, "Accounting and Reporting for Special Assessments," GASBS 6) that discusses the accounting treatment for special assessments and their related debt. Prior to GASBS 6, there was a special fund type that accounted for special assessments, so the good news is that there is one less type of fund to learn about. The big issue with how special assessments are recorded is whether the government is obligated in any manner for the debt.

- If the government is obligated in some manner to assume the payment of the debt related to the special assessment in the event of default by the property owners, all transactions related to the capital improvements related to the special assessment are accounted for in the same manner as any other capital improvement and financing of the government. Transactions of the construction phase of the project should be reported in the capital projects fund (assuming one is being used), meaning the proceeds from the bonds would be recorded as an "other financing source" and spending on the project would be recorded as expenditures. However, one other set of accounting entries is required. At the time of the levy of the special assessment, a receivable for special assessments should be recorded in the capital projects fund. Because this receivable is not a current financial resource, a deferred revenue amount should also be recorded. As the payments are collected from the property owners, the receivable amount is reduced. As the receivable is reduced, the deferred revenue account is also reduced with a corresponding amount of revenue being recognized.

- If the government is not obligated in any manner for the debt related to a special assessment, the construction phase is treated like other capital projects, meaning that expenditures are recognized in the capital projects fund. The source of the funds in the capital projects fund, however, should be identified by a description other than "bond proceeds," for example, "contributions from property owners." Although in both cases the capital projects fund receives the proceeds from debt, in the case where the government is not obligated in any manner for the debt, the accounting reflects the fact that conceptually the property owners are receiving the debt proceeds and then turning them over to the government. The government records the receipt of these funds in the capital projects fund as a contribution from the property owners. In addition, the government will not use a debt service fund (discussed in the next section) to record the collection of special assessments and their payment to bondholders, because the debt is not a debt of the government.

Debt Service Funds

Debt service funds are a type of governmental fund that is used to account for resources that are restricted, committed or assigned for debt service. Debt service is simply a fancy way of saying "making principal and interest payments on the government's debt." Once again, the government should determine whether it is legally obligated to establish debt service funds. If it is not, the government should decide whether it would be useful from a managerial perspective to establish such a fund or funds. From a practical perspective, most governments that have long-term debt outstanding do use debt service funds. Where resources are being accumulated for principal and interest maturing in future years, those financial resources should be reported in a debt service fund.

One thing to keep in mind is that establishing debt service funds as an accounting and financial reporting tool is different from the requirement in many bond indentures or similar agreements that establishes reserve funds, or other financial requirements. For example, a bond indenture (contract) may require that one year's worth of debt service be maintained in a restricted cash account to be used only in the event of default by the government on the debt. This is not a debt service fund. This is a restricted cash account often called a debt service reserve fund. A debt service fund is an accounting mechanism used to account for transactions involving making normal principal and interest payments on a government's debt. A debt service reserve fund is money kept out of the reach of the government that will be used to pay bondholders in the event that a government defaults on its debt.

As a governmental fund, the debt service fund uses the modified accrual basis of accounting and the current financial resources measurement focus. There are three accounting issues that are often encountered relating to debt service funds.

1. Whether and when tax revenues should be recorded directly in a debt service fund
2. Expenditure recognition for debt service payments
3. Advance refunding of debt issues

Each of these will be discussed briefly in the following sections.

Whether and When Tax Revenues Should Be Recorded Directly in a Debt Service Fund

This is a fairly narrow issue of situations where a specific revenue source, such as property taxes or sales taxes, is restricted for debt service on general long-term debt. Assuming that the government has established a debt service fund, the accounting question is whether these restricted tax revenues should be recorded directly as revenue of the debt service fund or whether they should be recorded as revenue of the general fund and then re-corded as a transfer to the debt service fund.

When taxes are specifically restricted for debt service, they may be reported directly as revenue in the debt service fund, ra-ther than in the general fund with a subsequent transfer to the debt service fund. However, circumstances such as a legal re-quirement to account for all revenues, including restricted taxes, in the general fund may sometimes require that restricted taxes be first reported in the general fund. In this case, an operating trans-fer from the general fund to the debt service fund would be re-corded for the amount of the specific tax. The accounting may be influenced by the manner in which these revenues are budgeted. For example, the restricted tax revenue and the transfer to the debt service fund may both be part of the budget of the general fund, in which case it may make more sense to have the ac-counting follow that track than to record the revenue directly in the debt service fund. This will also be true for taxes that are par-tially restricted for debt service. For example, a property tax may be used to fund current debt service requirements, with any excess property tax revenue over the amount needed for debt ser-vice to be used for general operations or other functions of the government. Accounting for the entire property tax in the general fund, with a transfer of the required debt service amount to the debt service fund makes more sense than splitting the tax reve-nues into two funds. It will also facilitate a financial statement reader's being able to determine how much property tax revenue was recognized during the year without having to add up amounts from two different funds.

Expenditure Recognition for Debt Service Payments

As mentioned, the debt service fund, as a governmental fund, uses the modified accrual basis of accounting. However, gener-ally accepted accounting principles for governments result in debt service expenditures being recorded on an accounting basis sim-ilar to the cash basis. Unmatured (meaning that they are not yet due) principal and interest payments on general long-term debt, including special assessment debt for which the government is obligated in some manner, are not recorded as a liability and ex-penditure of the debt service fund. In other words, if a government with a June 30, 20X1, fiscal year-end makes a debt service principal and interest payment on July 1, 20X1, the principal payment would not be recorded as a liability and an expenditure for the year that ends June 30, 20X1. Nor would the government accrue interest expense for this payment for the year ended June 30, 20X1. Interest would not be accrued at June 30, 20X1, even if the interest paid on July 1, 20X1 was earned by the bond-holders during the previous six months, which is often the case. As long as the interest and principal payment is not due until July 1, 20X1, neither would be recorded as a liability and expenditure of a debt service fund on June 30, 20X1.

The preceding discussion assumes that debt service payments are being made on a timely basis. If the principal and interest payment became due and were not paid, the debt service fund would record a liability for the due but unpaid debt service payment. One other consideration is the situation where a government has transferred resources into a debt service fund before the debt service payment has become due. In this case, the debt service fund would reflect the resources available for the debt service payment, but not the liability for the payment itself. Generally accepted accounting principles permit governments to record the liability and expenditure for the debt service payment in this case. Given that the fund has the resources, the liability will be satisfied with current financial resources, consistent with recording a liability in the fund under the current financial resources measurement focus. It is important to note that recording the liability and expenditure for debt service in this limited exception is optional and not required.

Advance Refunding of Debt Issues

Transactions known as advance refundings of debt are one of the unique types of accounting transactions often found in the debt service funds. This topic is closely related to the requirements of GAAP as to when the refunded debt can be removed from the government-wide statement of net assets. Statement No. 7 of the GASB, "Advance Refundings Resulting in Defeasance of Debt" (GASBS 7), provides the accounting rules for these types of transactions.

An advance refunding transaction typically involves a government issuing new debt and using the proceeds to pay off (refund in advance) an existing debt issue. Since the bonds for the existing debt issue have not matured, the government takes the proceeds from the new bonds and places a sufficient amount of these funds in a trust to pay the interest and principal on the existing bonds. As the bonds and debt service from the existing bonds become due, they are paid with the funds that the government had put in the trust. Basically, the government has substituted the new debt for the existing debt.

There are two ways that the government could remove the liability for the old debt from the statement of net assets. The first, called a legal defeasance, occurs when debt is legally satisfied based on provisions of the debt instrument or contract even though the debt has not actually been paid. This situation does not occur frequently. The second, called an in-substance defeasance, is far more common. An in-substance defeasance occurs when debt is considered defeased for accounting purposes even though a legal defeasance has not occurred.

Statement No. 7 of the GASB sets the rules for when the debt can be removed from the statement of net assets as a result of an in-substance defeasance. The government must irrevocably place cash or other assets with an escrow agent in a trust to be used solely for satisfying scheduled payments of both interest and principal of the defeased debt, and the possibility that the government will be required to make future payments on that debt is remote. The trust is restricted to owning only monetary assets that are essentially risk-free as to the amount, timing, and collection of interest and principal. The monetary assets should be denominated in the currency in which the debt is payable. Statement No. 7 also prescribes that for debt denominated in US dollars, risk-free monetary assets are essentially limited to

- Direct obligations of the US government (including state and local government securities, which are a type of investment that the US Treasury issues specifically to provide state and local governments with required cash flows at yields that do not exceed the Internal Revenue Service's arbitrage limits)
- Obligations guaranteed by the US government

- Securities backed by US government obligations as collateral and for which interest and principal payments generally flow immediately through to the security holder

For advance refunding transactions that result in defeasance of debt reported in the government-wide statement of net assets, the proceeds from the new debt should be reported as "other financing source—proceeds from refunding bonds" in the fund receiving the proceeds, which this discussion is assuming is the debt service fund. Payments to the escrow from resources provided by the new debt should be reported as "other financing use—payment to the refunded bond escrow agent." Payments to the escrow agent made from other resources of the government should be reported as debt service expenditures.

Permanent Funds

One additional type of governmental fund that was defined by GASBS 34 is the permanent fund. Permanent funds are used to report resources that are legally restricted to the extent that only the earnings, and not the principal, may be used for purposes that support the government's programs, meaning programs that are for the benefit of the government or its citizens. Permanent funds operate in a manner similar to endowments, where the investment earnings, and not the principal, can be spent. Note that the earnings of a permanent fund are used to support the government's activities. This is in contrast to a type of fiduciary fund, discussed later in this chapter, called the private-purpose trust fund, in which the principal may be spent, but not for activities or programs normally carried on by the government. An example of a permanent fund is a cemetery perpetual-care fund, which provides resources for the ongoing maintenance of a public cemetery.

PROPRIETARY FUNDS

The next type of fund that we will examine is the proprietary fund. There are two types of proprietary funds—enterprise funds and internal service funds. Specific uses for these two types of proprietary funds will also be examined.

The first thing to realize about proprietary funds is that they use a different basis of accounting and measurement focus than the governmental funds than have been discussed in this chapter so far. Proprietary funds use the accrual basis of accounting and the economic resources measurement focus. This means that the balance sheets of proprietary funds will reflect both current and noncurrent assets and liabilities. In other words, capital assets (such as infrastructure, buildings, equipment, etc.) are recorded as assets by the fund. In addition, debt issued related to the activities of the proprietary fund is recorded as a liability on the balance sheet of the proprietary fund. (Keep in mind that the assets and liabilities of the proprietary funds are also included in the assets and liabilities of the government-wide statement of net assets.) In addition to recording noncurrent assets and liabilities, which is basically a result of their measurement focus, proprietary funds also recognize revenues and expense on the accrual basis of accounting, which means that revenues and expenses are recorded in different accounting periods than they would be by governmental funds. Chapter 2 describes the accrual basis of accounting that is used by proprietary funds.

One overly simplified way of viewing the accounting used by proprietary funds is that it is basically the same as that used by commercial enterprises and not-for-profit organizations. However, since commercial enterprises and not-for-profit organizations follow the accounting rules set by the Financial Accounting Standards Board (FASB), does that mean that proprietary funds should also follow those rules? Not exactly. GASB Statement No. 20, "Accounting and Financial Reporting for Proprietary Funds and Other Governmental Entities That Use Proprietary Fund Accounting" (GASBS 20), sets the rules in this area and they can be slightly confusing. Statement No. 20 requires that proprietary funds apply all applicable GASB pronouncements, as well as the following pronouncements issued on or before November 30, 1989, unless those pronouncements conflict with or contradict GASB pronouncements:

- FASB Statements
- FASB Interpretations

- Accounting Principles Board (APB) Opinions
- Accounting Research Bulletins (ARBs)

Proprietary funds have the option to apply all FASB Statements and Interpretations, APB Opinions, and ARBs issued after November 30, 1989, except for those that conflict with or contradict GASB pronouncements. (The significance of the November 30, 1989 date is that it is the date of SAS 69 which previously set the GAAP hierarchy for governments and nongovernments and is discussed in Chapter 1.) Note that once a proprietary fund elects to apply or not apply these FASB and other pronouncements it must be consistent from year to year. A proprietary fund cannot apply the FASB pronouncements one year and not the next. Nor can a proprietary fund pick and choose the pronouncements that it likes to apply and ignore the others. The election must be applied consistently and uniformly from year to year. The GASB Web site (www.gasb.org) has a useful list of these FASB pronouncements with a brief explanation as to whether they would be applicable to proprietary funds. The list is updated as the FASB issues new pronouncements.

The following sections describe the actual uses of the two types of proprietary funds—enterprise funds and internal service funds.

Enterprise Funds

Enterprise funds are used to account for operations that fall within two basic categories:

1. Activities that are financed and operated in a manner similar to private business enterprises, where the intent of the governing body is to finance or recover costs of providing goods or services to the general public on a continuing basis primarily through user charges
2. Operations where the governing body has decided that periodic determination of revenues earned, expenses incurred, and/or net income is appropriate for capital maintenance, public policy, management control, accountability or other purposes

Enterprise funds are primarily used to account for activities that are financed through user charges. However, the total cost of the activity does not have to be paid for by the user charges. The government (or other governmental entity) may subsidize a significant portion of the costs of the enterprise fund. Typical activities accounted for in enterprise funds include those that are similar to utilities, such as water and sewer funds and electric utility funds. Parking lots operated by governments are another example of proprietary activities accounted for in a proprietary fund.

Statement No. 34 of the GASB continued the previous practice that an enterprise fund may be used to report any activity for which a fee is charged to external users of goods and services. However, GASBS 34 also specifies three situations where the use of an enterprise fund is required. The criteria are to be applied to the activity's principal revenue sources, meaning that insignificant activities where fees are charged would not automatically require the use of an enterprise fund. An enterprise fund is required to be used if one or more of the following criteria are met:

- The activity is financed with debt that is secured solely by a pledge of the revenues from fees and charges of the activity. Often proprietary funds use revenue bonds to finance their capital activities. The revenue stream from the proprietary activity (such as water and sewer charges received from customers) is pledged to provide for the annual debt service on the revenue bonds. However, if the debt is secured by a pledge of the revenues of the activity and the full faith and credit of the related government or component unit, the debt is not considered to be payable solely from the fees of the activity, even if it is not expected that the primary government or component unit would actually make any payments on the debt. In this case, the criterion is not met and the use of an enterprise fund would not be required.
- Laws or regulations require that the activity's costs of providing services (including capital costs such as depreciation or debt service) be recovered from fees and charges, rather than taxes or similar revenues.
- The pricing policies of the activity establish fees and charges designed to recover its costs, including capital costs such as depreciation or debt service.

Two accounting features of enterprise funds that are important to understanding an enterprise fund's financial statements
involving capital contributions and recording defeasances of debt
are discussed in the following sections.

Contributed Capital

Because enterprise funds use an accounting and financial reporting model that resembles the commercial accounting and reporting model, the concept of "capital" or how the funds obtain their
resources for operations (other than the issuance of debt) must be
addressed. The net assets of the proprietary fund (assets less liabilities) are categorized as

• Invested in capital assets, net of related debt
• Restricted
• Unrestricted

Additional discussion of these classifications will be provided in
later chapters. At this point, it is important simply to understand
that the proprietary funds define their net assets in different categories.

One of the more significant changes in this area brought
about by GASBS 34 is the accounting for capital contributed by a
government into the proprietary fund. Previously, these capital
contributions were recorded directly as additions to net assets.
Statement No. 34 requires that these capital contributions flow
through the statement of revenues, expenses, and changes in net
assets, where they are reported separately from operating revenues and expenses, but not directly as an addition to net assets. A
too-quick read of this statement of a proprietary fund may cause
the reader to think that the proprietary activity "made more
money" than it actually did because some of the increase in net
assets may not be from its proprietary activity, but rather from a
capital contribution from the primary government.

Refundings of Debt

The previous section on debt service funds described advance
refundings of debt as they impacted the debt service fund and

government-wide financial statements as they relate to governmental activities. However, since the debt that is refunded is actually recorded on the financial statements of the proprietary funds, there are some different rules for accounting for these defeasances. The rules are set by GASBS 23, "Accounting and Financial Reporting for Refundings of Debt Reported by Proprietary Activities" (GASBS 23).

This can be a fairly complex accounting area that is beyond the scope of this book. The reader should be aware of one or two simple concepts as to these refundings that will be helpful in understanding a proprietary fund's financial statements. When a government refunds debt in a proprietary fund, it incurs an accounting gain or loss. This gain or loss is calculated as the difference between the carrying amount of the old debt (that is, the amount recorded on the balance sheet) and the reacquisition price (that is, how much the government had to pay or place in escrow to repay the refunded debt). This gain or loss is not recognized immediately in the period that the refunding occurred. Rather, the gain or loss is spread out (or amortized, using the correct accounting term) over the life of the new debt or old debt, whichever is shorter. As the gain or loss is spread out over future years, it is treated as an adjustment of interest expense in each of the future years.

Internal Service Funds

Internal service funds are used to account for the financing of goods or services provided by one department or agency of a governmental unit to other departments or agencies of the same governmental unit on a cost-reimbursement basis. Because internal service funds use the economic resources measurement focus and the accrual basis of accounting, they allow the full cost of providing goods or services to other departments or agencies to be charged to the receiving department or agency.

As the main purpose of internal service funds is to identify and allocate costs of goods or services to other departments, it is generally recommended that governments use separate internal service funds for different activities. Keep in mind, however, the GAAP does not require the use of internal service funds, nor does it require that the internal service fund include the full cost of services that are provided. A government may choose to leave some of the related costs out of the internal service fund, such as a rent charge or a utility charge.

Internal service funds are often used to determine and allocate the costs for a diverse group of activities, such as

- Duplicating and printing services
- Motor pools
- Central garages
- Information processing
- Purchasing
- Central stores and warehousing

Clearly, combining the costs of providing motor pool services with the costs of providing information processing services in the same internal service fund will not result in a very useful basis to allocate costs. Establishing separate funds will result in a more effective cost-allocation process.

While an internal service fund in some cases is used for goods and services provided on a cost-reimbursement basis to quasi-governmental or not-for-profit organization, GAAP requires that if the reporting government itself is not the predominant participant in the activity, the activity should be reported as an enterprise fund. In other words, the "internal" in internal service funds means that the predominant activity of the fund should be internal to the reporting entity.

Many of the transactions between internal service funds and other funds take the form of quasi-external transactions. The funds receiving the goods or services from the internal service fund report an expenditure or an expense, while the internal service fund reports revenue. The consequence of this approach is that there is a duplicate reporting of revenues and expenditures. For example, an internal service fund records an expense to recognize the cost of providing goods or services to another fund. This same expense is then duplicated in the other funds when the funds that received the goods and services are charged for their share of the cost. Elimination entries should be made in the financial statements to remove the "doubling-up" effect of internal service activities.

Internal service funds should be set up so that they break even. The costs that they incur are charged to other funds. There should not be a profit or loss built into the charges to the other fund. Of course, the internal service fund will never exactly break even and small deficits or surpluses in an internal service fund generally does not present a financial reporting problem. However, when an internal service fund has a significant surplus or deficit, the government should adjust the charges made to the other funds in order to more accurately reflect the true costs of the goods or services used by those other funds.

There is an interesting twist for reporting internal service fund asset and liability balances on the government-wide statement of net assets. Any asset or liability balances not eliminated would be reported in the governmental activities column of the statement. While one would expect that internal service fund balances would be reported in the business-type activities column, the rationale for including them in the governmental column is that the activities accounted for in an internal service fund are usually more governmental than business-type in nature. However, if enterprise funds are the predominant or only participant in an internal service fund, the government would report the internal service fund's residual assets and liabilities within the business-type activities column in the statement of net assets.

FIDUCIARY FUNDS

The last major group of funds that need to be examined is the fiduciary funds. Since the fiduciary funds account for "other people's money," their assets, liabilities, revenues, and expenses are not included in the government-wide financial statements. This is certainly different from the assets, liabilities, revenues, and expenditures/expenses of the governmental and proprietary funds, which, after any required adjustment to the accrual basis of accounting and economic resources measurement focus, are reported as part of the government-wide financial statements. You will find fiduciary funds presented as a separate group of funds only within the fund financial statements reported as part of a government's basic financial statements.

There are four types of fiduciary funds, each of which will be briefly described in this section.

1. Pension (and other employee benefit) trust funds
2. Investment trust funds
3. Private-purpose trust funds
4. Agency funds

Pension (and Other Employee Benefit) Trust Funds

Governments almost always offer pension benefits to their employees. The pension plans related to these benefits are reported as pension trust funds in the government's financial statements if either of the following criteria is met:

- The pension plan qualifies as a component unit of the government (this will be discussed further in Chapter 5 on the reporting entity).
- The pension plan does not qualify as a component unit of the government, but the plan's assets are administered by the government.

Pension (and other employee benefit) trust funds use the accrual basis of accounting and the economic resources measurement focus. A separate pension (and other employee benefit) trust fund should be used for each separate plan. Accounting and financial reporting for pension trust funds is discussed in later chapters of this book. For now, it is sufficient to understand when these funds are reported as part of a government's fund financial statements and that these funds use the accrual basis of accounting and the economic resources measurement focus.

In addition to pension plans, there may be other types of pension and employee benefit funds that would be reported along with the pension funds described above. For example, governments sometimes have funds that supplement pension benefits that would be reported in this category. In addition, some governments report deferred compensation plans, including those governed by Internal Revenue Code Section 457, as part of the pension (and other employee benefit) trust funds. In practice, many governments find that they do not meet the criteria for including Section 457 deferred compensation within their fiduciary fund financial statements. This results because governments often have little administrative involvement with these plans and do not perform the investing functions for these plans. If governments do administer a Section 457 plan and/or do the investing for the plan, the pension (and other employee benefit) trust fund type of fund is where the plan would be reported.

One other type of pension (and other employee benefit) trust fund that has seen some increase in use is a trust fund set up to accumulate resources to pay for postemployment benefits other than pensions (OPEBs). As governments implemented the requirements of GASB Statement No. 45, "Accounting and Financial Reporting by Employers for Postemployment Benefits Other Than Pensions," the magnitude of many governments' liability for these types of benefits (which usually include health-care coverage and other benefits for retirees) became alarmingly clear. The vast majority of governments had not been setting aside resources currently to fund these future obligations, as they typically do for pensions. Accordingly, in some cases, governments began to set aside some resources for these future obligations in OPEB trusts, which would be accounted for as a pension (and other employee benefit) trust fund type.

Investment Trust Funds

A special type of trust fund, the investment trust fund, is used by governments that sponsor external investment pools and that provide individual investment accounts to other legally separate entities that are not part of the same financial reporting entity. For these cases there is GASB Statement No. 31, "Accounting and Financial Reporting for Certain Investments and for External Investment Pools" (GASBS 31), which requires that investment trust funds be established. These rules are described as follows:

- *External portion of external investment pools.* An external investment pool commingles the funds of more than one legally separate entity and invests on the participants' behalf in an investment portfolio; GASBS 31 specifies that the external portion of each pool should be reported as a separate investment trust fund. The external portion of an external investment pool is the portion of the pool that belongs to legally separate entities that are not part of the sponsoring government's financial reporting entity.

- *Individual investment accounts.* Governmental entities that provide individual investment accounts to other legally separate entities that are not part of the same financial reporting entity must report those investments in one or more separate investment funds. In the way that the individual investment accounts function, specific investments that are required for individual entities and the income from and changes in the fair value of those investments affect only the entity for which they were acquired.

In other words, if a government invests funds on behalf of others, these funds should be reported in an investment trust fund. This is regardless of whether the government combines the other entity's money with its own or whether it gives the other entity its own separate account.

Investment trust funds use the accrual basis of accounting and the economic resources measurement focus. A typical example of where an investment trust fund is used is where one level of government, such as a state, pools the investment assets of local governments, and invests those funds on behalf of the local governments.

Private-Purpose Trust Funds

A private-purpose trust fund is a type of fiduciary fund that is used to report all trust arrangements (other than pension and other employee benefit and investment trust funds) under which the principal and income benefit individuals, private organizations, and other governments. Similar to other fiduciary funds, private-purpose trust funds cannot be used to support a government's own programs. It is important, therefore, to make sure that an activity is absent any public purpose of the government before it is accounted for as a private-purpose trust fund, even if individuals, private organizations, or other governments received direct or indirect benefit from the activity. Private-purpose trust funds use the accrual basis of accounting and the economic resources measurement focus.

Agency Funds

Agency funds are used to account for assets held solely in a custodial capacity. As a result, the assets of agency funds are always equal to their liabilities to the owners of the assets. Agency funds typically involve only the receipt, temporary investment, and remittance of assets to their respective owners. Agency funds are often used by school districts to account for student activity funds that are held by the school district but whose assets legally belong to the students. Another common example of agency funds is to account for taxes collected by one government on behalf of other governments. The collecting government has virtually no discretion in how the funds in the agency fund are to be spent. They are simply collected and then remitted to the government on whose behalf they were collected.

There are two instances in GAAP where the use of agency funds is required. First, when a government receives a grant and acts solely as a cash conduit to pass the funds along to others, GASB Statement No. 24, "Accounting and Financial Reporting for Certain Grants and Other Financial Assistance" (GASBS 24), requires that an agency fund be used. However, the use of an agency fund in these instances is infrequent because the government would have to *not* have any administrative requirements for the grant in order to account for it in an agency fund. In most instances, the government that receives a grant that will be passed through to other entities will have administrative requirements, so that the grant will be accounted for in another fund and revenues and related expenditures will be recorded for the grant activities.

The second instance where an agency fund is required is where a government collects special assessments (described earlier in this chapter) but the government is not obligated in any manner for the debt related to the capital improvements. In this instance, it is merely collecting money and passing it along to the paying agent that will make the principal and interest payments to the holders of the special assessment debt.

SUMMARY

This chapter presents an overview of the various funds that governments use and looks at some of the typical or unique transactions that are accounted for by those funds. It has crammed a lot of information into a (relatively) short space. The reader should have a feel for the complexity of transactions accounted for in funds and be aware of some of the issues that are often required to be addressed in using funds effectively for management purposes, while still accounting for and reporting fund information in accordance with generally accepted accounting principles.

CHAPTER 4

Basics of Governmental Financial Statements

One of the more frustrating experiences for nonaccountants (and for many accountants, as well) is trying to make some sense out of a government's various financial statements. Readers of this book who have read the financial statements of commercial organizations may not have understood every item in those statements, but may have felt at least somewhat comfortable in understanding the basic framework of what was presented—a balance sheet (what is owned and owed), an income statement (how much money the company made), and a cash flow statement (how much cash the company collected and what it spent it on). Pick up a set of governmental financial statements and you are confronted with government-wide financial statements, fund financial statements (with separate sets of financial statements for governmental activities, business-type activities, and fiduciary funds), required supplemental information, and component unit financial statements. What do all of these statements mean? How can the same government's assets or results of operations be presented two or three different ways? Which are the real numbers? Why does the income statement look like it is upside down? What is the difference between financial statements and a comprehensive annual financial report? This chapter will attempt to sort out these statements to give the reader at least a fighting chance in wading through a set of governmental financial statements. It will also help the reader understand the difference between a government's general-purpose financial statements and a government's comprehensive annual financial report.

GENERAL-PURPOSE FINANCIAL STATEMENTS

The general-purpose financial statements of a government prepared in accordance with generally accepted accounting principles includes both information reported on a government-wide basis and information presented on a fund basis. The basic components of the general-purpose financial statements are as follows:

- Management's discussion and analysis
- The basic financial statements (including government-wide financial statements, fund financial statements, and notes to the financial statements)
- Required supplementary information

Each of these will be discussed and illustrated in this chapter. As the reader gets further along in the details presented in this chapter, it will be helpful to keep this relatively simple list in mind to understand exactly where we are in the financial reporting maze.

MANAGEMENT'S DISCUSSION AND ANALYSIS

Management's discussion and analysis (MD&A) is an introduction to the financial statements that provides readers with a brief, objective, and easily readable analysis of the government's financial performance for the year and its financial position at year-end. The analysis included in MD&A is based on currently known facts, decisions, or conditions. For a fact to be currently known, it should be based on events or decisions that have already occurred, or have been enacted, adopted, agreed upon, or contracted. This means that governments should not include discussions about the possible effects of events that might happen. (Discussion of possible events that might happen in the future may be discussed in the letter of transmittal that is prepared as part of a Comprehensive Annual Financial Report, discussed later in this chapter.) MD&A should contain a comparison of current year results with those of the prior year.

Statement No. 34 of the GASB provides a listing of very specific topics to be included in MD&A, although governments are encouraged to be creative in presenting the information using graphs, charts, and tables. The GASB would like MD&A to be a useful analysis that is prepared with thought and insight, rather than boiler-plate material prepared by rote every year. However, the phrase "the minimum is the maximum" applies. This means that MD&A should address all of the applicable topics listed in GASBS 34, but MD&A should address only these topics. Of course, governments preparing Comprehensive Annual Financial Reports can include in the Letter of Transmittal any topic that would be precluded from being included in MD&A.

Current year information is addressed in comparison with the prior year, although the current year information should be the focus of the discussion. If the government is presenting comparative financial data with the prior year in the current year financial statements, the requirements for MD&A apply to only the current year. However, if the government is presenting comparative financial statements, that is, a complete set of financial statements for each year of a two-year period, then the requirements of MD&A must be met for each of the years presented.

In addition, MD&A focuses on the primary government. For fund information, the analysis of balances and transactions of individual funds would normally be confined to major funds, although discussion of nonmajor fund information is not precluded. Governments use judgment in determining whether discussion and analysis of discretely presented component unit information is included in MD&A. The judgment is based on the significance of an individual component unit's significance to the total of all discretely presented component units, as well as its significance to the primary government. (Chapter 5 explains component units.)

The minimum requirements for MD&A are as follows:

1. Brief discussion of the basic financial statements, including the relationships of the statements to each other and the significant differences in the information that they provide. (This is where governments should explain the differences in results and measurements in the govern-

ment-wide financial statements and the fund financial statements.)

2. Condensed financial information derived from the government-wide financial statements, comparing the current year to the prior year. GASBS 34 specifies that the following elements are included:

   a. Total assets, distinguishing between capital assets and other assets
   b. Total liabilities, distinguishing between long-term liabilities and other liabilities
   c. Total net assets, distinguishing among amounts invested in capital assets, net of related debt; restricted amounts; and unrestricted amounts
   d. Program revenues, by major source
   e. General revenues, by major source
   f. Total revenues
   g. Program expenses, at a minimum by function
   h. Total expenses
   i. The excess or deficiency before contributions to term and permanent endowments or permanent fund principal, special and extraordinary items
   j. Contributions
   k. Special and extraordinary items
   l. Transfers
   m. Change in net assets
   n. Ending net assets

3. Analysis of the government's overall financial position and results of operations. This information should assist users in determining whether financial position has improved or deteriorated as a result of the current year's operations. GASBS 34 requires that reasons for significant changes from the prior year be described, not simply the computation of percentage changes.

4. Analysis of the balances and transactions of individual funds.

5. Analysis of significant variations between original and final budgeted amounts and between financial budget amounts and actual budget results for the general fund (or

its equivalent). MD&A discusses the reasons for significant budget variances, such as why the significant variance occurred.

6. Description of significant capital asset and long-term debt activity during the year.

7. For governments that use the modified approach to report some or all of their infrastructure assets (i.e., when they do not record depreciation expense on their infrastructure assets), the following is discussed:

   a. Significant changes in the assessed condition of eligible infrastructure assets

   b. How the current assessed condition compares with the condition level the government has established

   c. Significant differences from the estimated annual amount to maintain/preserve eligible infrastructure assets compared with the actual amounts spent during the year.

8. Description of currently known facts, decisions or conditions that are expected to have a significant effect on financial position or results of operations.

Some of the terms and phrases included in the preceding list of MD&A requirements will become clearer as we cover these topics later in this chapter. At first glance, it appears that MD&A is a fairly complicated narrative. As governments have gained experience in preparing their MD&A, one can still see a diversity in practice as to how much information is provided in the MD&A. The size of the government does not seem to determine the size of the MD&A. Small governments may provide a fifteen- or twenty-page MD&A, while larger governments may use ten pages or less. What is important are the quality and usefulness of the information presented, and this will clearly vary by government. Many governments seem to have done a good job of using MD&A as a mechanism to explain the various financial statements that are presented. This can really help readers get through the statements with a high level of understanding.

One thing to keep in mind is that the GASB considers MD&A to be required supplementary information, or RSI as it is commonly called. While there are additional disclosures that are considered RSI (which are discussed after the basic financial statements), MD&A is RSI that should precede the financial statements. This fact is more important for the coverage of MD&A by independent auditors, which provide the same audit coverage of MD&A as they do of other RSI. By the way, the audit coverage provided by independent auditors of RSI, including MD&A, is virtually *none*, so the reader should not assume that MD&A and RSI are actually audited. Auditors are basically checking that the discussion contains all the required parts and there is nothing in the RSI that is inconsistent with the basic financial statements.

THE BASIC FINANCIAL STATEMENTS

The basic financial statements are the core of the general-purpose financial statements. Remember that the basic financial statements, which include the notes to the financial statements, plus the RSI, which includes MD&A, equal the general-purpose financial statements. The basic financial statements include the government-wide financial statements, the fund financial statements, and the notes to the financial statements. Each of these elements is described in the following sections.

Government-Wide Financial Statements

The government-wide financial statements present financial information about the government as a whole. They include the financial information of the governmental activities of the government (which are basically the same as the activities accounted for in the governmental funds described in Chapter 3) and the business-type activities of the government (which are basically the enterprise activities accounted for in the enterprise funds also described in Chapter 3). The total of the governmental activities and the business-type activities comprise the activities of what is known as the primary government. Note that the fiduciary fund activities that were discussed in Chapter 3 are *not* included in the government-wide financial statements.

The government-wide financial statements also include financial information about component units, which are legally separate entities that because of their relation to the government are included in the financial statements of the government. It is not a pure analogy, but component units (which are described in Chapter 5) are like subsidiaries that are reported in consolidated financial statements of a commercial company. Some component units are called "blended component units." Their financial activities are treated similar to funds that are included (blended) in the governmental or business-type activity amounts in the government-wide financial statements. (Extra credit is given to readers that figured out that since blended component units are included in the governmental and business-type activities, they are considered to be part of the primary government.) Other component units are called "discretely presented component units" and their financial activities are reported in separate columns on the government-wide financial statements.

The government-wide financial statements are prepared using the accrual basis of accounting and the economic resources measurement focus. Again remember that for governmental activities, the government will need to convert the governmental fund financial information from the modified accrual accounting basis and the current financial resources measurement focus to the accrual accounting basis and economic resources measurement focus. If this concept is grasped, it will go a long way to understanding why governments seem to present "two sets of books." It is the same financial activity presented in two perspectives—one in the government-wide financial statements and one (as we will see later in this chapter) in the fund financial statements.

Note that the enterprise funds already use the accrual accounting basis and economic resources measurement focus. Their financial results do not need to be converted when they are presented in the government-wide financial statements—they are already on the same basis of accounting and measurement focus as the government-wide financial statements.

There are two financial statements that comprise the government-wide financial statements.

1. Statement of net assets
2. Statement of activities

Each of these statements is described below. Readers familiar with commercial organization financial statements will notice that a government-wide statement of cash flows is not required.

Statement of Net Assets

This is the government's balance sheet. It presents the government's assets and liabilities as of a specific point in time, which is the government's fiscal year-end. The difference between the government's assets and liabilities is known as its net assets. A government's net assets on the statement of net assets need to be divided into three categories.

1. Invested in capital assets, net of related debt
2. Restricted net assets (distinguishing among major categories of restrictions)
3. Unrestricted net assets

These net asset components require some additional explanation and analysis.

- *Invested in capital assets, net of related debt.* This amount represents capital assets net of accumulated depreciation, and reduced by the outstanding bonds, mortgages, notes or other borrowings that are attributable to the acquisition, construction or improvement of those assets. Note that if the amount of debt issued for capital purposes exceeds the amount of the net book value of capital assets, this number will be reported as a negative amount.
- *Restricted net assets.* This amount represents those net assets that should be reported as restricted because constraints are placed on the net asset use that are either

  - Externally imposed by creditors (such as those imposed through debt covenants), grantors, contributors, or laws or regulations of other governments

- Imposed by law through constitutional provisions or enabling legislation

Basically, restrictions are not unilaterally established by the reporting government itself and cannot be removed without the consent of those imposing the restrictions or through formal due process. Restrictions can be broad or narrow, provided that the purpose is narrower than that of the reporting unit in which it is reported. Legislation that earmarks that a portion of a tax be used for a specific purpose does not constitute "enabling legislation" that would result in those assets being reported as restricted. However, a general state statute pertaining to local governments that provides that revenues derived from a fee or charge not be used for any purpose other than for which the fee or charge was imposed creates a legally enforceable restriction on the use of the resources raised through fees and charges.

When permanent endowments or permanent fund principal amounts are included in restricted net assets, restricted net assets should be displayed in two additional components—expendable and nonexpendable. Nonexpendable net assets are those that are required to be retained in perpetuity.

- *Unrestricted net assets.* This amount consists of net assets that do not meet the definition of restricted net assets or net assets invested in capital assets, net of related debt.

Exhibit 4.1 presents a sample statement of net assets, based on the examples provided in GASBS 34.

EXHIBIT 4.1 Sample statement of net assets

City of Anywhere
Statement of Net Assets
June 30, 20XX

| | Primary Government | | | |
	Governmental activities	Business-type activities	Total	Component units
Assets				
Current assets:				
Cash and cash equivalents	$ xx,xxx	$ xx,xxx	$ xx,xxx	$ xx,xxx
Investments	xx,xxx	xx,xxx	xx,xxx	xx,xxx
Receivables (net)	xx,xxx	xx,xxx	xx,xxx	xx,xxx
Internal balances	xx,xxx	(xx,xxx)	--	--
Inventories	xx,xxx	xx,xxx	xx,xxx	xx,xxx
Total current assets	xxx,xxx	xxx,xxx	xxx,xxx	xxx,xxx
Noncurrent assets:				
Restricted cash and cash equivalents	xx,xxx	xx,xxx	xx,xxx	--
Capital assets				
Land and infrastructure	xx,xxx	xx,xxx	xx,xxx	xx,xxx
Depreciable buildings, property, and equipment, net	xx,xxx	xx,xxx	xx,xxx	xx,xxx
Total noncurrent assets	xxx,xxx	xxx,xxx	xxx,xxx	xxx,xxx
Total assets	$xxx,xxx	$xxx,xxx	$xxx,xxx	$xxx,xxx
Liabilities				
Current liabilities:				
Accounts payable	$ xx,xxx	$ xx,xxx	$ xx,xxx	$ xx,xxx
Deferred revenue	xx,xxx	xx,xxx	xx,xxx	xx,xxx
Current portion of long-term obligations	xx,xxx	xx,xxx	xx,xxx	xx,xxx
Total current liabilities	xxx,xxx	xxx,xxx	xxx,xxx	xxx,xxx
Noncurrent liabilities:				
Noncurrent portion of long-term obligations	xx,xxx	xx,xxx	xx,xxx	xx,xxx
Total liabilities	xxx,xxx	xxx,xxx	xxx,xxx	xxx,xxx
Net Assets				
Invested in capital assets, net of related debt	xx,xxx	xx,xxx	xx,xxx	xx,xxx
Restricted for:				
Capital projects	xx,xxx	--	xx,xxx	xx,xxx
Debt service	xx,xxx	xx,xxx	xx,xxx	--
Community development projects	xx,xxx	--	xx,xxx	--
Other purposes	xx,xxx	--	xx,xxx	--
Unrestricted	xx,xxx	xx,xxx	xx,xxx	xx,xxx
Total net assets	xxx,xxx	xxx,xxx	xxx,xxx	xxx,xxx
Total liabilities and net assets	$xxx,xxx	$xxx,xxx	$xxx,xxx	$xxx,xxx

Statement of Activities

The statement of activities is roughly the equivalent of an invoice statement. A better way to view it, however, is as a summary of the transactions (activities) the sum of which takes you from the beginning net asset number to the ending net asset number reported on the statement of net assets.

The statement of activities should use the net (expense) revenue format, which is easier to view than describe. See Exhibit 4.2 for an example of a statement of activities based on the examples provided in GASBS 34.

The objective of this format is to report the relative financial burden of each of the reporting government's functions on its taxpayers. The format identifies the extent to which each function of the government draws from the general revenues of the government or is self-financing through fees or intergovernmental aid.

The statement of activities presents governmental activities by function or program and business-type activities at least by segment. Segments are identifiable activities reported as or within an enterprise fund or another standalone entity for which one or more revenue bonds or other revenue-backed debt instrument are outstanding.

Expense presentation. The statement of activities presents expenses of governmental activities by function in at least the level of detail required in the governmental fund statement of revenues, expenditures, and changes in fund balances (described later in this chapter). Expenses for business-type activities are reported in at least the level of detail as by segment, which is defined as an identifiable activity reported as or within an enterprise fund or another stand-alone entity for which one or more revenue bonds or other revenue-backed debt instruments are outstanding. A segment has a specific identifiable revenue stream pledged in support of revenue bonds or other revenue-backed debt and has related expenses, gains and losses, assets, and liabilities that can be identified.

Governments should report all expenses by function except for those expenses that meet the definitions of special items or extraordinary items, discussed later in this chapter. Governments

EXHIBIT 4.2 Sample statement of activities

City of Anywhere
Statement of Activities
For the Fiscal Year Ended June 30, 20XX

| | | Program revenues | | | Net (expense) revenue and changes in net assets | | | |
| | | | | | Primary government | | | |
Functions/Programs	Expenses	Charges for services	Operating grants and contributions	Capital grants and contributions	Governmental activities	Business-type activities	Total	Component units
Primary government:								
Governmental activities								
General government	$ xx,xxx	$ xx,xxx	$ xx,xxx	$ —	$ (xx,xxx)	$ —	$(xx,xxx)	$ —
Public safety	xx,xxx	xx,xxx	xx,xxx	xx,xxx	(xx,xxx)	—	(xx,xxx)	—
Public works	xx,xxx	xx,xxx	—	xx,xxx	(xx,xxx)	—	(xx,xxx)	—
Health and sanitation	xx,xxx	xx,xxx	xx,xxx	—	(xx,xxx)	—	(xx,xxx)	—
Community development	xx,xxx	—	—	xx,xxx	(xx,xxx)	—	(xx,xxx)	—
Education	xx,xxx	—	—	—	(xx,xxx)	—	(xx,xxx)	—
Interest on long-term debt	xx,xxx	—	—	—	(xx,xxx)	—	(xx,xxx)	—
Total governmental activities	xxx,xxx	xxx,xxx	xxx,xxx	xxx,xxx	(xxx,xxx)	—	(xxx,xxx)	—
Business-type activities:								
Water and sewer	xx,xxx	xx,xxx	—	xx,xxx	—	xx,xxx	xx,xxx	—
Parking facilities	xx,xxx	xx,xxx	—	—	—	(xx,xxx)	(xx,xxx)	—
Total business-type activities	xxx,xxx	xxx,xxx	—	xx,xxx	—	xxx,xxx	xxx,xxx	—
Total primary government	$xxx,xxx	$xxx,xxx	$xxx,xxx	$xx,xxx	xxx,xxx	xxx,xxx	xxx,xxx	—
Component units:								
Parking Authority	$xx,xxx	$xx,xxx	$xx,xxx	$xx,xxx				$ xx,xxx
Water Authority	xx,xxx	xx,xxx	$ xx,xxx	—				(xx,xxx)
Total component units	$xx,xxx	$xxx,xxx	$xx,xxx	$xx,xxx				$(xx,xxx)

General revenues:
Taxes:
Property taxes — — — xx,xxx — xx,xxx xx,xxx
Franchise taxes — — — xx,xxx — xx,xxx xx,xxx
Payment from City of Anywhere — — — — — — xx,xxx
Grants and contributions not restricted to specific programs — — — xx,xxx — xx,xxx xx,xxx
Investment earnings — — — xx,xxx xx,xxx xx,xxx xx,xxx
Miscellaneous — — — xx,xxx xx,xxx xx,xxx xx,xxx
Special item—Gain on sale of baseball stadium — — — xx,xxx — xx,xxx —
Transfers — — — xx,xxx (xx,xxx) — —
Total general revenues, special items, and transfers — — — xxx,xxx (xxx,xxx) xxx,xxx xxx,xxx
Change in net assets — — — xxx,xxx xxx,xxx xxx,xxx xxx,xxx
Net assets—beginning — — — xxx,xxx xxx,xxx xxx,xxx xxx,xxx
Net assets—ending — — — $xxx,xxx $xxx,xxx $xxx,xxx $xxx,xxx

are required, at a minimum, to report the direct expenses for each function. Direct expenses are those that are specifically associated with a service, program, or department and, accordingly, can be clearly identified with a particular function.

There are numerous government functions—such as the general government, support services, and administration—that are actually indirect expenses of the other functions. For example, the police department of a city reports to the mayor. The direct expenses of the police department would likely be reported under the function "public safety" in the statement of activities. However the mayor's office (along with payroll, personnel, and other departments) supports the activities of the police department although they are not direct expenses of the police department. Governments are permitted, but not required, to allocate these indirect expenses to other functions. Governments may allocate some but not all indirect expenses, or they may use a full-cost allocation approach and allocate all indirect expenses to other functions. If indirect expenses are allocated, they are displayed in a column separate from the direct expenses of the functions to which they are allocated. Governments that allocate central expenses to funds or programs, such as through the use of internal service funds, are not required to eliminate these administrative charges when preparing the statement of activities, but should disclose in the summary of significant accounting policies that these charges are included in direct expenses.

The reporting of depreciation expense in the statement of activities requires some careful analysis. (Depreciation expense is described in Chapter 7.) Depreciation expense for the following types of capital assets is included in the direct expenses of functions or programs:

- Capital assets that can be specifically identified with a function or program
- Capital assets that are shared by more than one function or program, such as a building in which several functions or programs share office space

Some capital assets of a government may essentially serve all of the functions of a government, such as a city hall or county administrative office building. There are several options for presenting depreciation expense on these capital assets.

- Include the depreciation expense in an indirect expense allocation to the various functions or programs.
- Report the depreciation expense as a separate line item in the statement of activities (labeled in such a way as to make clear to the reader of the financial statements that not all of the government's depreciation expense is included on this line).
- Report as part of the general government (or its equivalent) function.

Depreciation expense for infrastructure assets associated with governmental activities should be reported in one of the following ways:

- Report the depreciation expenses as a direct expense of the function that is normally used for capital outlays for and maintenance of infrastructure assets.
- Report the depreciation expense as a separate line item in the statement of activities (labeled in such a way as to make clear to the reader of the financial statements that not all of the government's depreciation expense is included on this line).

Interest expense on general long-term liabilities should be reported as an indirect expense.

Revenue presentation. Revenues on the statement of activities are distinguished between program revenues and general revenues.

- Program revenues are those derived directly from the program itself or from parties outside the government's taxpayers or citizens, as a whole. Program revenues reduce the net cost of the program that is to be financed from the government's general revenues. On the statement of activities, these revenues are deducted from the expenses of the functions and programs discussed in the previous section. There are three categories into which program revenues should be distinguished.

1. *Charges for services*. These are revenues based on exchange or exchange-like transactions. This type of program revenues arises from charges to customers or applicants who purchase, use, or directly benefit from the goods, services, or privileges provided. Examples include water use charges, garbage collection fees, licenses and permits such as dog licenses or building permits, and operating assessments, such as for street cleaning or street lighting.

2. *Program-specific operating grants and contributions*. (See the following discussion on program-specific capital grants and contributions.)

3. *Program-specific capital grants and contributions*. Both program-specific operating and capital grants and contributions include revenues arising from mandatory and voluntary nonexchange transactions with other governments, organizations, or individuals, that are restricted for use in a particular program. Some grants and contributions consist of capital assets or resources that are restricted for capital purposes, such as purchasing, constructing, or renovating capital assets associated with a particular program. These revenues are reported separately from grants and contributions that may be used for either operating expenses or capital expenditures from a program, at the discretion of the government receiving the grant or contribution. Sometimes the accounting for revenues that meet the definition of program revenues presents a question where the grants specify amounts for specific programs, but the programs are spread in the statement of activities over several functions. If a grant meets the definition of program revenue, it should be recorded as such. If the grant is detailed by program and the statement of activities is detailed by function, a reasonable allocation method should be used to assign the program revenues to the appropriate functions. This issue, however, is different from when a government has the discretion to use a particular grant for more than one program or function.

In this case, the grant would be considered a general revenue instead of a program revenue because of the discretion that the government can exert in how the grant amounts are used.

- General revenues are all those revenues that are not required to be reported as program revenues. All taxes, regardless of whether they are levied for a specific purpose, should be reported as general revenues. Taxes should be reported by type of tax, such as real estate taxes, sales tax, income tax, franchise tax, etc. (Although operating special assessments are derived from property owners, they are not considered taxes and are properly reported as program revenues.) General revenues are reported after total net expense of the government's functions on the statement of activities.

A government's statement of activities may report extraordinary and special items. Extraordinary items are those that are unusual in nature and infrequent in occurrence. This tracks the private sector accounting definition of this term.

Special items were a new concept introduced by GASBS 34. They are defined as "significant transactions or other events within the control of management that are either unusual in nature or infrequent in occurrence." Special items are reported separately in the statement of activities before any extraordinary items.

The following events or transactions may qualify as extraordinary or special items and are used by the GASB as examples:

Extraordinary Items

- Costs related to an environmental disaster caused by a large chemical spill in a train derailment in a small city
- Significant damage to the community or destruction of government facilities by natural disaster or terrorist act. However, geographic location of the government may determine if a weather-related natural disaster is infrequent.
- A large bequest to a small government by a private citizen

Special Items

- Sales of certain general government capital assets
- Special termination benefits resulting from workforce reductions due to sale of the government's utility operations
- Early retirement program offered to all employees
- Significant forgiveness of debt

Certainly understanding the statement of activities is far more difficult than understanding the statement of net assets. While GASBS 34 introduced kind of an upside-down format for this statement and created a host of rules and requirements that are summarized above, the important thing is to not get lost in the details and to understand what the statement is trying to present. The basic intent of the statement is to enable readers to determine

- The total direct costs of each of the major functions or programs
- The net costs of these programs and functions after considering how much money each of them actually brings into the government in the form of user charges or grants
- How much general revenues (mostly taxes) the government gets each year to pay for the net costs of the programs and functions
- Whether the government's net program cost is covered by its general revenues—another way of saying whether overall, the government's net assets increased or decreased during the year

To accomplish this, the statement of activities presents the following information. First, start with the direct expense of a government's major programs (public safety, transportation, health, education, parks, general government, etc.) and certain expenses that do not relate to programs, specifically interest expense on long-term debt. Reduce those expenses by revenues that are brought in by each of those programs. This represents the net cost to the government for each of these programs and the non-program expenses. The difference between this amount and the general revenues of the government (all of its tax revenue as well as other revenues not related to specific programs) represents the change in the net assets of the government. (This change may also be affected by extraordinary items and special items, as well as transfers with the discretely presented component units.)

Fund Financial Statements

The next set of statements that are part of the basic financial statements of a government are the fund financial statements. There are fund financial statements for each of the following types of funds:

- Governmental funds
- Proprietary funds
- Fiduciary funds

Remember that the same set of activities that are reported in the governmental funds and proprietary funds are reported in the government-wide financial statements. The assets, liabilities, and activities of the fiduciary funds are reported only in the fund financial statements and do not find their way into the government-wide financial statements.

Before describing the statements presented for each of these fund types, the concept of "major fund" must be understood. Many governments have large numbers of funds, some numbering into the hundreds. The governmental financial reporting model recognizes that presenting exactly the same information for all of these funds in financial statements would be unwieldy. Statement No. 34 of the GASB introduced the concept of major fund so that when reporting governmental and proprietary funds, only information for each of the major funds is required to be presented. All of the other funds that are not considered major funds can be combined together and reported in one column in the fund financial statements.

So how does a fund get to be a major fund? It is basically an arithmetical calculation based on the size of the fund, but there are some exceptions. First, the general fund (as the main operating fund of the government) is always considered to be a major fund. Other funds are considered major funds if they meet both of the following criteria:

- Total assets, liabilities, revenues, or expenditures/expenses of the fund are at least 10% of the corresponding total (assets, liabilities, revenues, or expenditures/expenses) for all funds in that category (i.e., either governmental or proprietary).
- Total assets, liabilities, revenues, or expenditures/expenses of the fund are at least 5% of the corresponding total for all governmental and enterprise funds combined.

For example, say that total assets of a special revenue fund are $125. Total assets for all governmental funds are $1,000. Total assets for all enterprise funds are $250. This special revenue fund is a major fund. Its assets are more than 10% of the total assets for all governmental funds ($125 divided by $1,000, or 12.5%). Its assets are more than 5% of the total assets of all governmental and enterprise funds combined ($125 divided by $1,000 + $250, or 10%).

Notice that the fund type of enterprise funds is used in this calculation and not the total for all proprietary funds, which means that the totals for internal service funds are not considered in the calculation. In addition, the government may choose to report any fund that it believes to be particularly important or of interest to readers as a major fund even if it does not meet the monetary criteria discussed above.

The following sections describe the financial statements presented for each of these fund types.

Governmental Funds

Chapter 3 discussed the specific types of funds that are considered governmental funds. They are the general fund, special revenue funds, capital projects funds, debt service funds, and permanent funds. Governmental funds are required to present two financial statements.

1. Balance sheet
2. Statement of revenues, expenditures, and changes in fund balances

In each of these statements, a separate column is presented for each major governmental fund. A single column is presented for all of the nonmajor governmental funds that combines all of the amounts for all of the nonmajor funds. A total is presented on each statement reflecting the total amounts for all governmental funds.

The balance sheet presents the assets, liabilities, and fund balances of the governmental funds. An example balance sheet is presented as Exhibit 4.3. The balance sheet is presented in a "balanced" format, meaning that the total of assets equals the total of liabilities plus the total fund balances. Notice also that the term "fund balances" is to be used to connote the difference between assets and liabilities, instead of the net asset term used for a similar balance in the government-wide financial statements. Remember that governmental funds use the modified accrual basis of accounting and current financial resources measurement focus. Therefore, in general, the balance sheet of these funds will not contain long-term assets (such as capital assets) or long-term liabilities (such as long-term debt).

Note that in Exhibit 4.3, the fund balances of the funds presented are categorized as reserved and unreserved. Under current accounting standards, the term "reserved" is used. There are two reasons why a portion of fund balance is reported as reserved. The first is to the portion of the fund balance that is not available to appropriate for expenditure. An example is a reserve for inventories, which indicates that the portion of fund balance that is represented by inventories is not available for expenditure. (Very simply stated, you cannot write a check based on the amount of inventory.)

The second reason for reporting a reserve is a reserve for the portion of fund balance that is legally segregated for a specific future use. An example of this is a reserve for encumbrances, which indicates that a portion of the fund balance has already been committed and is not available to spend on something else. For example, a purchase order may have been sent to a vendor and the government is waiting for the vendor to deliver the goods or services. Since the goods or services have not been received, there is no expenditure to record in the financial statements, but the "encumbrance" indicates that the funds are already committed for this particular purchase.

EXHIBIT 4.3 Governmental funds balance sheet

City of Anywhere
Governmental Funds
Balance Sheet
June 30, 20XX

	General	Capital projects	Debt service	Nonmajor governmental funds	Total governmental funds
Assets					
Cash and cash equivalents	$xx,xxx	$xx,xxx	$xx,xxx	$xx,xxx	$xx,xxx
Investments	xx,xxx	--	xx,xxx	xx,xxx	xx,xxx
Receivables					
Real estate taxes	xx,xxx	--	--	--	xx,xxx
Federal, state, and other aid	xx,xxx	xx,xxx	--	--	xx,xxx
Taxes other than real estate	xx,xxx	--	--	xx,xxx	xx,xxx
Other	xx,xxx	--	--	xx,xxx	xx,xxx
Due from other funds	xx,xxx	xx,xxx	xx,xxx	xx,xxx	xx,xxx
Due from component units	xx,xxx	xx,xxx	--	xx,xxx	xx,xxx
Restricted cash and investments	--	xx,xxx	--	xx,xxx	xx,xxx
Total assets	$xx,xxx	$xx,xxx	$xx,xxx	$xx,xxx	$xx,xxx
Liabilities and fund balances					
Liabilities:					
Accounts payable and accrued liabilities	$xx,xxx	$xx,xxx	$xx,xxx	$xx,xxx	$xx,xxx
Bond anticipation notes payable	--	--	--	xx,xxx	xx,xxx
Accrued tax refunds:					
Real estate taxes	xx,xxx	--	--	--	xx,xxx
Other	xx,xxx	--	--	--	xx,xxx
Accrued judgments and claims	xx,xxx	xx,xxx	--	--	xx,xxx

	General	Capital projects	Debt service	Nonmajor governmental funds	Total governmental funds
Deferred revenues:					
Prepaid real estate taxes	xx,xxx	--	--	--	xx,xxx
Uncollected real estate taxes	xx,xxx	--	--	--	xx,xxx
Taxes other than real estate	xx,xxx	--	--	xx,xxx	xx,xxx
Other	xx,xxx	xx,xxx	--	xx,xxx	xx,xxx
Due to other funds	xx,xxx	xx,xxx	xx,xxx	xx,xxx	xx,xxx
Due to component units	XX,XXX	--	--	--	XX,XXX
Total liabilities	XX,XXX	XX,XXX	XX,XXX	XX,XXX	XX,XXX
Fund balances					
Reserved for:					
Debt service	--	--	xx,xxx	xx,xxx	xx,xxx
Noncurrent mortgage loans	--	--	--	xx,xxx	xx,xxx
Unreserved reported in:					
General fund	xx,xxx	--	--	--	xx,xxx
Capital Projects Fund	--	xx,xxx	--	--	xx,xxx
Nonmajor funds	XX,XXX	XX,XXX	XX,XXX	XX,XXX	XX,XXX
Total fund balances (deficit)	XX,XXX	XX,XXX	XX,XXX	XX,XXX	XX,XXX
Total liabilities and fund balances	$XX,XXX	$XX,XXX	$XX,XXX	$XX,XXX	$XX,XXX

Tip The GASB recently issued Statement No. 54, "Fund Balance Reporting and Governmental Fund Type Definitions" (GASBS 54), which will essentially be required for governments to adopt for fiscal years ending June 30, 2011, and thereafter. One purpose of this new statement is to update the manner in which fund balance is categorized and displayed. The classifications of fund balances had not been changed in many years and were due for an update, particularly in light of the many changes made to the government financial reporting model. Upon implementation of GASBS 54, fund balances of governmental funds will be classified as follows:

- Nonspendable—This will represent amounts that cannot be spent because they are either in nonspendable form or legally or contractually required to be maintained intact. Examples would include the amounts for inventories (as described above) that are nonspendable and the corpus of a permanent fund, which contractually cannot be spent.
- Restricted—Restricted for the governmental funds will now have the same definition of restricted that is used in preparing the government-wide financial statements. Accordingly, fund balances will be reported as restricted when constraints are placed on the use of resources that are either

  - Externally imposed by creditors, grantors, contributors, or laws or regulations of other governments, or
  - Imposed by law through constitutional provisions or enabling legislation

- Committed—These are amounts that can be used for specific purposes because of constraints imposed by the government's highest decision-making authority. To use the resources for something else, the government would have to take the same type of action (for example, legislation, resolution or ordinance) as it did to originally impose the constraint on the resources.
- Assigned—These are amounts constrained by the government's intent to use them for specific purposes. Intent should be expressed by the governing body itself or a body

(for example, a budget or finance committee) that has been delegated the authority to assign amounts for specific purposes.

- Unassigned—After applying all of the other classifications, this will essentially represent the remaining fund balance of the general fund.

A couple of important additional points that will assist in understanding the requirements of GASBS 54:

- By reporting amounts that are not committed or restricted in special revenue, capital project, debt service or permanent funds, the government has assigned those amounts for specific purposes and those amounts would be reported as assigned in those funds.
- Stabilization funds (often called "rainy day funds") should be reported in the general fund as restricted or committed if they meet the criteria discussed above. Stabilization agreements that do not meet these criteria should be reported as unassigned in the general fund. In other words, stabilization funds should not be reported as assigned fund balance.

The statement of revenues, expenditures, and changes in fund balances is the second financial statement presented for governmental funds. An example of this statement is presented in Exhibit 4.4. This statement is broken into three main categories: revenues, expenditures, and other financing sources (uses) of funds. Revenues are presented by source, such as taxes, grants, and charges for services. Expenditures are presented by function or program, such as general government, public safety, social services, and so forth. Expenditures not assigned to an individual program are reported as additional line items. Debt service expenditures (including both interest payments and principal redemptions) are reported separately. Other financing sources and uses include all types of transactions that are not considered revenues and expenditures. These include transfers between funds and component units and proceeds from the sales of bonds. The

EXHIBIT 4.4 Governmental funds statement of revenues, expenditures, and changes in fund balance

City of Anywhere
Governmental Funds
Statement of Revenues, Expenditures, and Changes in Fund Balances
For the Year Ended June 30, 20XX

	General	Capital projects	Debt service	Nonmajor governmental funds	Total governmental funds
Revenues					
Real estate taxes	$xx,xxx	$ --	$ --	$ --	$ xx,xxx
Sales and use taxes	xx,xxx	--	--	--	xx,xxx
Other taxes	xx,xxx	--	--	--	xx,xxx
Federal, state, and other categorical aid	xx,xxx	xx,xxx	--	xx,xxx	xx,xxx
Unrestricted federal and state aid	xx,xxx	--	--	--	xx,xxx
Charges for services	xx,xxx	--	--	--	xx,xxx
Investment income	xx,xxx	--	xx,xxx	--	xx,xxx
Other revenues	xx,xxx	xx,xxx	xx,xxx	xx,xxx	xx,xxx
Total revenues	xx,xxx	xx,xxx	xx,xxx	xx,xxx	xx,xxx
Expenditures					
Current operations:					
General government	xx,xxx	xx,xxx	--	xx,xxx	xx,xxx
Public safety and judicial	xx,xxx	xx,xxx	--	--	xx,xxx
Education	xx,xxx	xx,xxx	--	xx,xxx	xx,xxx
Social services	xx,xxx	xx,xxx	--	--	xx,xxx
Environmental protection	xx,xxx	xx,xxx	--	--	xx,xxx
Transportation services	xx,xxx	xx,xxx	--	--	xx,xxx
Parks, recreational, and cultural activities	xx,xxx	xx,xxx	--	--	xx,xxx
Housing	xx,xxx	xx,xxx	--	--	xx,xxx
Health (including payments to HHC)	xx,xxx	xx,xxx	--	--	xx,xxx
Pensions	xx,xxx	--	--	--	xx,xxx

	General	Capital projects	Debt service	Nonmajor governmental funds	Total governmental funds
Debt service:					
Interest	--	--	xx,xxx	xx,xxx	xx,xxx
Redemptions	--	--	xx,xxx	xx,xxx	xx,xxx
Total expenditures	xx,xxx	xx,xxx	xx,xxx	xx,xxx	xx,xxx
Excess (deficiency) or revenues over expenditures	xx,xxx	(xx,xxx)	(xx,xxx)	(xx,xxx)	(xx,xxx)
Other financing sources (uses)					
Transfers from (to) General Fund	--	xx,xxx	xx,xxx	(xx,xxx)	xx,xxx
Proceeds from sale of bonds	--	xx,xxx	--	xx,xxx	xx,xxx
Capitalized leases	--	xx,xxx	--	--	xx,xxx
Transfer from Capital Projects Fund	--	--	--	--	--
Transfer to Debt Service Fund	(xx,xxx)	--	--	(xx,xxx)	(xx,xxx)
Transfer to component units for debt service	(xx,xxx)	--	--	--	(xx,xxx)
Transfers to Nonmajor Debt Service Fund	--	--	--	--	(xx,xxx)
Total other financing sources (uses)	(xx,xxx)	xx,xxx	xx,xxx	(xx,xxx)	xx,xxx
Net change in fund balances	xx,xxx	xx,xxx	xx,xxx	(xx,xxx)	(xx,xxx)
Fund Balances at Beginning of Year	xx,xxx	xx,xxx	xx,xxx	xx,xxx	xx,xxx
Fund Balances at End of Year	$xx,xxx	$xx,xxx	$xx,xxx	$(xx,xxx)	$(xx,xxx)

bottom line for the governmental funds, representing all the revenues, expenditures, and other financing sources and uses of funds, represents the change in the fund balances for the fiscal year. The ending fund balance of the prior fiscal year, plus or minus this bottom line for all of the governmental funds reported on the statement of revenues, expenditures, and changes in fund balances, has to equal the ending fund balance reported on the balance sheet.

Remember that the "governmental" activities on both the government-wide financial statements and the fund financial statements represent the same activities presented on two different accounting bases and measurement focuses. Statement No. 34 of the GASB requires that governments reconcile these two sets of statements. Basically, the reconciliations detail all of the areas where the different accounting bases and measurement focuses cause the numbers to be different on the government-wide statements and the fund financial statements for the governmental activities. Most of the reconciling items have to do with the fact that the funds do not record long-term assets and long-term liabilities related to the governmental activities, whereas the government-wide financial statements do record these items. An example of the reconciliation of the governmental fund balance sheet fund balance amounts to the net assets of the "governmental activities" column of the government-wide statement of net assets is presented as Exhibit 4.5. An example of the reconciliation of the net change in fund balances reported on the governmental fund statement of revenues, expenditures, and changes in fund balance to the change in net assets for governmental activities reported on the government-wide statement of activities is presented as Exhibit 4.6.

EXHIBIT 4.5 Reconciliation of the fund balances of governmental funds to the net assets of governmental activities

City of Anywhere
Reconciliation of the Balance Sheet of Governmental Funds to the Statement of Net Assets
June 30, 20XX

Amounts reported for *governmental activities* in the Statement of Net Assets are different because:

Total fund balances—governmental funds	$(xx,xxx)
Inventories recorded in the Statement of Net Assets are recorded as expenditures in the governmental funds	xx,xxx
Capital assets used in governmental activities are not financial resources and therefore are not reported in the funds	xx,xxx
Other long-term assets are not available to pay for current period expenditures and therefore are deferred in the funds	xx,xxx
Long-term liabilities are not due and payable in the current period and accordingly are not reported in the funds:	
Bonds and notes payable	(xx,xxx)
Accrued interest payable	(xx,xxx)
Other long-term liabilities	(xx,xxx)
Net assets (deficit) of governmental activities	$(xx,xxx)

EXHIBIT 4.6 Reconciliation of the net change in governmental fund balances with the change in net assets of governmental activities

City of Anywhere
Reconciliation of the Statement of Revenues, Expenditures, and Changes in Fund Balances of Governmental Funds to the Statement of Activities
For the Year Ended June 30, 20XX

Amounts reported for *governmental activities* in the Statement of Activities are different because:

Net change in fund balances—total governmental funds		$(xx,xxx)
Governmental funds report capital outlays as expenditures. However, in the statement of activities the cost of those assets is allocated over their estimated useful lives and reported as depreciation expense. This is the amount by which capital outlays exceeded depreciation in the current period.		
Purchases of fixed assets	$xx,xxx	
Depreciation expense	(xx,xxx)	xx,xxx
The net effect of various miscellaneous transactions involving capital assets and other (i.e., sales, trade-ins, and donations) is to decrease net assets		(xx,xxx)
The issuance of long-term debt (e.g., bonds, leases) provides current financial resources to governmental funds, while the repayment of the principal of long-term debt consumes the current financial resources of governmental funds. Neither transaction, however, has any effect on net assets. Also, governmental funds report the effect of issuance costs, premiums, discounts, and similar items when debt is first issued, whereas these amounts are deferred and amortized in the statement of activities. This amount is the net effect of these differences in the treatment of long-term debt and related items.		
Proceeds from sales of bonds	(xx,xxx)	
Principal payments of bonds	xx,xxx	
Other	(xx,xxx)	(xx,xxx)

Some expenses reported in the statement of activities do not require the use of current financial resources and therefore are not reported as expenditures in governmental funds	(xx,xxx)
Revenues in the statement of activities that do not provide current financial resources are not reported as revenues in the funds	(xx,xxx)
Change in net assets—governmental activities	$(xx,xxx)

These examples of reconciliations also provide the reader with some of the more common reasons why the different accounting bases and measurement focuses cause differences for governmental activities between the government-wide and fund financial statements.

Proprietary Funds

The second set of fund financial statements included in a government's basic financial statements are the proprietary fund financial statements. Since the proprietary funds report activities using the same accounting basis and measurement focus as is used in the government-wide financial statements, their presentation resembles that of the government-wide statements much more than the governmental fund statements. Remember from Chapter 3 that there are two types of proprietary funds— enterprise funds and internal service funds—and it is these funds that are reported in the proprietary fund financial statements. Proprietary funds are required to present three financial statements.

1. Statement of net assets
2. Statement of revenues, expenses, and changes in fund net assets
3. Statement of cash flows

Each of these statements will have individual columns for each of the major enterprise funds of the government. A single column is used to report all of the enterprise funds that are nonmajor. A total column for all enterprise funds (major and nonmajor) is also required. In addition, each of these statements will have a single column to report all of the government's internal service funds.

The statement of net assets presents the assets, liabilities and net assets of the proprietary funds. It is presented in a classified format. This does not mean that it is top secret. It means that current assets are presented separately from noncurrent assets and current liabilities are presented separately from long-term liabilities. Generally, a current asset is an asset that is cash or will be turned into cash within a one-year period. A current liability is a liability that is expected to be paid within one year. As can be implied from the classification requirement, since proprietary funds use the accrual basis of accounting and the economic resources measurement focus, the statement of net assets includes long-term assets and liabilities.

The net assets presented in the statement of net assets are categorized as invested in capital assets, net of related debt, restricted, and unrestricted, similar to the presentation discussed earlier in the chapter on the government-wide statement of net assets. Again, the invested in capital assets, net of related debt represents the book value of capital assets purchased or constructed with debt (book value is the cost less accumulated depreciation) reduced by the amount of debt outstanding that was used to purchase or construct the assets. Where there are different types of restrictions on net assets (such as restricted for debt service or restricted for capital programs), the restricted asset amount should disclose the amounts that are restricted for each major type of restriction. Exhibit 4.7 provides an example of the proprietary funds statement of net assets.

EXHIBIT 4.7 Proprietary funds classified statement of net assets

City of Anywhere
Statement of Net Assets
Proprietary Funds
June 30, 20XX

| | Enterprise Funds | | | |
	Water and sewer	Electric utility	Total	Internal service funds
Assets				
Current assets:				
Cash and cash equivalents	$xx,xxx	$xx,xxx	$xx,xxx	$xx,xxx
Investments	--	--	--	xx,xxx
Receivables, net	xx,xxx	xx,xxx	xx,xxx	xx,xxx
Due from other governments	xx,xxx	--	xx,xxx	--
Inventories	xx.xxx	--	xx.xxx	xx.xxx
Total current assets	xx.xxx	xx.xxx	xx.xxx	xx.xxx

Noncurrent assets:				
Restricted cash and cash equivalents	--	xx,xxx	xx,xxx	--
Capital assets:				
Land and improvements	xx,xxx	xx,xxx	xx,xxx	--
Construction in progress	xx,xxx	--	xx,xxx	--
Distribution and collection systems	xx,xxx	--	xx,xxx	--
Buildings and equipment	xx,xxx	xx,xxx	xx,xxx	xx,xxx
Less accumulated depreciation	(xx,xxx)	(xx,xxx)	(xx,xxx)	(xx,xxx)
Total noncurrent assets	xx,xxx	xx,xxx	xx,xxx	xx,xxx
Total assets	xx,xxx	xx,xxx	xx,xxx	xx,xxx
Liabilities				
Current liabilities:				
Accounts payable	xx,xxx	xx,xxx	xx,xxx	xx,xxx
Due to other funds	xx,xxx	--	xx,xxx	xx,xxx
Compensated absences	xx,xxx	xx,xxx	xx,xxx	xx,xxx
Claims and judgments	--	--	--	xx,xxx
Bonds, notes, and loans payable	xx,xxx	xx,xxx	xx,xxx	xx,xxx
Total current liabilities	xx,xxx	xx,xxx	xx,xxx	xx,xxx
Noncurrent liabilities:				
Compensated absences	xx,xxx	xx,xxx	xx,xxx	--
Claims and judgments	xx,xxx	xx,xxx	xx,xxx	xx,xxx
Bonds, notes, and loans payable	xx,xxx	xx,xxx	xx,xxx	--
Total noncurrent liabilities	xx,xxx	xx,xxx	xx,xxx	xx,xxx
Total liabilities	xx,xxx	xx,xxx	xx,xxx	xx,xxx
Net Assets				
Invested in capital assets, net of related debt	xx,xxx	xx,xxx	xx,xxx	xx,xxx
Restricted for debt service	--	xx,xxx	xx,xxx	--
Unrestricted	xx,xxx	xx,xxx	xx,xxx	xx,xxx
Total net assets	$xx,xxx	$xx,xxx	$xx,xxx	$xx,xxx

The statement of revenues, expenses, and changes in net assets for proprietary funds is the operating statement for these funds. It includes the following main categories of activities: operating revenues, operating expenses, and nonoperating revenues and expenses. Operating revenues are listed by the source of the revenues, which in the case of proprietary funds is usually charges for services. Operating expenses are listed by the main types of expenses incurred by the funds. Sometimes this categorization of expenses is referred to as the natural classification, such as personnel costs, rent, utilities, and so on. (Remember this is different from the governmental fund statement of revenues, expenditures, and changes in funds balance, in which expenditures are categorized by program, such as public safety, social services, education, etc.) The nonoperating revenues and expenses category includes, generally, investment income and interest expense. After the total of nonoperating expenses, proprietary funds report any capital contributions that they have received, usually from the governmental funds of the government. Previous to GASBS 34, these capital contributions were added directly to the net assets of proprietary funds. In other words, they did not appear in the calculation of the change in net assets for the year, which many equate to the bottom line of the proprietary fund. Using the GASBS 34 reporting model, these capital contributions, while not considered operating revenues, are included in the calculation of the change in net assets for the year, meaning that they are included in the bottom line of the proprietary fund.

Expert Tip In considering whether a proprietary fund makes money from its activities, the financial statement reader needs to consider that capital contributions from the government are not the same as revenues earned from charges for services. To see whether the proprietary fund is making or losing money from its activities, removing the amount of capital contributions as an addition to the net assets of the proprietary fund presents what many might argue is a better picture of the results of the activities of the proprietary fund.

Note also that the change in net assets displayed on the statement of revenues, expenses, and changes in net assets added to (or subtracted from) the beginning net assets for the fiscal year (which are the ending net assets of the previous fiscal year) equals the ending net assets, which must be the same as the net assets at the end of the fiscal year reported on the statement of net assets. An example of the statement of revenues, expenses, and changes in net assets for proprietary funds is presented in Exhibit 4.8.

Expert Tip It may appear strange that sometimes the word "expenditures" is used and sometimes the word "expenses" is used on an operating statement to represent what appears on the surface to be the same thing. Actually, there is a distinction. The term "expenditure" is used when the modified accrual basis of accounting and current financial resources measurement focus are used. Therefore, governmental fund financial statements report expenditures. The term "expense" is used when the accrual basis of accounting and the economic resources measurement focus are used. Therefore, proprietary fund financial statements and the government-wide financial statements report expenses.

EXHIBIT 4.8 Proprietary funds statement of revenues, expenses, and changes in fund net assets

City of Anywhere
Statement of Revenues, Expenses, and Changes in Fund Net Assets
Proprietary Funds
For the Year Ended June 30, 20XX

| | *Enterprise Funds* | | | |
	Water and sewer	*Electric utility*	*Total*	*Internal service funds*
Operating Revenues				
Charges for services	$xx,xxx	$xx,xxx	$xx,xxx	$xx,xxx
Miscellaneous	--	xx,xxx	xx,xxx	xx,xxx
Total operating revenues	xx,xxx	xx,xxx	xx,xxx	xx,xxx
Operating Expenses				
Personal services	xx,xxx	xx,xxx	xx,xxx	xx,xxx
Contractual services	xx,xxx	xx,xxx	xx,xxx	xx,xxx
Utilities	xx,xxx	xx,xxx	xx,xxx	xx,xxx
Repairs and maintenance	xx,xxx	xx,xxx	xx,xxx	xx,xxx
Other supplies and expenses	xx,xxx	xx,xxx	xx,xxx	xx,xxx
Insurance claims and expenses	--	--	--	xx,xxx
Depreciation	xx,xxx	xx,xxx	xx,xxx	xx,xxx
Total operating expenses	xx,xxx	xx,xxx	xx,xxx	xx,xxx
Operating income (loss)	xx,xxx	(xx,xxx)	xx,xxx	(xx,xxx)
Nonoperating Revenues (Expenses)				
Interest and investment revenue	xx,xxx	xx,xxx	xx,xxx	xx,xxx
Miscellaneous revenue	--	xx,xxx	xx,xxx	xx,xxx
Interest expense	(xx,xxx)	(xx,xxx)	(xx,xxx)	(xx,xxx)
Miscellaneous expense	--	(xx,xxx)	(xx,xxx)	(xx,xxx)
Total nonoperating revenue (expenses)	(xx,xxx)	(xx,xxx)	(xx,xxx)	(xx,xxx)
Income (loss) before contributions and transfers	xx,xxx	(xx,xxx)	xx,xxx	(xx,xxx)
Capital contributions	xx,xxx	--	xx,xxx	xx,xxx
Transfers in	--	--	--	xx,xxx
Transfers out	(xx,xxx)	(xx,xxx)	(xx,xxx)	(xx,xxx)
Change in net assets	xx,xxx	(xx,xxx)	xx,xxx	(xx,xxx)
Total net assets—beginning	xx,xxx	xx,xxx	xx,xxx	xx,xxx
Total net assets—ending	$xx,xxx	$xx,xxx	$xx,xxx	$xx,xxx

The statement of cash flows is a type of financial statement that has not been mentioned so far in this book. While the names are different, each of the financial statements described to this point can be categorized as either a balance sheet or an income statement. The cash flow statement is really a completely different type of statement that provides information about proprietary funds' inflows and outflows of cash. Since the cash flow statement has received virtually no attention to this point, the following paragraphs will explain what the statement is and how it should be read. Exhibit 4.9 presents an example of proprietary funds' statement of cash flows. Readers who are familiar with cash flow statements from commercial enterprises will notice that the cash flow statements prepared by governments are quite similar, with two important differences. These main differences are that governments must always prepare the statement on the "direct method," and capital activities are reported in two categories—capital and noncapital. Both of these differences will be discussed later in this section.

Expert Tip It may seem that the cash flow statement does not appear often in government financial statements, because it relates only to proprietary funds. In practice, many public authorities that issue separate financial statements use proprietary fund accounting, and cash flow statements will be found in these stand-alone financial statements for these types of entities. It is interesting to note that most times, these entities using proprietary fund accounting are reported as discretely presented component units (explained in Chapter 5) that appear only in the government-wide financial statements. Since there is no cash flow statement as part of the government-wide financial statements, there would be no cash flow statement for these entities when reporting as part of the primary government's financial statements. However, when these entities issue their own financial statements, they fall within the requirements of proprietary fund accounting, and a statement of cash flows would be required in their separately issued financial statements.

EXHIBIT 4.9 Proprietary funds statement of cash flows

City of Anywhere
Statement of Cash Flows
Proprietary Funds
For the Year Ended June 30, 20XX

	Enterprise Funds			Internal service funds
	Water and sewer	Electric utility	Total	
Cash Flows from Operating Activities				
Receipts from customers	$xx,xxx	$ xx,xxx	$xx,xxx	$ xx,xxx
Payments to suppliers	(xx,xxx)	(xx,xxx)	(xx,xxx)	(xx,xxx)
Payments to employees	(xx,xxx)	(xx,xxx)	(xx,xxx)	(xx,xxx)
Internal activity—payments to other funds	(xx,xxx)	--	(xx,xxx)	(xx,xxx)
Claims paid	--	--	--	(xx,xxx)
Other receipts (payments)	(xx,xxx)	--	(xx,xxx)	xx,xxx
Net cash provided by operating activities	xx,xxx	xx,xxx	xx,xxx	xx,xxx
Cash Flows from Noncapital Financing Activities				
Operating subsidies and transfers to other funds	(xx,xxx)	(xx,xxx)	(xx,xxx)	xx,xxx
Cash Flows from Capital and Related Financing Activities				
Proceeds from capital debt	xx,xxx	xx,xxx	xx,xxx	--
Capital contributions	xx,xxx	--	xx,xxx	--
Purchases of capital assets	(xx,xxx)	(xx,xxx)	(xx,xxx)	(xx,xxx)
Principal paid on capital debt	(xx,xxx)	(xx,xxx)	(xx,xxx)	(xx,xxx)
Interest paid on capital debt	(xx,xxx)	(xx,xxx)	(xx,xxx)	(xx,xxx)
Other receipts (payments)	--	xx,xxx	xx,xxx	xx,xxx
Net cash (used) by capital and related financing activities	(xx,xxx)	(xx,xxx)	(xx,xxx)	(xx,xxx)
Cash Flows from Investing Activities				
Proceeds from sales of investments	--	--	--	xx,xxx
Interest and dividends	xx,xxx	xx,xxx	xx,xxx	xx,xxx
Net cash provided by investing activities	xx,xxx	xx,xxx	xx,xxx	xx,xxx
Net (decrease) in cash and cash equivalents	(xx,xxx)	(xx,xxx)	(xx,xxx)	(xx,xxx)
Balances—beginning of the year	xx,xxx	xx,xxx	xx,xxx	xx,xxx
Balances—end of the year)	$xx,xxx	$ xx,xxx	$xx,xxx	$ xx,xxx
Reconciliation of operating income (loss) to net cash provided by operating activities:				
Operating income (loss)	$xx,xxx	$(xx,xxx)	$xx,xxx	$(xx,xxx)
Adjustments to reconcile operating income to net cash provided by operating activities:				
Depreciation expense	xx,xxx	xx,xxx	xx,xxx	xx,xxx

Change in assets and liabilities:				
Receivables, net	xx,xxx	xx,xxx	xx,xxx	xx,xxx
Inventories	xx,xxx	--	xx,xxx	xx,xxx
Accounts and other payables	(xx,xxx)	(xx,xxx)	(xx,xxx)	xx,xxx
Accrued expenses	(xx,xxx)	xx,xxx	(xx,xxx)	(xx,xxx)
Net cash provided by operating activities	$xx,xxx	$ xx,xxx	$xx,xxx	$ xx,xxx

Noncash capital financing activities:
Capital assets of $xx,xxx were acquired through contributions from developers.

Information about cash receipts and disbursements presented in a statement of cash flows is designed to help the reader of the financial statements assess (1) an entity's ability to generate future net cash flows, (2) its ability to meet its obligations as they come due, (3) its needs for external financing, (4) the reasons for differences between operating income or net income, if operating income is not separately identified on the operating statement, and (5) the effects of the entity's financial position on both its cash and its noncash investing, capital, and financing transactions during the period.

While a statement of cash flows refers to and focuses on cash, included in the definition of the term *cash* for purposes of preparing the statement are cash equivalents. Cash equivalents are short-term, liquid investments that are so close to cash in characteristics that for purposes of preparing the statement of cash flows, they should be treated as if they were cash. *Cash equivalents* are defined as short-term, highly liquid investments that are

- Readily convertible to known amounts of cash
- So near their maturity that they present insignificant risk of changes in value because of changes in interest rates

In general, only those investments with original maturities of three months or less are considered to meet this definition. Common examples of cash equivalents are Treasury bills, commercial paper, certificates of deposit, money-market funds, and cash management pools.

A statement of cash flows classifies cash receipts and disbursements into the following categories:

- Cash flows from operating activities
- Cash flows from noncapital financing activities
- Cash flows from capital and related financing activities
- Cash flows from investing activities

The following paragraphs provide guidance on how transactions are classified into these categories and provide examples of the types of cash inflows and outflows that should be classified.

Cash flows from operating activities. Operating activities generally result from providing services and producing and delivering goods. On the other hand, operating activities include all transactions and other events that are not defined as capital and related financing, noncapital financing, or investing activities, and therefore could be viewed as a "catchall" for transactions that don't meet the definition of the other cash flow classifications. Cash flows from operating activities are generally the cash effects of transactions and other events that enter into the determination of operating income.

The following are examples of cash inflows from operating activities:

- Cash inflows from sales of goods and services, including receipts from collection of accounts receivable and both short- and long-term notes receivable arising from those sales
- Cash receipts from grants for specific activities considered to be operating activities of the grantor government (A grant agreement of this type is considered to be essentially the same as a contract for services.)
- Cash receipts from other funds for reimbursement of operating transactions
- All other cash receipts that do not result from transactions defined as capital and related financing, noncapital financing, or investing activities

Some examples of cash outflows from operating activities are the following:

- Cash payments to acquire materials for providing services and manufacturing goods for resale, including principal payments on accounts payable and both short- and long-term notes payable to suppliers for those materials or goods
- Cash payments to other suppliers for other goods or services
- Cash payments to employees for services
- Cash payments for grants to other governments or organizations for specific activities considered to be operating activities of the grantor government
- Cash payments for taxes, duties, fines, and other fees or penalties
- All other cash payments that do not result from transactions defined as capital and related financing, noncapital financing, or investing activities

Cash flows from noncapital financing activities. As its title indicates, cash flows from noncapital financing activities include borrowing money for purposes other than to acquire, construct, or improve capital assets and repaying those amounts borrowed, including interest. This category should include proceeds from all borrowings, including revenue anticipation notes not clearly attributable to the acquisition, construction, or improvement of capital assets, regardless of the form of the borrowing.

The following are examples of cash inflows from noncapital financing activities:

- Proceeds from bonds, notes, and other short- or long-term borrowing not clearly attributable to the acquisition, construction, or improvement of capital assets
- Cash receipts from grants or subsidies (such as those provided to finance operating deficits), except those specifically restricted for capital purposes and specific activities that are considered to be operating activities of the grantor government
- Cash received from property and other taxes collected for the governmental enterprise and not specifically restricted for capital purposes

Examples of cash outflows for noncapital purposes include the following:

- Repayments of amounts borrowed for purposes other than acquiring, constructing, or improving capital assets
- Interest payments to lenders and other creditors on amounts borrowed or credit extended for purposes other than acquiring, constructing, or improving capital assets
- Cash paid as grants or subsidies to other governments or organizations, except those for specific activities that are considered to be operating activities for the grantor government
- Cash paid to other funds, except for interfund services

Cash flows from capital and related financing activities. This classification of cash flows includes those cash flows for (1) acquiring and disposing of capital assets used in providing services or producing goods, (2) borrowing money for acquiring, constructing, or improving capital assets and repaying the amounts borrowed, including interest, and (3) paying for capital assets obtained from vendors on credit.

The following are examples of cash inflows from capital and related financing activities:

- Proceeds from issuing or refunding bonds, mortgages, notes, and other short- or long-term borrowing clearly attributable to the acquisition, construction, or improvement of capital assets
- Receipts from capital grants awarded to the governmental enterprise
- Receipts from contributions made by other funds, other governments, and the cost of acquiring, constructing, or improving capital assets
- Receipts from sales of capital assets and the proceeds from insurance on capital assets that are stolen or destroyed
- Receipts from special assessments or property and other taxes levied specifically to finance the construction, acquisition, or improvement of capital assets

Examples of cash outflows for capital and related financing activities include the following:

- Payments to acquire, construct, or improve capital assets
- Repayments or refundings of amounts borrowed specifically to acquire, construct, or improve capital assets
- Other principal payments to vendors who have extended credit to the governmental enterprise directly for purposes of acquiring, constructing, or improving capital assets
- Cash payments to lenders and other creditors for interest directly related to acquiring, constructing, or improving capital assets

Cash flows from investing activities. The final category of cash flows is cash flows from investing activities. Investing activities include buying and selling debt and equity instruments and making and collecting loans (except loans considered part of the governmental enterprise's operating activities, as described above.)

The following are examples of cash inflows from investing activities:

- Receipts from collections of loans (except program loans) made by the governmental enterprise and sales of the debt instruments of other entities (other than cash equivalents) that were purchased by the governmental enterprise
- Receipts from sales of equity instruments and from returns on the investments in those instruments
- Interest and dividends received as returns on loans (except program loans), debt instruments of other entities, equity securities, and cash management or investment pools
- Withdrawals from investment pools that the governmental enterprise is not using as demand accounts

Examples of cash outflows that should be categorized as cash flows from investing activities include the following:

- Disbursements for making loans (except program loans) made by the governmental enterprise and payments to acquire debt instruments of other entities (other than cash equivalents)
- Payments to acquire equity instruments
- Deposits into investment pools that the governmental enterprise is not using as demand accounts

Statement No. 34 of the GASB requires that the direct method be used for reporting cash flows from operating activities. The direct method reports the major classes of gross cash receipts and gross cash payments; the sum (the total receipts less the total payments) equals the net cash provided by operating activities. The term *net cash used by* operating activities should be used if the total of the gross cash payments exceeds the amount of gross cash receipts.

The other method for reporting cash flows is known as the "indirect" method and is not permitted for use by governments in preparing cash flow statements. (Commercial entities have the option of using either the direct method or the indirect method, with the indirect method the one used most often.) The indirect method determines cash provided or used by operations by starting out with the "net income" amount and backing into the cash that would have been provided or used by operations in a manner similar to the reconciliation discussed in the next paragraph.

When using the direct method as described above, the statement of cash flows should also present a reconciliation between the net cash flows provided or used by operations with the amount of net operating income. This reconciliation requires adjusting operating income to remove the effects of depreciation, amortization, or other deferrals of past operating cash receipts and payments, such as changes during the period in inventory, deferred revenue, and similar accounts. In addition, accruals of expected future operating cash receipts and payments must be reflected, including changes in receivables and payables.

While the above discussion may seem complicated, keep in mind that the statement of cash flows is basically concerned with displaying cash inflows and outflows in the four categories described above. What simplifies the reading of the statement of cash flows is that it deals with a relatively simple concept—cash coming into the government and cash going out of the government. There is no accounting basis or measure focus to worry about.

Fiduciary Funds

The final set of fund financial statements left to discuss are the fiduciary fund financial statements. Remember from Chapter 3 that fiduciary funds include pension (and other employee benefit) trust funds, investment trust funds, private-purpose trust funds, and agency funds. There are two fiduciary fund financial statements:

1. Statement of fiduciary net assets
2. Statement of changes in fiduciary net assets

The fiduciary fund financial statements present a separate column for each fund type. For simplicity's sake, Exhibits 4.10 and 4.11 provide examples of these two statements using only the pension (and other employee benefit) trust fund and the agency fund.

EXHIBIT 4.10 Statement of fiduciary net assets

City of Anywhere
Fiduciary Funds
Statement of Fiduciary Funds
June 30, 20XX
(in thousands)

	Pension and other employee benefit trust funds	Agency fund
Assets		
Cash and cash equivalents	$xx,xxx	$xx,xxx
Receivables:		
Receivable for investment securities sold	xx,xxx	--
Accrued interest and dividend receivable	xx,xxx	--
Investments:		
Other short-term investments	xx,xxx	--
Debt securities	xx,xxx	xx,xxx
Equity securities	xx,xxx	--
Guaranteed investment contracts	xx,xxx	--
Mutual funds	xx,xxx	--
Collateral from securities lending transactions	xx,xxx	--
Due from other funds	xx,xxx	--
Other	xx,xxx	xx,xxx
Total assets	xx,xxx	xx,xxx
Liabilities		
Accounts payable and accrued liabilities	xx,xxx	xx,xxx
Payable for investment securities purchased	xx,xxx	--
Accrued benefits payable	xx,xxx	--
Due to other funds	xx,xxx	--
Securities lending transactions	xx,xxx	--
Other	xx,xxx	xx,xxx
Total liabilities	xx,xxx	xx,xxx
Net Assets		
Held in trust for benefit payments	$xx,xxx	$___ --

EXHIBIT 4.11 Fiduciary funds statement of changes in fiduciary net assets

City of Anywhere
Fiduciary Funds
Statement of Changes in Fiduciary Net Assets
For the Year Ended June 30, 20XX

	Pension and other employee benefit trust funds
Additions	
Contributions:	
Member contributions	$xx,xxx
Employer contributions	xx,xxx
Total contributions	xx,xxx
Investment income:	
Interest income	xx,xxx
Dividend income	xx,xxx
Net depreciation in fair value of investments	(xx,xxx)
Less investment expenses	xx,xxx
Investment loss, net	(xx,xxx)
Payments from other funds	xx,xxx
Other	xx,xxx
Total additions	(xx,xxx)
Deductions	
Benefit payments and withdrawals	xx,xxx
Payments to other funds	xx,xxx
Administrative expenses	xx,xxx
Total deductions	xx,xxx
Decrease in plan net assets	(xx,xxx)
Net Assets	
Held in trust for benefit payments	
Beginning of year	xx,xxx
End of year	$xx,xxx

In reviewing these two sample statements, the reader may think that the column for agency funds was mistakenly left off the statement of changes in fiduciary net assets. This is not the case. The net assets of agency funds are always zero. The agency fund's assets always equal its liabilities because whatever assets it holds are owed back to someone or some organization. Whatever the assets of an agency fund are at year-end, they are reported, along with the corresponding liability, on the statement of fiduciary net assets. No activity is displayed for agency funds on the statement of changes in fiduciary funds net assets.

Keep in mind that the assets, liabilities, and changes in net assets for fiduciary funds are reported only in these fiduciary fund financial statements. They are not included in the government-wide financial statements. The reason is that they are "other people's money" and do not represent assets or liabilities of the government.

Notes to the Financial Statements

The notes to the financial statements are an important part of the financial statements. They are designed to provide the reader with information that is useful in understanding the basic financial statements and to provide information that is not evident from the financial statements. It is hard, if not impossible, to read and understand financial statements without reading the notes. Unfortunately, the notes to the financial statements of governments tend to be very long and very complex. My friends at the GASB will be mad at me, but, as the saying goes, the GASB never saw a disclosure that they didn't like. In other words, the recent trend in note disclosure is an increase in disclosure requirements rather than a decrease in disclosure requirements.

To understand the notes to the financial statements, the reader really needs to understand the accounting concepts that underlie the basic financial statements as well as the accounting principles that apply to specialized areas, such as accounting for leases, pensions, landfill closure costs, derivatives, and so on. Hopefully, the discussion of accounting principles presented throughout this book will help the reader plow through the notes to government financial statements.

Exhibit 4.12 provides a listing of some of the disclosure items from the GASB's Codification of its accounting and financial reporting standards that should convey a good sense of the information that can be learned from the notes to the financial statements.

Exhibit 4.12 GASB Codification listing of topics included in the notes to the financial statements

I. Summary of significant accounting policies (including departures from GAAP, if any)

    A. Description of the government-wide financial statements and exclusion of fiduciary activities and similar component units

B. A brief description of the component units of the financial reporting entity and their relationships to the primary government. This should include a discussion of the criteria for including component units in the financial reporting entity and how the component units are reported. Also include information about how the separate financial statements for the individual component units may be obtained. In component unit separate reports, identification of the primary government in whose financial report the component unit is included and a description of its relationship to the primary government.

C. Basis of presentation—government-wide financial statements

1. Governmental and business-type activities, major component units
2. Policy for applying FASB pronouncements issued after November 30, 1989, to business-type activities
3. Policy for eliminating internal activity
4. Effect of component units with differing fiscal year-ends

D. Basis of presentation—fund financial statements

1. Major and nonmajor governmental and enterprise funds, internal service funds, and fiduciary funds by fund type
2. Descriptions of activities accounted for in the major funds, internal service fund type, and fiduciary fund types
3. Policy for applying FASB pronouncements issued after November 30, 1989, to enterprise funds
4. Interfund eliminations in fund financial statements not apparent from headings

E. Basis of accounting.

1. Accrual—government-wide financial statements

     2. Modified accrual—governmental fund financial statements, including the length of time used to define *available* for purposes of revenue recognition

     3. Accrual—proprietary and fiduciary fund statements

F. Assets, liabilities, and net assets and fund balances described in the order of appearance in the statements of net assets/balance sheet

     1. Definition of cash and cash equivalents used in the proprietary fund statement of cash flows

     2. Disclosure of valuation bases

     3. Capitalization policy, estimated useful lives of capital assets

     4. Description of the modified approach for reporting infrastructure assets (if used)

     5. Significant or unusual accounting treatment for material account balances or transactions

     6. Policy regarding whether to first apply restricted or unrestricted resources when an expense is incurred for purposes for which both restricted and unrestricted net assets are available

G. Revenues, expenditures/expense

     1. Types of transactions included in program revenues in the government-wide statement of net assets

     2. Policy for allocating indirect expense to functions in the government-wide statement of activities

     3. Unusual or significant accounting policy for material revenue, expenditures, and expenses

     4. Property tax revenue recognition

     5. Vacation, sick leave, and other compensated absences

     6. Policy for defining operating revenues and operating expenses in proprietary fund statements or revenues, expenses, and changes in fund net assets

II.   Stewardship, compliance, and accountability

A. Significant violations of finance-related legal and contractual provisions and actions taken to address such
violations
B. Deficit fund balance or fund net assets of individual
funds

III. Detail notes on all activities and funds

A. Assets

1. Cash deposits and pooling of cash and investments
2. Investments, including discussion of various risks
3. Reverse repurchase agreements
4. Securities lending transactions
5. Receivable balances
6. Property taxes
7. Due from other governments—grants receivable
8. Required disclosures about capital assets

B. Liabilities

1. Payable balances
2. Pension plan obligations and postemployment
benefits other than pension benefits
3. Other employee benefits
4. Construction and other significant commitments
5. Claims and judgments
6. Lease obligations (capital and operating)
7. Short-term debt and liquidity
8. Long-term debt

a. Description of individual bond issues and
leases outstanding
b. Required disclosures about long-term liabilities
c. Summary of debt service requirements to maturity
d. Terms of interest rate changes for variable-rate
debt

e.   Disclosure of legal debt margin
f.   Bonds authorized but unissued
g.   Synopsis of revenue bond covenants
h.   Special assessment debt and related activities
i.   Debt Refundings and extinguishments
j.   Demand bonds
k.   Bond, tax, and revenue anticipation notes

9. Landfill closure and postclosure care

C. Interfund receivables and payables and interfund elim-
    inations
D. Revenues and expenditures/expenses

1. On-behalf payments for fringe benefits and sala-
    ries
2. Significant transactions that are either unusual or
    infrequent, but not within the control of manage-
    ment

E. Donor-restricted endowment disclosures
F. Interfund transfers
G. Encumbrances outstanding

IV.   Segment information—enterprise funds
V.   Individual major component unit disclosures (if not re-
      ported on the face of the government-wide statements or
      in combining statements)
VI.   The nature of the primary government's accountability for
      related organizations
VII. Summary disclosure of significant contingencies

A. Litigation
B. Federally assisted programs—compliance audits

VIII. Significant effects of subsequent events

REQUIRED SUPPLEMENTARY INFORMATION

Required supplementary information (RSI) consists of schedules, statistical data, and other information that the GASB has determined are an essential part of financial reporting and should be presented with, but not as a part of, the basic financial statements of a governmental entity. The rules set by the GASB as to what is reported as RSI are specific. In other words, the government does not have the option to include other information that it would like to include in RSI. The RSI under current accounting standards consists of the following:

- Management's Discussion and Analysis
- Budgetary comparison schedules
- Information on the modified approach for reporting infrastructure assets
- Employee benefit-related information

Each of these components of RSI will be discussed briefly in the following sections.

Management's Discussion and Analysis

Management's Discussion and Analysis (MD&A) was discussed earlier in this chapter. It is considered by the GASB to be RSI and should precede the presentation of the basic financial statements.

Budgetary Comparison Schedules

Budgetary comparison statements are required to be presented for certain funds. While governments have the option to include this information as a statement within the fund financial statements, the GASB prefers that this information be included in RSI. The funds required to present budgetary comparison schedules are the general fund and each major special revenue fund that has a legally adopted budget.

The budgetary comparison schedules should include the adopted budget amounts, the final budget amounts (which is the budget after whatever modifications have been made), and the actual results. It is important to note that the actual results are presented on whatever basis of accounting is used by the budget. Usually this is not the modified accrual basis of accounting, because governments' budgets often reflect certain revenues and expenditures differently from what would be required by GAAP. Yes, this is a *third* way to present the *same* information (budgetary basis) in addition to the accrual basis of accounting used in the government-wide financial statements and the modified accrual basis of accounting used in the fund financial statements. (Remember that the general fund and special revenue funds are considered governmental funds.) Assuming that the budgetary basis of accounting is different from the modified accrual basis for a fund under GAAP, the government has to reconcile the two different accounting bases either as a separate schedule or as a note to the RSI.

Information on the Modified Approach for Reporting Infrastructure Assets

Chapter 7, which covers capital assets, will describe the requirement information that needs to be included in RSI when the modified approach for reporting infrastructure assets is used in lieu of depreciating those assets.

Employee Benefit-Related Information

Governments that sponsor pension plans and other postemployment benefit plans in which they are the sole employer are required to present certain information as RSI that helps readers to understand the funded status of those pension plans. (These plans will be discussed in greater detail in Chapter 8.) The information presented should include, for the most recent and two preceding actuarial valuations of the plan, the following:

- The actuarial valuation date, the actuarial value of the plan's assets, the actuarial accrued liability, the total unfunded liability, the actuarial value of assets as a percentage of the actuarial accrued liability, the annual payroll for the

employees covered by the plan, and the ratio of the un-funded actuarial liability to the annual covered payroll
- Factors that affect the identification of trends in these amounts, including changes in benefit provisions, the size or composition of the population covered by the plan, as well as changes in the actuarial assumptions

COMPREHENSIVE ANNUAL FINANCIAL REPORT

The general-purpose financial statements discussed so far in this chapter reflect the minimum financial reporting requirements for governments presenting financial statements in accordance with GAAP. Often these are the financial statements included in Official Statements, which are the documents prepared when governments are selling debt to the public. There is a broader level of reporting for governments, however, known as the comprehensive annual financial report, commonly called the CAFR. The CAFR includes the general-purpose financial statements, and a great deal more information. The CAFR is the document that the GASB prefers governments to use for their external financial reporting, although as described above, that does not preclude a government from issuing stand-alone general-purpose financial statements. The GASB defines the CAFR to include the following:

- Introductory section
- Financial section
- Statistical tables

Each of these components of the CAFR will be described in the following sections.

Expert Tip Many readers may be confused about the role of the Government Finance Officers Association (GFOA) as to the requirements of the CAFR. The GFOA administers an awards program known as the Certificate of Achievement for Excellence in Financial Reporting. Governments may choose to annually submit their CAFRs to the GFOA, and if the CAFR meets the GFOA's requirements, a Certificate of Achievement will be awarded to the government for that year's CAFR. The GFOA's requirements go beyond the GAAP requirements of the GASB, not so much as to substantive content, but as to the details of presentation of the CAFR. Accordingly, governments desiring to obtain the GFOA Certificate of Achievement must meet not only the requirements of the GASB, but also those of the GFOA. The GFOA's guidelines are published in its *Governmental Accounting, Auditing, and Financial Reporting* publication, commonly referred to as the GAAFR. In practice, even governments that do not participate in the Certificate of Achievement program can still look to the GAAFR for helpful guidance on accounting and financial reporting issues.

The sections that follow also include some of the more common requirements of the GAAFR, since these are the common disclosures likely to be found in a government's CAFR.

Introductory Section

The introductory section is generally excluded from the scope of the independent audit and includes the following:

- *Report cover and title page*
- *Table of contents* listing the various statements and schedules included in the CAFR, broken down by location in the introductory, financial, and statistical sections
- *Letter of transmittal.* The GASB requires that the introductory section include a letter of transmittal, but the GAAFR provides significant guidance on the topics to include in the letter of transmittal.

The following are the basic requirements for the letter of transmittal as contained in the GAAFR:

- *Formal transmittal of the CAFR.* This section is the actual communication of the CAFR to its intended users. For example, the letter of transmittal might cite the legal requirements for preparing the CAFR and then indicate that the submission of the CAFR is in fulfillment of those requirements. Other topics that are suggested for inclusion are

- Management's framework of internal controls
- Independent audit of the financial statements, including limitations inherent in a financial statement audit
- Reference to other independent auditor reports, such as those resulting from a single audit of federal awards programs
- Direction of readers' attention to the MD&A contained in the financial section of the CAFR

- *Profile of the government.* This would include a brief description of the government's structure and the types of services it provides. This section might also briefly discuss the inclusion of component units and the budget process.
- *Information useful in assessing the government's financial position.* The GAAFR distinguishes financial condition from financial position in that financial condition focuses on both existing and future resources and claims on those resources. Because this future-looking information is generally precluded from inclusion in the MD&A, the letter of transmittal should serve as a vehicle to discuss these subjective factors affecting financial condition.
- *Awards and acknowledgements.* This would include any Certificate of Achievement from the GFOA received by the previous year's CAFR, as well as other awards and acknowledgments of those contributing to the preparation of the CAFR.

The GASB encourages governments to include "other material deemed appropriate by management" in the introductory section. The GAAFR includes the following suggestions:

- A reproduction of the Certificate of Achievement on the prior year's financial statements, if this award was in fact obtained
- A list of the principal officials of the government
- An organizational chart of the government showing the assignment of responsibilities of personnel
- Audit committee letter that may be issued by a government's audit committee

Financial Section

The financial section of the CAFR is composed of these main components.

- The independent auditor's report
- Management's Discussion and Analysis
- The basic financial statements
- Required supplementary information (RSI)
- The combining and individual nonmajor fund and component unit financial statements and schedules

The following discussion provides additional detail on the independent auditor's report and the combining and individual fund financial statements and schedules. The contents of the general-purpose financial statements were described in detail in the previous sections of this chapter.

Independent Auditor's Report

The independent auditor's report should be the first item included in the financial section of the CAFR. The independent auditor should report on whether the financial statements are fairly presented in accordance with GAAP. The auditor may also provide an opinion on the combining financial statements and schedules "in relation to" the financial statements. The auditor should also indicate whether he or she has audited the other financial information in the CAFR. The independent auditor generally indicates that the information in the statistical section of the CAFR has not been audited.

Combining and Individual Nonmajor Fund and Nonmajor Component Unit Financial Statements and Schedules

The combining and individual fund financial information prepared in a CAFR focuses on information about nonmajor fund and nonmajor component unit financial information. Since the basic financial statements provide information about major funds, the combining and individual fund presentation completes the financial reporting picture by providing information about nonmajor funds and nonmajor component units. A government with a full range of fund types and component units would conceivably have the following sets of combining statements:

- Nonmajor governmental funds
- Nonmajor enterprise funds
- Internal service funds
- Private-purpose trust funds
- Pension (and other employee benefit) trust funds
- Investment trust funds
- Agency funds
- Nonmajor discretely presented component units

Statistical Tables

The third section of the CAFR is the statistical section. The statistical section provides both financial and nonfinancial information that is often very useful to investors, creditors, and other CAFR users. The statistical section presents certain information on a trend basis; that is, summary information is provided for each year in a ten-year period.

The GASB has updated the information required for the statistical section through Statement No. 44, "Economic Condition Reporting—The Statistical Section—An Amendment of NCGA Statement 1" (GASBS 44). The update was needed to include certain information that related to the current financial reporting model as well as to refresh an reevaluate the information that was previously required. The statistical schedules under GASBS 44 are grouped into the following categories:

- Financial trends information
- Revenue capacity
- Debt capacity
- Demographic and economic information
- Operating information

While the purpose of this book is not to provide a complete disclosure checklist of what is contained in the statistical section, the following discussion will give a reader a sense of the breadth of information that is available in this section. There are often many pieces of fascinating information that can be obtained from the statistical section, and a reader of a government's CAFR would do well to spend some time in looking through this information. The following are some of the types of information that you can expect to find in the statistical section. Although the reader might think that a good deal of this information is available from the financial statements, in many cases it is trend information provided for the last ten years that makes the statistical section useful.

Financial trends information

- Information about net assets—the three components of net assets (invested in capital assets, net of related debt, restricted, and unrestricted) are shown separately for governmental activities, business-type activities, and in total for the primary government.
- Information about changes in net assets, shown separate for governmental and business-type activities such as expenses by function, program revenues by category, general revenues, etc. (Basically, this information presents a summarized activities statement for the last ten years.)
- Information about governmental funds—information about fund balances and changes in fund balances, similar to that required for net assets above, for governmental funds

Revenue base

- Information about the bases on which revenue is derived shown by major component (for example, different types of real estate on which real estate taxes are based)
- Information about revenue rates (i.e., the tax rates that are applied to the revenue bases discussed above)
- Information about overlapping taxing authorities, where multiple layers of government are taxing the same base
- Principal revenue payers
- Property tax levies and collections, including trend information as to how much and when a tax levy actually is collected

Debt Capacity

- Each type of debt (general obligation bonds, revenue bonds, loans, capital leases, etc.) divided between governmental and business activities
- Ratio of total outstanding debt to total personal income and a per capita ratio of total debt outstanding
- Calculation of net general bonded debt—usually general obligation bonds less resources restricted to paying the principal of these outstanding bonds
- Ratio of general bonded debt to the total estimated actual value of taxable property
- Direct and overlapping debt which provides information about the debt of other governments that overlap the same geographic area as the reporting government (i.e., the taxpayers are supporting debt of a government outside the reporting entity of the government preparing the CAFR)
- Information about debt limitations, which provides a calculation of how close a government is to reaching the limit on debt that it may issue
- Pledged revenue coverage which essentially applies to revenue bonds and compares the amount of revenues pledged for debt service on these bonds to the principal and interest payments on this debt

Demographic and Economic Information

- Demographic and economic indicators, such as population, total personal income, per capita personal income and the unemployment rate
- Identification of the ten principal employers and number of persons they employ

Operating Information

- Number of employees by function or program
- Indicators of demand or level of service provided
- Indicators of the volume, usage, or nature of the government's capital assets

The GASB permits governments to add additional information into the statistical section, as long as it is consistent with the objectives of GASBS 44. In addition to the pure statistical information provided above, the government is also required to provide certain narrative information that is meant to assist readers in understanding this information. While normal year-to-year changes do not require explanations, governments are required to provide information about atypical trends and other anomalies that the reader might not otherwise understand. These would include changes in assumptions or accounting methods, organization restructuring, major policy changes, and other similar events.

SUMMARY

It has taken a long chapter to describe the lengthy, complex, and often difficult-to-understand financial reporting model for governments. The key to understanding this reporting model is to remember its main components (government-wide or fund financial statements) and not get lost in the details or lose sight of the broader picture of the information being presented.

CHAPTER 5

Understanding the Reporting Entity

The concept of a government's *reporting entity* is important to understand in order to understand what a government's financial statements represent. In a nutshell, the concept of reporting entities deals with determining what legal entities that are separate from the government should be included in the financial statements of the government. Outside of governmental accounting, the parallel question is what subsidiaries are included in the consolidated financial statements of the parent company. For example, The Walt Disney Company (parent company) owns several companies, including the ABC network, ESPN, and Touchstone Pictures (subsidiaries). If each of these companies is a separate legal entity, should the financial statements of the subsidiaries be combined (or consolidated, to use the correct nongovernmental term) with those of Disney when Disney prepares its own financial statements? The answer is yes. Governments need to make similar decisions as to what separate legal entities are combined with those of the government when the government prepares its financial statements.

Governments have a different basis on which to make this inclusion decision. In the private sector, the decision is based on control, which is usually determined by the amount of voting stock the parent holds in the subsidiary. Does the parent own enough stock of the subsidiary so that it controls it in a way defined in accounting rules? Governments do not hold shares of stock in their related, but legally separate, governmental entities. They need another basis for deciding whether to include another entity within their financial statements. That is what the rules described in this chapter are all about. The rules, by the way, are established by GASB Statement No. 14, "The Financial Reporting Entity," and will be discussed throughout this chapter.

BACKGROUND

Governments often create separate legal entities to perform some of the functions normally associated with or performed by government. These separate entities may themselves be governmental entities or they may be not-for-profit or for-profit organizations. Sometimes these separate organizations are created to enhance revenues or reduce debt service costs of governments. Other times, these separate organizations are created to circumvent restrictions to which the state or local government would be subject. The following are some examples of these other organizations that are commonly created by a government:

- A separate public authority that operates as a utility, such as a water and sewer authority, may be created as a separate legal entity. Because a utility such as the water and sewer authority has a predictable revenue stream (the water and sewer charges to its customers), the utility will likely be able to sell debt in the form of revenue bonds, pledging the water and sewer charge revenues to the debt service on the revenue bonds. Because of this identification of a specific revenue stream, it is likely that the revenue bonds issued by the authority will carry a lower interest rate than general obligation bonds issued by the local government.
- A housing finance authority may be created to finance the construction of moderately priced housing. The rental income on the constructed rental units can be correlated with the debt of the housing finance authority, again resulting in a lower interest cost to the government. The debt issued by the housing finance authority is likely to be issued without requiring a bond resolution approved by the voters of the jurisdiction. The existence of the housing finance authority expedites the government's flexibility as to when and how much debt it issues. In a related use of a financing agency,

the state or local government may be approaching its statutory limit on its ability to issue debt. If the housing finance authority's debt is not included in the state or local government's debt limit calculation, the state or local government avoids having the debt issued by the housing finance authority count against its debt limit, even though the state or local government may have chosen to issue the debt itself.

• In some instances, a not-for-profit organization can be invested with powers that might require a constitution or charter amendment. For example, an economic development authority may be established to buy, sell, or lease land and facilities, assist businesses within the jurisdiction, or negotiate and facilitate tax rate reductions to encourage businesses to remain in or relocate to the jurisdiction. Usually this separately incorporated entity is able to assume more powers and operate with greater flexibility than the state or local government itself.

The types and purposes of these entities continue to expand as governments seek to facilitate operations and to enter new service areas needed by their constituents. The above are but a few examples of the types of entities and areas of responsibility that the financial statement preparer and auditor are likely to encounter.

ACCOUNTABILITY FOCUS

In developing accounting principles relative to defining the reporting entity for state and local governments, the GASB focused on the concept of "accountability." The GASB has defined *accountability* as the cornerstone of governmental financial reporting because the GASB believes that financial reporting plays a major role in fulfilling government's responsibility to the public.

Despite the outward appearance of autonomy, the organizations described above are usually administered by governing bodies appointed by the elected officials of the state or local government or by the government's officials servicing in *ex officio* capacities of the created entities. These officials of the state or local government are accountable to the citizens for their public policy decisions, regardless of whether they are carried out by the state or local government itself or by the specially created entity. This broad-based notion of the accountability of government officials led the GASB to the underlying concept of the governmental financial reporting entity. GASBS 14 states that "Governmental organizations are responsible to elected governing officials at the federal, state, or local level; therefore, financial reporting by a state or local government should report the elected officials' accountability for those organizations."

Because one of the key objectives of financial reporting as defined by the GASB is accountability, it became logical for the GASB to define the financial reporting entity in terms of the accountability of the government officials (and ultimately to the elected officials that appointed these government officials). The GASB also concluded that the users of financial statements should be able to distinguish between the financial information of the primary government and its component units (these terms are discussed in more detail below).

To accomplish the objectives and goals described above, the reporting entity's financial statements should present the fund types and account groups of the primary government (including certain component units whose financial information is blended with that of the primary government, because in substance, they are part of the primary government) and provide an overview of the other component units, referred to as discretely presented component units.

FINANCIAL REPORTING ENTITY DEFINED

The GASBS 14 definition of the financial reporting entity is as follows:

> ... the financial reporting entity consists of (a) the primary government, (b) organizations for which the primary government is financially accountable, and (c) other organizations for which the nature and significance of their relationship with the primary government are such that exclusion would cause the reporting entity's financial statements to be misleading or incomplete.

Primary Government

The *primary government* is defined as a government that has a separately elected governing body; that is, one that is elected by the citizens in a general, popular election. A primary government is any state or local government (such as a municipality or county). A primary government may also be a special-purpose government, such as a school district, if it meets all of the following criteria:

- It has a separately elected governing body
- It is legally separate
- It is fiscally independent of other state and local governments (defined below)

A primary government consists of all of the organizations that make up its legal entity. This would include all funds, organizations, institutions, agencies, departments, and offices that are not legally separate. If an organization is determined to be part of the primary government, its financial information should be included with the financial information of the primary government.

It is important to note that a governmental organization that is not a primary government (including component units, joint ventures, jointly governed organizations, or other stand-alone governments) will still be the nucleus of its own reporting entity when it issues separate financial statements. These other organizations should apply the guidance of GASBS 14 as if they were a primary government when issuing separate financial statements. For example, assume that a city located on a major river establishes a separate legal entity to manage its port operations and foster shipping and other riverfront activities. The port authority is a separate legal entity, although its governing board is appointed by the city's mayor, that is, the governing board is not elected. The port authority is not a primary government.

However, assume the port authority itself sets up two additional separate legal entities: an economic development authority (to promote economic activity on the riverfront) and a souvenir shop (to raise funds as well as to publicize the riverfront activities). If these two separate entities meet the tests described in the chapter to be considered component units of the port authority, they would be included in the port authority's reporting entity, even though the port authority is not a primary government.

Component Units

Component units are organizations that are legally separate from the primary government for which the elected officials are financially accountable. A component unit may be a governmental organization (except a governmental organization that meets the definition of a primary government), a not-for-profit organization, or even a for-profit organization. In addition to qualifying organizations that meet the "financial accountability" criteria (described more fully below), a component unit can be another type of organization whose relationship with the primary government requires its inclusion in the reporting entity's financial statements. Once it is determined that the organization is a component unit included in the reporting entity, the financial statement preparer decides whether the component unit's financial information should be "blended" with that of the primary government or "discretely presented."

Financial Accountability

The GASB is careful to distinguish accountability from financial accountability. Elected officials are accountable for an organization if they appoint a voting majority of the organization's governing board. However, these appointments are sometimes not substantive because other governments, usually at a lower level, may have oversight responsibility for those officials. GASBS 14 uses the term *financial accountability* to describe the relationship that is substantive enough to warrant the inclusion of the legally separate organization in the reporting entity of another government. The criteria for determining whether a legally separate organization is financially accountable to a government, and therefore must be considered a component unit of the government's reporting entity, are

    A. The primary government is financially accountable if it appoints a voting majority of the organization's governing body, and (1) it is able to impose its will on that organization or (2) there is a potential for the organization to provide specific financial benefits to, or impose specific financial burdens on, the primary government. (In determining whether the primary government appoints a majority of the organization's board, the situation may be encountered where the members of the organization's governing body consist of the primary government's officials serving as required by law, that is, as ex officio members. While not technically "appointed" [because the individuals serve on the organization's board because their positions make them board members by law], this situation should be treated as if the individuals were actually appointed by the primary government for purposes of determining financial accountability.)

B. The primary government may be financially accountable if an organization is fiscally dependent on the primary government regardless of whether the organization has (1) a separately elected governing board, (2) a governing board appointed by a higher level of government, or (3) a jointly appointed board.

To apply these rules, governments need to understand some specific definitions of terms provided by the GASB, such as

- Appointment of a voting majority (used in A. above)
- Imposition of will (used in A. above)
- Financial benefit to or burden on the primary government (used in A. above)
- Fiscal dependency (used in B. above)

The following sections further describe these concepts as contemplated by GASBS 14.

Appointment of a voting majority. A primary government generally has a voting majority if it appoints a simple majority of the organization's governing board members. However, if more than a simple majority of the governing board is needed to approve financial decisions, the criterion for appointing the majority of the board to determine accountability has not been met.

The primary government's ability to appoint a voting majority of the organization's governing board must have substance. For example, if the primary government must appoint the governing board members from a list or slate of candidates that is very narrow and controlled by another level of government or organization, it would be difficult to argue that the primary government actually appointed a voting majority of a governing board, since the freedom of choice is so limited. A primary government's appointment ability would also not be substantive if it consisted only of confirming candidates to the governing board that were actually selected by another individual or organization.

Imposition of will. If, in addition to its ability to appoint a voting majority of an organization's governing board, a primary government is able to impose its will on the organization, the primary government is financially accountable for the organization. GASBS 14 provides guidance on when a primary government can impose its will on another organization. Generally, a primary government has the ability to impose its will on an organization if it can significantly influence the programs, projects, activities, or level of services performed or provided by the organization. Imposition of will can be demonstrated by the existence of any one of the following conditions:

- The ability to remove appointed members of the organization's governing board
- The ability to modify or approve the budget of the organization
- The ability to modify or approve rate or fee changes affecting revenues, such as water usage rate increases
- The ability to veto, overrule, or modify the decisions (other than the budget and rates or fee changes listed above) of the organization's governing body
- The ability to appoint, hire, reassign, or dismiss those persons responsible for the day-to-day operations or management of the organization

GASBS 14 acknowledges that there are other conditions that may exist that also indicate that the primary government has the capability to impose its will on another organization. As with the previously described tests, the focus should be on substance rather than on insignificant or ministerial approvals.

Financial benefit to or burden on the primary government. If the primary government appoints a voting majority of the organization's governing board and there is a potential for the organization to either provide specific financial benefits to or impose specific financial burdens on the primary government, the primary government is financially accountable for the organization.

The benefit or burden to the primary government may be demonstrated in several ways, such as legal entitlements or obligations or reflection of the benefit or burden in decisions made by the primary government or agreements between the primary government and the organization.

Any one of the following conditions could demonstrate that the primary government and the organization have a financial burden or benefit relationship:

- The primary government is legally entitled to or can otherwise access the organization's resources
- The primary government is legally obligated or has otherwise assumed the obligation to finance the deficits of, or provide financial support to, the organization
- The primary government is obligated in some manner for the debt of the organization

The financial burden or benefit may be direct or indirect. A direct financial burden or benefit occurs when the primary government is entitled to the resources or is obligated for the deficits or debts of the organization. An indirect benefit or burden exists if one or more of the primary government's component units is entitled to the resources or is obligated for the deficits or debts of the organization.

GASBS 14 provides additional guidance in applying the financial benefit and burden provisions listed above. The following paragraphs describe this guidance and highlight some considerations for the financial statement preparer.

- *Legally entitled to or can otherwise access the organization's resources.* To meet this test, the important factor to consider is whether the primary government has the ability to access the resources of the organization, not whether the primary government has actually exercised this ability by extracting resources from the organization in the past. In determining whether this ability exists, it is necessary to evaluate whether the organization would continue to exist as a going concern. In other words, if the primary government can only access the organization's assets in the event of the liquidation of the organization, it would not be considered an ability to access the resources of the organization for purposes of applying this test.

In some cases, the ability to access the assets of the organization is fairly obvious. For example, if an organization is established to administer a lottery for a state or local primary government, the primary government is likely to have easy access to the assets of the lottery authority. In fact, there are likely to be daily, weekly, or monthly transfers of revenues from the lottery authority to the primary government. However, sometimes the access to assets is less clear. For example, a state government may be able to access excess reserve funds held by a state housing finance authority. While there may be no strong precedent for the state to take the excess reserve funds from the housing finance authority, and such an event might be rare, the state's right to do so would be adequate to meet the test.

- *Legally obligated or has otherwise assumed the obligation to finance the deficits of, or provide financial support to, the organization.* It is important to note that the primary government may either be legally obligated to provide the financial support, or it may choose to be obligated to provide the financial support, for a variety of reasons. GASBS 14 provides two examples of when a primary government assumes the obligation to financially support another organization.

  - Organizations are sometimes established to provide public services financed by user charges that are not expected to be sufficient to sustain their operations. Typical examples include higher education, mass transportation, and health care services. In these cases, a public policy decision is

made to require a state or local government to provide
financial support to the organization to increase the availability and affordability of the service to a broader segment of citizens. The support from the primary government may take a number of forms, including annual
appropriations to meet operating costs, periodic capital
grants, or payments of debt service on behalf of the organization.

• A primary government may also assume the obligation to
finance the deficits of an organization. These deficits
may or may not be expected to recur annually. A financial burden exists, for the purposes of applying this test,
regardless of whether the primary government has ever
actually financed the organization's deficit, or even if the
organization has never actually had a deficit. The key is
the *obligation* to finance the deficit, not whether it has
actually occurred.

In other cases, organizations' operations are funded fully
or partially by revenues generated through tax increment financing. Legally separate development or redevelopment authorities sometimes receive the incremental taxes resulting
from tax increment financing arrangements. In this case, a
taxing government temporarily waives its right to receive the
incremental taxes from its own levy. The incremental taxes
instead are remitted to the separate organization. This type of
tax increment financing should be considered evidence of an
obligation to provide financial support to an organization
(that is, a financial burden).

• *Obligated in some manner for the debt of the organization.*
The concept of a primary government being obligated in
some manner for the debt of the organization is similar to
that of the primary government being responsible for operating deficits in determining whether the organization
should be included in the reporting entity of the primary
government. The obligation on the part of the primary government for the debt of the organization can be either expressed or implied. A primary government is considered to
be obligated in some manner for the debt of an organization
if

- It is legally obligated to assume all or part of the debt in the event of default by the organization on the debt, or
- It may take certain actions to assume secondary liability for all or part of the debt, and the primary government takes (or has given indications that it will take) those actions.

GASBS 14 notes the following conditions that would indicate that the primary government is obligated in some manner for the debt of the organization:

- The primary government is legally obligated to honor deficiencies to the extent that proceeds from other default remedies are insufficient.
- The primary government is required to temporarily cover deficiencies with its own resources until funds from the primary repayment source or other default remedies are available.
- The primary government is required to provide funding for reserves maintained by the debtor organization, or to establish its own reserve or guarantee fund for the debt.
- The primary government is authorized to provide funding for reserves maintained by the debtor organization or to establish its own reserve or guarantee fund and the primary government establishes such a fund. (If the fund is not established, the considerations of the conditions listed below in which the government "may" cover the deficiencies nevertheless provide evidence that the primary government is obligated in some manner.)
- The primary government is authorized to provide financing for a fund maintained by the debtor organization for the purpose of purchasing or redeeming the organization's debt, or to establish a similar fund of its own, and the primary government establishes such a fund.
- The debtor government explicitly indicates by contract, such as a bond agreement or offering statement, that in the event of a default, the primary government may cover deficiencies, although it has no legal obligation to do so. The bond offering statement may specifically refer to a law that authorizes the primary government to include an

appropriation in its budget to provide funds, if necessary, to honor the debt of the organization.

- Legal decisions within the state or previous actions by the primary government related to actual or potential defaults on another organization's debt make it probable that the primary government will assume responsibility for the debt in the event of default.

If the primary government appoints a voting majority of the organization's governing body and is obligated in some manner for the debt of the organization, the primary government is financially accountable for that organization.

Concept of fiscal dependency. A primary government may be fiscally accountable for another organization regardless of whether the other organization has a separately elected governing board, a board appointed by another government, or a jointly appointed board. The fiscal accountability in these cases results from the organization's fiscal dependency on the primary government. GASBS 14 describes the circumstances for each of the three examples of the origins of the governing board listed above.

1. Special-purpose governments with separately elected governing boards. Special-purpose governmental entities with separately elected governments may be fiscally dependent on a primary government. The best example of a fiscally dependent special-purpose government is a school district. For example, a school board may be separately elected; however, if the primary government approves the school board's budgets and levies taxes to fund the school district, the school district is fiscally dependent on the primary government and should be included as a component unit in the primary government's reporting entity.
2. Governmental organizations with boards appointed by another government. Fiscal dependency may also exist even when the organization's governing board is appointed by a higher-level government. Continuing with the school district example, the local school board may be appointed by state officials, although the local primary government approves the school board's budgets, autho-

rizes the school board's issuance of debt, and levies property taxes on the citizens of the primary government to financially support the school board. In this case, the school board would usually be included as a component unit of the local primary government. The school board is fiscally dependent on the local primary government, even though it does not appoint a voting majority of the members of the school board.

3. Governmental organizations with jointly appointed boards. The type of governmental entity with a jointly appointed board is often a port authority, river authority, transportation authority, or other regional government that adjoins several governments. Sometimes these governmental organizations are governed by boards in which none of the participating primary governments appoints a majority of the voting board members. If this type of governmental organization is fiscally dependent on only one of the participating primary governments, it should be included as a component unit of the reporting entity of that primary government. For example, if a port authority serves two states and is governed by a board appointed equally by the two states, and is empowered to issue debt with the substantive approval of only one of the states, the port authority should be included in the reporting entity of that state government.

Other Organizations that Are Included in the Reporting Entity

In applying the criteria and conditions that indicate financial accountability, a significant amount of judgment is required on the part of the financial statement preparer, because the breadth of variation in the "typical" governmental reporting entity is wide. In addition, GASBS 14 specifies that certain organizations should be included in the reporting entity of a primary government even if the financial accountability test is not met. These organizations should be included as component units if the nature and significance of their relationships with the primary government are such that exclusion from the financial reporting entity of the primary government would make the primary government's financial statements incomplete or misleading. Clearly, a significant amount of judgment is required for compliance with this provision by the primary government.

DISPLAY OF COMPONENT UNITS

The issue of which organizations should be included in the financial reporting entity of a state or local government is the first of a two-step process in addressing the financial statements of a state or local government. After determining which component units to include in the financial reporting entity of the government, the second step is to determine how the financial information of those component units (and their related disclosures) will be presented. This section addresses this second step of presenting the financial information of the component units as part of the financial statements of the reporting entity of the state or local government.

Overview of Reporting Component Units

An objective of the financial statements of the reporting entity should be to provide an overview of the entity based on financial accountability, while at the same time allowing financial statement users to distinguish among the financial information of the primary government and the financial information of the component units. As will be more fully described later in this chapter, some component units are so closely related to the primary government that their information is combined (i.e., blended) with that of the primary government. Other component units, which generally comprise the majority of component units, should be presented separately (i.e., discretely) from the primary government.

In addition, the determination of whether an organization is a component unit and whether it should be blended or discretely presented is a process independent of the considerations that governments make in reporting fiduciary funds. There may be organizations that do not meet the definition for inclusion in the financial reporting entity. These organizations should be reported as fiduciary funds of the primary government if the primary government has a fiduciary responsibility for them. For example, pension funds or deferred compensation plans are not evaluated as component units. Rather, they are included in a government's reporting entity because of the government's fiduciary role and responsibility.

Discrete Presentation of Component Units

Most component units will be included in the financial statements of the reporting entity using discrete presentation. The reporting entity's government-wide statement of net assets should include a column to display the combined balance sheet of the discretely presented component units. The presentation of discretely presented component units in the government-wide financial statements under GASBS 34 is discussed in Chapter 4. Discretely presented component units are presented only in the government-wide financial statements. There is no reporting of discretely presented component units at the fund level.

Similarly, the reporting entity's government-wide statement of activities should include one column to display the activities for discretely presented component units that use governmental fund accounting.

GASBS 34's requirements for providing information in the basic financial statements about component units of a reporting entity government can be met in one of three ways (note that these requirements do not apply to component units that are fiduciary in nature). These options are discussed later in this chapter.

Blended Component Units

The preceding discussion focused on the presentation and disclosures required for discretely presented component units. This section will focus first on the determination of whether a component unit's financial information should be "blended" with that of the primary government. When there are blended component units, the use of the term "primary government" is meant to refer to the reporting government *and* the blended component units.

Why Blend Some Component Units?

One of the objectives of the financial reporting for the reporting entity described earlier was to be able to distinguish the financial information of the primary government from its component units. A question arises of why this objective seems to be abandoned in order to blend certain component units so that they are less distinguishable from the primary government. The answer to this is that the GASB concluded that there are component units that, despite being legally separate from the primary government, are so intertwined with the primary government that they are, in substance, the same as the primary government. It is more useful to report these component units as part of the primary government. These component units should be reported in a manner similar to the balances and transactions of the primary government itself, a method known as "blending." This view was reinforced by GASBS 34, which made the primary government, including blended component units, the focus of financial reporting in the basic financial statements and required supplementary information.

Determination of Blended Component Units

There are two circumstances in which a component unit should be blended.

1. The component unit's governing board is substantively the same as the governing body of the primary government. *Substantively the same* means that there is sufficient representation of the primary government's entire governing body on the component unit's governing body to allow complete control of the component unit's activities. For example, the board of a city redevelopment authority may be composed entirely of the city council and the mayor, serving in an ex officio capacity. The primary government is, essentially, serving as the governing body of the component unit.
2. The component unit provides services entirely (or almost entirely) to the primary government, or otherwise exclusively (or almost exclusively) benefits the primary gov-

ernment even though it does not provide services directly to it. The nature of this type of arrangement is similar to that of an internal service fund. The goods and services are provided to the government itself, rather than to the individual citizens. GASBS 14 provides the example of a building authority created to finance the construction of office buildings for the primary government. If the component unit provides services to more than just the primary government, it should still be blended if the services provided to others are insignificant to the overall activities of the component unit. Other component units that should be blended are those that exclusively (or almost exclusively) benefit the primary government by providing services indirectly. GASBS 14 provides the example of a primary government that establishes a component unit to administer its employee benefit programs. In this case, the component unit exclusively benefits the primary government, even though the component unit provides services to the employees of the primary government, rather than to the primary government itself.

In some cases, the component units that are to be blended with the primary government have funds of different fund types. For example, a component unit may have a general fund and a capital projects fund. If they meet the definition of major funds, they would be reported as such. If they are nonmajor funds, they would be blended with those of the primary government by including them in the appropriate nonmajor fund combining statements of the primary government. In addition, since the primary government's general fund is usually the main operating fund of the reporting entity and is a focal point for users of the financial statements, the primary government's general fund should be the only general fund for the reporting entity. The general fund of a blended component unit should be reported as a special revenue fund.

Reporting Discretely Presented Component Units

The requirements for presenting information about discretely presented component units can best be described by the term "overview." (Note that this discussion does not apply to blended component units, which are presented as if part of the primary government, and component units that are fiduciary in nature, which are included only in the fund financial statements with the primary government's fiduciary funds.)

Information about each major component unit is required to be presented. Information about nonmajor component units is aggregated in one column. The requirements for reporting can be accomplished by one of three alternatives.

1. Reporting each major component unit in a separate column in the government-wide statement of net assets and statement of activities.
2. Including combining statements of major component units in the reporting entity's basic statements after the fund financial statements. Aggregate totals would then be included in the government-wide financial statements for component units, supported by this combining schedule.
3. Presenting condensed financial statements in the notes to the financial statements.

If the government selects the alternative to present component unit information in the notes, the following details are provided:

1. Condensed statement of net assets

    a. Total assets—distinguishing between capital assets and other assets. Amounts receivable from the primary government or other component units should be reported separately.
    b. Total liabilities—distinguishing between long-term debt outstanding and other liabilities. Amounts payable to the primary government or to other component units should be reported separately.
    c. Total net assets—distinguishing between restricted, unrestricted and amounts invested in capital assets, net of related debt.

2. Condensed statement of activities

    a. Expenses (by major functions and for depreciation expense, if separately reported)
    b. Program revenues by type
    c. Net program (expense) revenue
    d. Tax revenues
    e. Other nontax general revenues
    f. Contributions to endowments and permanent fund principals
    g. Special and extraordinary items
    h. Change in net assets
    i. Beginning net assets
    j. Ending net assets

Budgetary Presentations

As described in Chapter 4, a government's basic financial statements must include a budgetary comparison (on the budget basis) for the general and special revenue for which annual budgets have been legally adopted either as part of the basic financial statements or as required supplementary information. This requirement would apply to blended component units as well. Budgetary data for the discretely presented component units that use governmental accounting are not required to be presented.

Intra-Entity Transactions and Balances

Special attention is required for transactions between and among the primary government, its blended component units, and its discretely presented component units.

For government-wide financial statements, resource flows between a primary government and a blended component unit should be reclassified as an internal activity in the financial statements of the reporting entity. Resource flows between a primary government and its discretely presented component units should be reported as if they were external transactions. However, receivable and payable balances between a primary government and a discretely presented component unit should be displayed on a separate line.

Note Disclosures

The notes to the financial statements of a financial reporting entity that includes many component units may be significantly expanded because of the need and requirements to disclose information about major component units.

The notes to the financial statements of the reporting entity should include a brief description of the component units of the financial reporting entity and their relationship to the primary government. The notes should include a discussion of the criteria for including the component units in the financial reporting entity and how the component units are reported. The notes should also include information about how the separate financial statements of the individual component units may be obtained.

Keep in mind when reading the note disclosures about component units in a government's financial statements that usually only fairly limited information is provided. In other words, a government does not have to include all of the disclosure requirements that it must meet for itself for all of the component units that are included in its reporting entity. If the reader needs detailed information about a component unit, it is best to get the separately issued financial statements of the component unit.

SUMMARY

This chapter addresses the somewhat complex issue of what entities make up a government's reporting entity. While there are detailed requirements as to which entities should be in and which entities should be left out, casual readers of financial statements do not have to be overly concerned with those decisions, unless of course they choose to be. Better to let the experts who prepared the financial statements worry about those details. What is important, however, is to understand what a component unit is, and to be able to distinguish between blended component units and discretely presented component units. This chapter should enable the reader to accomplish both of those objectives.

CHAPTER 6

Revenues from Nonexchange Transactions

The term *nonexchange transaction* has only recently gained wide use in government accounting and financial reporting, so governmental financial statement readers may at first think that this chapter will not have broad applicability. However, once the term is understood, it becomes clear that nonexchange transactions include accounting and financial reporting requirements for a significant part of a governmental entity's typical revenue transactions.

GASB Statement No. 33, "Accounting and Financial Reporting for Nonexchange Transactions" (GASBS 33), divides all transactions into two categories.

1. Exchange transactions, in which each party to a transaction receives and gives up something of essentially the same value (e.g., a government sells a homeowner water.)
2. Nonexchange transactions, in which a government gives or receives value without directly receiving or giving something equal in value in the exchange (e.g., a taxpayer pays his or her real estate taxes)

As will be more fully described below, nonexchange transactions therefore include very significant items of revenues and expenditures for governmental activities, such as taxes (including property, sales, and income taxes) as well as revenues provided by federal and state aid programs.

Note   The GASB issued Statement No. 33 because there was very little professional guidance in existence for recognizing nonexchange transactions on an accrual basis, which the GASB correctly anticipated was needed when the accrual basis of accounting is used in the government-wide financial statements. In addition, the GASB believed that the existing guidance for nonexchange transactions that are recorded on a modified accrual basis (which continues at the governmental fund level) could also use some clarification and standardization.

This chapter focuses on the accounting for nonexchange transactions from the revenue perspective. Keep in mind, however, that there are similar accounting questions that arise as to when a government would record an expense for a nonexchange transaction. This occurs when one government provides resources to another in a nonexchange transaction. The provider government has an expense and the recipient government has revenue. The concepts in this chapter will be helpful in understanding when provider governments record expenses for these types of transactions.

CLASSES OF NONEXCHANGE TRANSACTIONS

As if using a fancy term like "nonexchange" transactions was not enough to make accounting for these transactions sound complicated, the GASB went a little further by defining four different types of nonexchange transactions. Let us look at each of them.

Derived Tax Revenues

These are tax revenues that result from the government taxing an exchange transaction. There are at least three important types of taxes that would fall into this category.

1. Sales taxes
2. Personal income taxes
3. Corporate income taxes

Using sales tax as an example, a sale between, say, a retail store and its customer is the exchange transaction that "derives" the amount of the tax that the government is entitled to receive.

Imposed Nonexchange Revenues

This type of nonexchange transaction is the result of an assessment by a government on transactions other than exchange transactions. In other words, there is no exchange transaction that gives rise to the tax. Included in this category are the following:

- Real estate taxes
- Fines and penalties

In the case of real estate taxes, a government assesses the tax based on some measure, generally the assessed value of the property. There is no exchange transaction that gives rise to the tax revenue.

Government-Mandated Nonexchange Transactions

These are transactions that occur when one level of government (including the federal government) provides resources to a government at another level (such as a state providing a city with resources) and requires that the resources be used for a specific purpose (purpose restriction) or within a specified period of time (time restriction.) Basically, this category of nonexchange transactions includes government grants. However, to be technically accurate, this category of transactions should include those that have the following characteristics:

- A government mandates that a government at another level (the recipient government) must perform or facilitate a particular program in accordance with the providing government's enabling legislation, and provides resources for that purpose.
- There is a fulfillment of eligibility requirements (including time requirements) in order for a transaction to occur.

Later in this section, the impact of purpose and time requirements and other eligibility requirements on the accounting for these types of revenues will be discussed.

Voluntary Nonexchange Transactions

These are transactions that result from legislative or contractual agreements, other than exchanges, entered into willingly by two or more parties. This category of nonexchange transactions differs from the previous one in that these transactions are not imposed on the provider or the recipient. Included in this category are grants and entitlements as well as donations by other nongovernmental entities. While these transactions are not imposed on the provider or the recipient, the fulfillment of purpose and time requirements as well as eligibility requirements may be necessary for a transaction to occur.

ACCOUNTING REQUIREMENTS

The following paragraphs will briefly describe the accounting considerations for each of these categories of nonexchange transactions. Both the accrual basis of accounting and the modified accrual basis of accounting will be addressed. To clearly see how these principles are put into practice, the final section of this chapter discusses the accounting for the various types of nonexchange transaction revenues typically received by governments.

Derived Exchange Transactions

Accrual Basis of Accounting

Under the accrual basis of accounting, revenues from derived exchange transactions are recognized in the same period in which the exchange transaction takes place. In other words, when the retail sale is made that results in sales tax, the government should record the sales tax revenue in the same period as that in which the sale occurred. If the government has not received the sales tax by its fiscal year-end, it should record a receivable for all of the sales tax revenue that it is due for sales that occurred prior to its fiscal year-end. If the government has received any amounts in advance of the exchange transaction, it should record these amounts as deferred revenues, and not revenue.

Modified Accrual Basis of Accounting

The modified accrual basis of accounting works basically the same way as the accrual basis, but for revenues that have not been received by the fiscal year-end, only those amounts that are "available" to meet the current obligations of the government would be recorded as revenues. (Chapter 2 describes the concept of availability as it relates to the modified accrual basis of accounting.) Amounts that are receivable that are not considered available would be recorded as deferred revenue and not be recorded as revenue.

Imposed Nonexchange Revenues

Accrual Basis of Accounting

Under the accrual basis of accounting, revenues from imposed nonexchange transactions are generally recognized as revenues in the period when an enforceable legal claim to the assets arises. However, if the enabling legislation that gives rise to the tax has time requirements, revenues would not be recognized until the time requirements are met. In other words, if the enabling legislation specifies what time period the imposed tax relates to, revenues from this tax would not be recognized before this time period even if amounts have been received. Amounts received before the time requirement is met would be recorded as deferred revenue instead of revenue.

Modified Accrual Basis of Accounting

The modified accrual basis of accounting would recognize revenues in the same way as does the accrual basis of accounting except that, again, the availability criteria must be met. For property taxes, the most common type of imposed exchange transaction, the period of time that revenues collected after the fiscal year-end are considered available is defined as sixty days after the fiscal year-end. Property taxes that are receivable at the fiscal year-end but that will not be collected until more than sixty days after the fiscal year-end are recorded at year-end as deferred revenue.

Government-Mandated and Voluntary Nonexchange Transactions

The accounting rules work in a similar manner and will be discussed together.

Accrual Basis of Accounting

The accounting for government-mandated and voluntary nonexchange transactions centers on determining whether a transaction has occurred. One of the key determinants as to whether a transaction has occurred is whether all eligibility requirements to receive the revenue have been met. Compliance with time requirements is required for a transaction to have occurred. Accordingly, no revenues or receivables are recorded until any time requirements are met. In other words, a grant awarded to fund a program in the subsequent fiscal year does not meet the time requirements. The recipient government is not entitled to the resources until the next fiscal year. When the time requirements and any other eligibility requirements are met, the government would record the revenue (and any receivables) from the nonexchange transaction in the period that these requirements are met.

However, purpose restrictions ordinarily do not affect *when* a grant is recorded. If the government is entitled to the resources from a grant, when the grant is recorded is not affected by the fact that the use of the grant funds is restricted.

Many of the government-mandated nonexchange transactions are cost-reimbursable-type grants, or expenditure-driven grants as they are sometimes called. A government has to spend money in order to be eligible for reimbursement, so these types of transactions would not be recorded before the money is spent. If the government receives an advance of funds prior to spending the money, the receipt should be recorded as a deferred revenue, rather than as revenue.

Modified Accrual Basis of Accounting

Revenues are recognized when all eligibility requirements have been met and the resources are considered available. When the program is considered a cost-reimbursable program, the period of availability in practice may be longer than for other types of revenues. If the government has incurred costs under one of these programs, the revenues from the grant may be considered available to pay these costs, even if the grant revenue is not received until well after year-end. As a practical matter, when a government is relatively sure that it will be reimbursed for a cost incurred, it does not make much sense to recognize the cost in one fiscal year and the revenue in the next because the revenue did not meet an availability criteria.

The following sections describe the accounting for several of the more common types of revenues received by governments.

PROPERTY TAXES

Property taxes represent a significant source of revenue for many governments, particularly local governments. Property taxes recorded in a governmental fund should be accounted for as an imposed nonexchange revenue using the modified accrual basis. When a property tax assessment is made, it is to finance the budget of a particular period, meaning that the property taxes are intended to provide funds for the expenditures of that particular budget period. The revenue produced from any property tax assessment should be recognized in the fiscal period for which it is levied, provided that the "available" criterion of the modified accrual basis of accounting is met. (*Available* means that the property taxes are due to the government or past due and receivable within the current period, and are collected within the current period or expected to be collected soon enough thereafter to be used to pay current liabilities.) Property taxes due must be collected within sixty days after the period for which they were levied. For example, if property taxes are levied for a fiscal year that ends on June 30, 20X1, property taxes that were assessed and due for this period (and prior periods) can be recognized as revenue as long as they are collected by August 29, 20X1.

If unusual circumstances justify a period of greater than sixty days, the government should disclose the length of the period and the circumstances that justify its use. For example, in unusual circumstances, a government may be able to demonstrate that property taxes received after sixty days would be available to pay current liabilities if the current liabilities will be paid sometime after sixty days after year-end. Thus, there are two criteria that must be met before property tax revenue is to be recognized.

1. The property taxes are levied to finance the expenditures of the budget period reported.
2. The collections of these property taxes must take place no later than sixty days after the end of the reported period.

In recording property taxes, there is a difference as to when a receivable is recorded for property tax revenue and when the related revenue is recognized. A receivable should be recorded on the balance sheet for property tax receivables (net of estimated uncollectible property taxes receivable) on the date that the property taxes are levied. To the extent that property taxes receivable exceed the amount of revenue that may be recognized under the "available" criterion, the difference should be recorded as deferred revenue. Accordingly, revenue should only be recognized for the amount of the property taxes receivable amount on the balance sheet at the end of the fiscal year for the amounts of the property tax receivable that were collected sixty days after the balance sheet date. The difference between the property tax receivable at the fiscal year-end and the amount recognized as property tax revenue should be recorded as deferred property tax revenue. In the government-wide financial statements, even property tax revenues collected after the sixty-day period are recognized as revenues. The availability criteria do not apply to the accrual basis of accounting used in the government-wide financial statements.

In addition, when property taxes are collected in advance of the year for which they are levied, the advance collections should be recorded as deferred revenue. These advance collections should not be recognized as revenue until the period for which they were levied is reached.

INCOME AND SALES TAXES, AND OTHER DERIVED TAX REVENUES

Income taxes often represent a significant source of revenue to some governments. Sales taxes are another common form of significant revenue provider that are used by governments to fund operations. In addition, other forms of derived taxes, such as cigarette taxes, provide revenues to many state and local governments. What these taxes have in common is that they are derived from taxes imposed on exchange transactions. Prior to GASBS 33, these taxes were called taxpayer-assessed revenues, since they required some type of tax return or form on which the taxpayer calculated the amount of the tax due to the government.

On a modified accrual basis, the revenue from these taxes is fairly easy to determine because the availability criteria focus governments' attention on the collections from these taxes shortly after year-end. In practice, many governments have been using a one-month or two-month collection period after year-end (depending on the nature of the tax and how and when tax returns are filed) to determine the amounts that are recorded on the modified accrual basis. On the accrual basis, revenue recognition becomes more complicated in that estimates of what will be ultimately received for taxes imposed on exchange transactions occurring during the governments' fiscal year are required. Since many governments do not have fiscal years that match the calendar year and since many of these taxes are based on calendar-year tax returns, the calculations are further complicated.

These taxpayer-assessed revenues are difficult to measure for a number of reasons. First, the reporting period for these revenues is often a calendar year, and the majority of governments have a fiscal year that is other than the calendar year, and accordingly there are overlapping reporting periods. Second, the tax returns or remittance forms taxpayers use to remit these taxes are usually not due until several months after the calendar year-end and are subject to extension requests. Third, these types of taxes, particularly income taxes, are subject to estimated payment requirements throughout the year, and the final amount of the tax is determined when the tax return form is actually completed. Finally, since the revenues are taxpayer-assessed, it is sometimes difficult for the government to satisfactorily estimate the amount of tax it will ultimately receive based on historical information, because the taxes are generally based on the relative strength of the economy during the calendar year reported by the taxpayer. Historical information does not always have a direct correlation with the current status of the economy.

In some cases taxpayer-assessed revenues are collected by a level of government different from the government that is the actual beneficiary of the tax. For example, a state may be responsible for collecting sales taxes, although portions of the sales taxes collected are actually revenues of counties or cities located within the state. In these cases, the state will remit sales tax collections to the local governments (counties, cities, etc.) periodically. Similar situations exist where states collect personal income taxes imposed by major cities within the state.

The local governments receiving taxes collected by another level of government should apply the same criteria of recognizing these revenues (i.e., when they are measurable and available). If the collecting government remits the local government's portion of the taxes promptly, the local government is likely to recognize revenue in similar amounts to that which they would recognize if they collected the revenues themselves. On the other hand, if the collecting government imposes a significant delay until the time that it remits the portion of the collections due the local government to that local government, consideration must be given to when these revenues actually become available to the local government, given their delay in receiving the revenues from the collecting government.

While the measurable criterion can usually be met by effective use of accounting estimates, the available criterion is more direct. For reporting on the modified accrual basis of accounting, some governments choose to use the same sixty-day criterion used for property taxes collected after year-end for determining the amount of these revenues that should be considered available. Before adopting this general rule, the government should ensure that the tax relates back to the fiscal year for which the estimate is being made. For example, sales tax returns are often due monthly following the month of the sale. Assume that a government with a June 30 year-end requires sales tax returns to be filed and taxes remitted by the twentieth day of the month following the date of the sales. In this case, sales taxes remitted with the July 20 sales tax returns would relate to sales in June and would appropriately be accrued back to the fiscal year that ended June 30. However, the sales taxes remitted with the August 20 sales tax returns would relate to sales in July of the new fiscal year and would not be accrued back to the fiscal year that ended on June 30, despite being collected within sixty days of the June 30 year end.

In addition to accruing revenues for taxpayer-assessed taxes, governments must make the appropriate liability accruals for refunds that they are required to make based on tax returns that are filed. Governments generally use actual refunds made after the fiscal year-end, combined with estimates for refunds made using a combination of historical experience and information about the economy of the fiscal year reported. Tax refunds are likely to be a liability to be liquidated with current financial resources, and accordingly, a fund liability is recorded. The liability will also be recorded in the government-wide financial statements. Netting the tax refunds with the related tax revenues also provides a more accurate picture of the amount of tax revenues that should actually have been recorded by the government.

ADJUSTMENTS FOR THE ACCRUAL BASIS OF ACCOUNTING

In order to report the derived revenues from the taxes described in the previous paragraphs on the accrual basis of accounting and economic resources measurement focus used in the government-wide financial statements, the government needs to consider the taxes that will be collected after the availability period that is used for reporting these revenues on a modified accrual basis. The government needs to calculate how much revenue it "earns" during its fiscal year from exchange transactions that occurred during that fiscal year.

Consider the following example: A taxpayer prepares an income tax return for the calendar year ended December 31, 20X1. The taxpayer had withholdings taken from her salary during the year. In addition, the taxpayer made estimated tax payments throughout the year, with the final estimated payment made on January 15, 20X2. The taxpayer filed an extension request on April 15, 20X2, and paid an amount she estimated would be due with the final return. The return was filed on August 15, 20X2, which resulted in a refund that the taxpayer applied to her estimated payments for the calendar year ending December 31, 20X2. When completing her 20X2 tax return, the taxpayer discovers an error in the 20X1 return and files an amended return on May 15, 20X3, requesting an additional refund. How much would the government ultimately be entitled to receive in taxes from the earnings of the taxpayer during the government's fiscal year ended June 30, 20X1?

To approximate the answer to this question, a government would need to look at each component of the various tax events that are described above and determine how best to record the revenues (or refund) that occur from those events. The government has to assume that it is virtually impossible for it to have actual information in time for it to prepare its own financial statements on a timely basis. Furthermore, the fact that the tax year and the government's fiscal year are different essentially assures that some estimation process is required.

Each government's tax procedures and requirements are different, and different taxes work in different ways, so there is no set of prescribed procedures that can be suggested that will result in the best method in every case. Nevertheless, there are some general processes and procedures that might prove helpful. In the example described above, the government would probably be best off breaking the various tax events into groups and handling each in the most practical way. For example, withholding taxes are based on salary earnings and usually must be remitted to governments in a very short period of time. Perhaps withholding taxes received during the year should be recognized by the government in the year received. Similarly, estimated tax payments are often received quarterly and should correspond with estimates of earnings for each particular quarter. The estimated tax receipts related to the four quarters that comprise the government's fiscal year might be assumed to be recorded within that fiscal year. Tax payments received with returns and refunds made with returns filed on a timely basis (or received with extension request) might be aggregated and assumed to occur ratably over the calendar year. Accordingly, of the amounts received (or refunded) for calendar year 20X0, the government might assume that half were received in its 20X0 fiscal year and half in its 20X1 fiscal year. Projection of the first half of 20X2 would be needed and could be based on past history and adjusted for known factors, such as changes in tax rates or rising or declining incomes. Further, the government might determine that the amounts received or paid with amended returns is very small and may choose to simply account for these in the same period received or paid.

Note that not all derived tax revenues will be this difficult to calculate. For example, many governments require that sales taxes be remitted on a monthly basis. It should be fairly easy to match the receipts of sales tax revenues to the months of the fiscal year to which those taxes relate. For example, for a June 30 year-end, if sales taxes relating to the month of June are due to be remitted by July 20, the government would accrue the July receipts back to June, since that is when the sales on which the sales tax revenues were derived occurred.

GRANTS AND OTHER FINANCIAL ASSISTANCE

State and local governments typically receive a variety of grants and other financial assistance. At the state level, this financial assistance may be primarily federal financial assistance. At the local government level, the financial assistance may be federal, state, or other intermediate level of local government. Financial assistance generally is legally structured as a grant, contract, or cooperative agreement. The financial assistance might take the form of entitlements, shared revenues, pass-through grants, food stamps, and on-behalf payments for fringe benefits and salary.

What Financial Assistance Should Be Recorded?

Governments often receive grants and other financial assistance that they are to transfer to or spend on behalf of a secondary recipient of the financial assistance. These agreements are known as *pass-through grants*. All cash pass-through grants should be reported in the financial statements of the primary recipient government and should be recorded as revenues and expenditures of that government.

There may be some infrequent cases when a recipient government acts only as a cash conduit for financial assistance. Guidance on identifying these cases is provided by GASB Statement No. 24 (GASBS 24), "Accounting and Financial Reporting for Certain Grants and Other Financial Assistance." In these cases, the receipt and disbursement of the financial assistance should be reported as transactions of an agency fund. A recipient government serves as a cash conduit if it merely transmits grantor-supplied money without having administrative or direct financial involvement in the program. Some examples of a recipient government that would be considered to have administrative involvement in a program are provided by GASBS 24, as follows:

- The government monitors secondary recipients for compliance with program-specific requirements.
- The government determines eligibility of secondary recipients or projects, even if grantor-supplied criteria are used.

• The government has the ability to exercise discretion in how the funds are allocated.

A recipient government has direct financial involvement if, as an example, it finances some direct program costs because of grantor-imposed matching requirements or is liable for disallowed costs.

Revenue Recognition of Grants and Other Financial Assistance

Grants, entitlements, or shared revenues recorded in the general and special revenue funds should be recognized as revenue in the accounting period in which they become susceptible to accrual (they are measurable and available). In applying these criteria, the financial statement preparer must consider the legal and contractual requirements of the particular financial assistance being considered.

Financial assistance in the form of shared revenues and entitlements is often restricted by law or contract more in form than in substance. Only a failure on the part of the recipient to comply with prescribed regulations would cause a forfeiture of the resources. Such resources are often recorded as revenue at the time of receipt, or earlier if the susceptibility to accrual criteria are satisfied. If entitlements and shared revenues are collected in advance of the period that they are intended to finance, they are recorded as deferred revenue.

Grants are nonexchange transactions that would be classified as either government-mandated or voluntary nonexchange transactions. The accounting for both of these transactions is similar and is described earlier in this chapter. Many of the government-mandated grants that are received by governments are expenditure driven. These are covered later in this section. In many of the remaining grants, the key accounting component is when eligibility requirements are met, which determine when it is appropriate for the recipient government to recognize the grant as revenue. If the actual cash is received before the eligibility requirements have been met, the cash should be recorded as a deferred revenue until the eligibility requirements are met. On the other hand, if the eligibility requirements have been met and the cash has not yet been received by the recipient government, the recipient government would record a receivable and revenue for the grant revenue that it is owed. For recording this amount in a governmental fund on the modified accrual basis of accounting, the availability criteria should be examined to see if the revenue should be recognized or recorded as deferred revenue. In practice, grant revenue is usually received within a timeframe where the availability criteria are met (this is also discussed later, in the expenditure-driven revenue section).

One of the more important eligibility requirements is the time requirement, where the time period in which a grant is to be spent is specified. For example, if a state government provides formula-based education aid to a local government or a school district and specifies that the aid is for the school year that begins in September and ends in June, that is the period of time for which the grant revenue would be recognized. Few, if any, differences between the modified accrual basis of accounting on the fund level and the accrual basis of accounting at the government-wide level should arise. However, if no time period is specified (and all other eligibility requirements are met) the total amount of the grant would be recognized as revenue immediately. For example, assume that a state government with a December 31 year-end provides a grant to a local government in its budget for its fiscal year which begins on January 1, 20X1. The local government has a fiscal year of June 30. If there are no time requirements and all other eligibility criteria are met, the grant appropriation at the state level is available on January 1, 20X1, the first day of the state's fiscal year. In this case, the local government would recognize the revenue from the whole grant on January 1, 20X1.

This area has caused a somewhat unexpected surprise for some governments in implementing GASBS 33. In the above example, governments prior to adoption of GASBS 33 probably would have recognized half of the grant revenue in this example in the fiscal year ended June 30, 20X1, and half in the fiscal year ended June 30, 20X2. Under GASBS 33, the entire grant would be recognized in the fiscal year ended June 30, 20X1.

Expenditure-Driven Grants and Other Financial Assistance Revenue

Many grants and other financial aid programs are on a cost-reimbursement basis, whereby the recipient government "earns" the grant revenue when it actually makes the expenditures called for under the grant. This type of arrangement is described as "expenditure-driven" revenue, since the amount of revenue that should be recognized is directly related to the amount of expenditures incurred for allowable purposes under the grant or other contractual agreement. (Of course, the amount of revenue recognized under a grant or contract should not exceed the total allowable revenue for the period being reported, regardless of the amount of expenditures.) Using the terminology of GASBS 33, making the expenditure is simply an eligibility requirement. To be eligible for the grant revenue, you must make the expenditure.

In accounting for expenditure-driven revenue, governments typically make the expenditures first and then claim reimbursement from the grantor or other aid provider. In this case, a receivable should be established, provided that the criteria for recording revenue under the modified accrual basis of accounting are satisfied. For expenditure-driven revenues, determining whether the "available" criterion is met is difficult for some grants and other sources of aid. First, there will be a time lag from when the government actually makes the expenditures under the grant, accumulates the expenditure information to conform with some predetermined billing period, and submits the claim for reimbursement to the grantor or other aid provider. Sometimes the grantors and other aid providers delay disbursing payments to the recipient organizations while they review the reimbursement claims submitted by the recipient organization. In some cases, the aid providers even perform some limited types of audit procedures on claims for reimbursement. Often, the actual receipt of cash for expenditure-driven revenues exceeds the period normally considered "available" to pay current obligations. Governments, however, do record the receivable from the grantor or other aid provider and the related grant revenue, despite it being unclear as to whether the "available" criterion will be met. The reason for not requiring that the available criteria be met is that the government has already recognized the expenditures for these grants and other aid programs. Without recognizing the related grant revenue, the governmental fund's operating statements will indicate that there was a use of resources for these grants and other programs, when in fact, these programs are designed to break even and result in no drain of financial resources on the government. In practice, it is uncommon for the recognition of revenue related to reimbursement grants to be deferred based on the availability criterion of modified accrual accounting. Nevertheless, deferral may be considered in situations where reimbursement is not expected within a reasonable period.

SUMMARY

Understanding how governments record revenues from nonexchange transactions is key to understanding the government-wide and fund financial statements. This chapter addresses some of the more technical rules as to revenue recognition and discusses some of the more common nonexchange revenue transactions often found in a government's financial statements.

CHAPTER 7

Capital Assets

Governments often make significant investments in capital assets. Capital assets are the long-lived assets that require significant investments of resources. They include the assets often referred to as infrastructure assets (roads, bridges, parks, etc.) as well as land, buildings, and equipment. The term is frequently used that the costs of certain assets are "capitalized." This means that the costs at the time of purchase or construction are recorded as an asset on the statement of net assets or balance sheet rather than being charged to expense in the statement of activities or statement of revenues, expenses, and changes in fund balance. This chapter will examine some of the more common accounting issues relating to capital assets. The topics discussed include the following:

- Where are capital assets recorded in the financial statements?
- Recording and valuing capital assets
- Understanding depreciation
- Using the modified approach in lieu of depreciating infrastructure assets
- The basics of capitalized interest
- Capital assets resulting from capital lease transactions
- Intangible assets
- Impairments of capital assets

187

Understanding these topics is of key importance in understanding a government's financial statements.

WHERE ARE CAPITAL ASSETS RECORDED IN THE FINANCIAL STATEMENTS?

Answering this question requires distinguishing the recording of capital assets in the government-wide financial statements and in the fund financial statements.

Government-Wide Financial Statements

Capital assets are recorded as assets in the government-wide financial statements. (When an asset is referred to as being recorded, it means that the asset as well as accumulated depreciation and depreciation expense, if applicable, are also recorded.) The capital assets recorded in the government-wide financial statements include those used in governmental activities and those recorded for business-type activities. Capital assets relating to any fiduciary funds are not recorded in the government-wide financial statements.

Fund Financial Statements

Capital assets are not current financial resources. Accordingly, they are not recorded in the governmental funds. When a governmental fund purchases or constructs a capital asset, it is recorded as an expenditure rather than as an asset. Capital assets relating to governmental activities are recorded only in the government-wide financial statements.

Because proprietary funds record all economic resources, capital assets are recorded as assets in proprietary funds. When a proprietary fund purchases or constructs a capital asset, it is recorded as an asset on its balance sheet. Of course, these capital assets also carry forward to be recorded in the government-wide financial statements.

While one does not usually think of capital assets being bought or constructed by a fiduciary fund, these funds may have capital assets. For example, a large pension system reported as a pension (and other employee benefit) trust fund may own its own building, office equipment, computers, and so forth. These capital assets would be recorded in this particular fiduciary fund. Remember that the financial activities of the fiduciary funds do not carry forward to the government-wide financial statements. Accordingly, the capital assets recorded in fiduciary funds would not be part of the capital assets that are recorded in the government-wide financial statements.

RECORDING AND VALUING CAPITAL ASSETS

Governments determine what assets they will record as capital assets by using a capitalization policy, which is sometimes called a capitalization threshold. The purpose of using a capitalization policy is to avoid recording minor, short-lived assets.

To determine what assets will be treated as capital assets (regardless of whether it is a capital asset used in governmental or business-type activities or a capital asset of a proprietary fund) in practice, governments typically set monetary and useful life thresholds for when assets may be considered for capitalization. For example, a government may determine that in order to be treated as a capitalized asset, an asset should cost at least $5,000 and have a useful life of five years. Note that this threshold applies only to items that are appropriately capitalizable by their nature. For example, a repair or maintenance expenditure of $7,000 would not be capitalized even if the threshold were $5,000. The threshold would apply to items that would normally be capitalized and is used to prevent too many small assets from being capitalized, which becomes difficult for governments to manage. Continuing the $5,000 threshold example, a personal computer purchased for $4,000 would not be capitalized. However, ten personal computers purchased as part of the installation of an integrated computer network would be eligible for capitalization in this example.

Governments are notorious for having capitalization thresholds that are too low. Perhaps in their zeal to provide accountability for assets purchased with public resources, large governments exist that have capitalization thresholds of $100 to $500. Often, these thresholds have been in place for many years (sometimes from when the government first recorded capital assets) and have not been adjusted for inflation. This presents a waste of resources in accounting for the details of these numerous small assets. Governments should periodically review their capitalization thresholds to make sure that they make sense, given their significance to the government's financial statements. To address the accountability issue that is likely to arise in raising these thresholds, keep in mind that assets do not have to be recorded as capital assets to be safeguarded. In considering these accountability issues, the government must also consider that accountability standards may be imposed on the government from outside sources. For example, some federal and state contracts or grants may specify a capitalization level for tracking capital assets that are acquired with funds provided under the contract or grant. Although this level must be adhered to for contract or grant management purposes, the level should not determine the capitalization threshold established for financial reporting purposes.

Note Governments sometimes set or keep abnormally low capitalization rates because of sensitivity to their stewardship responsibilities for public resources. Other reasons, however, are more practical. For example, some governments can only issue general long-term debt for the acquisition or construction of capital assets. Therefore, the lower the capitalization threshold, the more assets can be purchased (for example, by a capital projects fund, which obtains its funds from the issuance of general long-term debt). These somewhat low dollar-amount items can be purchased and paid for over the life of the general long-term debt, with no impact on general fund resources, which are generally more subject to political sensitivities.

As a general rule, capital assets are initially recorded at cost. *Cost* is defined as the consideration that is given or received, whichever is more objectively determinable. In most instances, cost will be based on the consideration that the government gave for the capital asset, because that will provide the most objective determination of the cost of the asset.

The cost of a capital asset includes not only its purchase price or construction cost, but also any ancillary costs incurred that are necessary to place the asset in its intended location and in condition where it is ready for use. Ancillary charges will depend on the nature of the asset acquired or constructed, but typically include costs such as freight and transportation charges, site preparation expenditures, professional fees, and legal claims directly attributable to the asset acquisition or construction. An example of legal claims directly attributable to an asset acquisition is liability claims resulting from workers or others being injured during the construction of an asset, or damage done to the property of others as a direct result of the construction activities.

It is relatively easy for governments to ascertain the costs of capital assets that are purchased currently. Contracts, purchase orders, and payment information is available to determine the acquisition or construction costs. Again, the cost of a capital asset includes not only its purchase price or construction cost, but also whatever ancillary charges are necessary to place the asset in its intended location and in condition for its intended use. Thus, among the costs that should be capitalized as part of the cost of a capital asset are the following:

- Professional fees, such as architectural, legal, and accounting fees
- Transportation costs, such as freight charges
- Legal claims directly attributable to the asset acquisition
- Title fees
- Closing costs
- Appraisal and negotiation fees
- Surveying fees
- Damage payments
- Land preparation costs
- Demolition costs
- Insurance premiums during the construction phase
- Capitalized interest (discussed later in this chapter)

The reporting of capital assets by governments was not always common. As governments worked to adopt the requirements of early GAAP for governments, they were faced with the task of establishing capital asset records and valuation after many years of financial reporting without them. In these situations, many of the supporting documents and records that might contain original cost information were no longer available to establish the initial cost of these previously unrecorded assets.

Governments often found it necessary to estimate the original costs of these assets on the basis of such documentary evidence as may be available, including price levels at the time of acquisition, and to record these estimated costs in the appropriate capital asset records. While this problem will diminish in size as governments retire or dispose of these assets with estimated costs, the notes to the financial statements should disclose the extent to which capital asset costs have been estimated and the method (or methods) of estimation. Similar consideration is made for the retroactive recording of infrastructure assets under GASBS 34.

Governments sometimes acquire capital assets by gift. When these assets are recorded, they should be recorded at their estimated fair value at the time of acquisition by the government.

One of the most significant aspects of GASBS 34 is its definition of what is included in capital assets: land, improvements to land, easements, buildings, building improvements, vehicles, machinery, equipment, works of art and historical treasures, infrastructure, and all other tangible and intangible assets that are used in operations and that have initial useful lives extending to more than one year. The GASB 34 Implementation Guide defines land improvements to consist of betterments, other than building, that ready land for its intended use. Examples provided of land improvements include site improvements such as excavations, fill, grading, and utility installation; removal, relocation, or reconstruction of the property of others, such as railroads and telephone and power lines; retention walls; parking lots, fencing, and landscaping.

Included in the definition of capital assets are infrastructure assets. Previously, governments (not including proprietary funds) had the option of capitalizing infrastructure assets, and many, if not most, did not. (Infrastructure assets are defined by GASBS 34 as "long-lived capital assets that normally are stationary in nature and normally can be preserved for a significantly greater number of years than most capital assets.") Examples of infrastructure assets are roads, bridges, tunnels, drainage systems, water and sewer systems, dams, and lighting systems.

All governments are now required to report general infrastructure capital assets prospectively. Retroactive capitalization of major infrastructure assets required by GASBS 34 was more complicated. Governments with total annual revenues of less than $10 million did not have to retroactively record infrastructure assets, although they are encouraged to do so.

UNDERSTANDING DEPRECIATION

A useful way to think of depreciation is as a mechanism to spread the cost of an asset out over the life of the asset. Depreciation is recorded only in the financial statements described above that record capital assets. If capital assets are not recorded (such as on the governmental fund financial statements) do not expect to see depreciation expense recorded.

In the simplest example, say a government buys a $5,000 high-speed laser printer that it expects will have a useful life of five years and will have no salvage value at the end of the five years. When the printer is purchased, an asset for $5,000 is recorded. Assume that a simple method of depreciation known as "straight-line" is used in which the same amount of depreciation expense is recorded each year. A $5,000 asset divided by a five-year useful life means that $1,000 of depreciation expense will be recorded each year. Each year's statement of activities or statement of revenues, expenses, and changes in fund net assets will reflect depreciation expense of $1,000. At the same time the cost of the asset recorded will be reduced by an amount known as "accumulated depreciation," which, as its name implies, is the cumulative amount of depreciation expense recorded on this asset. At the end of the first year, $1,000 of depreciation expense will have been recorded. The asset will be reflected on the statement of net assets or balance sheet as $4,000, which is the $5,000 net of the accumulated depreciation of $1,000. This amount is sometimes referred to as the asset's net book value. At the end of year two, the asset will be reflected as $3,000, which is the $5,000 net of the accumulated depreciation of $2,000 ($1,000 from year one and $1,000 from year two). At the end of five years, the asset will be reflected as \$0, which is the \$5,000 net of accumulated depreciation of \$5,000. If at this time the government no longer uses the asset, it would remove the \$5,000 from its asset accounts and \$5,000 from its accumulated depreciation accounts, resulting in no net change to the statement of net assets or balance sheet—only the gross amount of assets and the accumulated depreciation accounts would change. If the government continues to use the asset beyond its five-year life, it would leave the \$5,000 recorded in the asset account and the \$5,000 in the accumulated depreciation account until such time as it stops using the asset. In addition, this example assumes that the asset has no salvage value (i.e., what the government could sell the asset for after using it for five years). Say the government could sell the asset for \$1,000 at the end of five years. The cost of the asset that would be depreciated would be reduced by the \$1,000. Only \$4,000 of the asset's cost (\$5,000 less the \$1,000 estimated salvage value) would be depreciated, meaning that the annual depreciation expense would be reduced to \$800 per year (\$4,000 divided by 5 years). At the end of the five years, the asset would be reflected on the statement of net assets or balance sheet at a net book value of \$1,000. Thinking about depreciation as a cost allocation tool, the real cost to the government in this case is \$4,000, because even though it paid \$5,000 for the asset, it expects to recover \$1,000 of that cost as salvage value at the end of the asset's useful life. The \$4,000 is the amount of cost that must be allocated to the years of service that the asset will provide.

In calculating depreciation, governments follow the same acceptable depreciation methods used by commercial enterprises. There is actually very little authoritative guidance issued by the FASB and its predecessor standard-setting bodies. In fact, the financial statement preparer would need to go back to AICPA Accounting Research Bulletin No. 43 (ARB 43), "Restatement and Revision of Accounting Research Bulletins," to find a definition of depreciation accounting, which is a system of accounting that aims to distribute the cost or other basic value of tangible capital assets, less any salvage value, over the estimated useful life of the unit (which may also be a group of assets) in a systematic and rational manner. Viewed differently, depreciation recognizes the cost of using up the future economic benefits or service potentials of long-lived assets.

In addition to obtaining the original cost information described in the preceding section to this chapter, a government must determine the salvage value (if any) of an asset, the estimated useful life of the asset, and the depreciation method that will be used. In practice, many governments usually assume that there will be no salvage value to the asset that they are depreciating. Governments tend to use things for a long time, and many of the assets that they record are useful only to the government, so there is no ready after-market for these assets. For example, what is the salvage value of a fully depreciated sewage treatment plant? Similarly, there is probably no practical use for used personal computer equipment, because governments are inclined to use these types of assets until they are virtually obsolete, which makes salvage value generally low. However, these governmental operating characteristics aside, if the government determines that there is likely to be salvage value for an asset being depreciated, the estimated salvage value should be deducted from the cost of the capital asset to arrive at the amount that will be depreciated.

Next, the government should determine the estimated useful lives of the assets that will be depreciated. Usually assets are grouped into asset categories and a standard estimated life or a range of estimated lives is used for each class.

Following are some common depreciable asset categories:

- Buildings
- Leasehold improvements
- Machinery and equipment
- Office equipment
- Infrastructure, including roads, bridges, parks, etc.

Two areas to keep in mind are that land is not depreciated, because it is assumed to have an indefinite life. In addition, as will be discussed later in this chapter, capital assets that are recorded as a result of capital lease transactions are also considered part of the depreciable assets of a governmental organization.

The final component of the depreciation equation that a government needs to determine is the method that it will use. The most common method used by governments is the straight-line method of depreciation in which the amount to be depreciated is divided by the asset's useful life, resulting in the same depreciation charge in each year.

Accelerated methods of depreciation, such as the sum-of-the-year's digits and the double-declining balance methods, may also be used. However, their use is far less popular than the straight-line method and the details of their calculation are beyond the scope of this book. Although proprietary funds do use a measurement focus and basis of accounting that result in a determination of net income similar to that of a commercial enterprise, there is less emphasis on the bottom line of proprietary activities than there would be for a publicly traded corporation, for instance. Reflecting this lower degree of emphasis, governments sometimes elect to follow the straight-line method of depreciation more for simplicity purposes, rather than for analyzing whether their assets actually do lose more of their value in the first few years of use.

Governments should also disclose their depreciation policies in the notes to the financial statements. For the major classes of fixed assets, the range of estimated useful lives that are used in the depreciation calculations should also be disclosed, as well as the depreciation method used in computing depreciation.

Since the government-wide financial statements are prepared using the economic resources measurement focus, depreciation on capital assets is recorded. This was another highly controversial issue of GASBS 34. In response to commentary that infrastructure assets do not depreciate in value in the traditional sense, GASBS 34 allows a "modified approach" as to depreciation on qualifying infrastructure assets, as discussed below.

Basically, depreciation rules for the government-wide financial statements (aside from the modified approach) follow those currently used by proprietary funds, as well as by commercial enterprises, which are described earlier in this section. Capital assets are reported in the statement of net assets net of accumulated depreciation. (Capital assets that are not depreciated, such as land, construction in progress, and infrastructure assets using the modified approach, should be reported separately from capital assets being depreciated in the statement of activities.) Depreciation expense is recorded in the statement of activities and is reported as an expense of the individual programs or functions that have identifiable depreciable assets. Capital assets are depreciated over their estimated useful lives, except for land and land improvements and infrastructure assets using the modified approach.

Depreciation expense may be calculated by individual assets or by classes of assets (such as infrastructure, buildings and improvements, vehicles, and machinery and equipment). In addition, depreciation may be calculated for networks of capital assets or for subsystems of a network of capital assets, which are described later in this chapter.

USING THE MODIFIED APPROACH IN LIEU OF DEPRECIATING INFRASTRUCTURE ASSETS

The GASBS 34 requirement to record infrastructure assets caused a huge change for governments in two ways. First, the retroactive recording of these assets was certainly a large challenge to implementing this aspect of the financial reporting model. Second, without the modified approach discussed in this section, governments would be required to depreciate the infrastructure assets that were recorded in the government-wide financial statements. (Note that infrastructure assets were always supposed to be recorded in proprietary funds, although some reporting model implementations found that this was not always the case in actual practice.) There are two basic schools of thought as to whether it makes sense to depreciate infrastructure assets. The first is that infrastructure assets are similar to other capital assets and should be treated consistently. Their costs should be allocated to the period of time that they are used by depreciating them in the same manner as other capital assets. The second school of thought is that infrastructure assets are unlike other capital assets. Their value does not diminish over time because governments spend money to maintain these assets in good working order. These expenses represent the true cost of the infrastructure asset and these costs, and not depreciation, should be charged to expense in the year that the costs are incurred. There may be no right or wrong answer to this question. What matters is that the debate resulted in the GASB allowing governments to use a modified method in lieu of depreciation expense for infrastructure assets when certain criteria are met.

To understand the modified approach a little better, recall the example of the $5,000 laser printer used in the previous section. It is reasonable that at the end of approximately five years the government will get rid of this printer and buy a new one. Depreciation for this type of asset seems fairly clear and logical. Contrast this with a major bridge that a government has built over a major waterway. The government estimates that the bridge will have a fifty-year useful life. At the end of fifty years, it is unlikely that the government will knock the old bridge down and build a new one. What is more likely to happen is that the government will make major renovations to the bridge over time and the bridge will be used indefinitely. The modified approach basically allows the government to not depreciate the bridge as long as it maintains the bridge at some stated level of condition. Any costs of renovations that are made to keep the bridge at that level of condition will be charged to expense as they are incurred. (If the bridge were being depreciated, major renovations would be added to the cost of the bridge and themselves depreciated.)

The GASB attached some strings as to when and how governments may use the modified approach. Infrastructure assets that are part of a network or subsystem of assets are not required to be depreciated if two requirements are met.

1. The government manages the eligible infrastructure assets using an asset management system that has the following characteristics:

    a. An up-to-date inventory of eligible infrastructure assets is maintained.
    b. Condition assessments of the eligible infrastructure assets are performed and summarized using a measurement scale.
    c. An estimate is made each year of the annual amount to maintain and preserve the eligible infrastructure assets at the condition level established and disclosed by the government.

2. The government documents that the eligible infrastructure assets are being preserved approximately at or above a condition level established and disclosed by the government. The condition level should be established and documented by administrative or executive policy, or by legislative action.

In applying these rules, a network of assets is composed of all assets that provide a particular type of service for a government. A network of infrastructure assets may be only one infrastructure asset that is composed of many components. A subsystem of a network of assets is composed of all assets that make up a similar portion or segment of a network of assets. In an Implementation Guide, the GASB provided the example of a water distribution system of a government, which would be considered a network. The pumping stations, storage facilities, and distribution mains could be considered subsystems of that network.

The requirements are designed to ensure that governments do in fact maintain the infrastructure assets for which they are using the modified approach at a stated condition level. If they do not, they will be required to stop using the modified approach and begin to depreciate the infrastructure asset. The government can use any number of rating systems to reflect the conditions of assets. For example, for a network of road, it may evaluate roads as being in "good," "adequate," or "poor" condition. The stated condition may be that 80% of the roads are evaluated in "good" condition. To continue to use the modified approach, the government would have to maintain its roads so that 80% of them would be evaluated as being in good condition. Note that the GASB does not set any qualitative rules for how well the infrastructure assets are maintained. If the government decided that 30% of its roads would be maintained in good condition, that is a policy decision of the government, not an accounting consideration.

Note that the GASB requires that the condition level be established by administrative or executive policy or by legislative action. This is meant to discourage governments from adjusting the condition assessment requirement arbitrarily. In the previous example, if the government finds that only 70% of its roads are evaluated to be in good condition, it should not be able to arbitrarily change the requirement to 70% from 80%.

In addition to the initial requirements for using the modified approach, governments using the modified approach also need to document that

- Complete condition assessments of eligible infrastructure assets are performed in a consistent manner at least every three years.
- The results of the most recent complete condition assessment provide reasonable assurance that the eligible infrastructure assets are being preserved approximately at or above the condition level established and disclosed by the government.

Governments are also required to present the following schedules, derived from asset management systems, as required supplemental information for all eligible infrastructure assets that are reported using the modified approach:

- The assessed condition, performed every three years, for at least the three most recent complete condition assessments, indicating the dates of the assessments
- The estimated annual amount calculated at the beginning of the fiscal year to maintain and preserve at (or above) the condition level established and disclosed by the government compared with the amounts actually expensed for each of the past five reporting periods

Governments that fail to meet the conditions described in this section are precluded from continuing to use the modified approach. Depreciation expense for the affected assets would need to begin to be recorded.

THE BASICS OF CAPITALIZED INTEREST

In answer to the question "Is the interest that a government pays on its debt an expense or an asset?" most people would probably say "an expense." For the most part, this would be a correct response. However, there is a limited situation where interest may be considered an asset—or more correctly part of the cost of an asset. This is the nature of capitalized interest. In a nutshell, interest costs related to monies paid during the period of time that an asset is being constructed (or otherwise readied for use) are considered part of the cost of the asset. This is the concept of capitalized interest. It is basically found in proprietary funds and in the business-type activities reported in the government-wide financial statements. As is usually the case, this simple concept is made more complicated when it is actually put into practice, as the following pages will describe.

Some assets that are reported in proprietary funds are constructed or take an extended period of time to prepare for use. These funds would include in the cost of those constructed assets any interest cost that would ordinarily be capitalized under the accounting rules for commercial enterprises. In other words, the requirements of Statement of Financial Accounting Standards No. 34 (SFAS 34), "Capitalization of Interest Cost," as adopted for application to the governmental accounting and financial reporting model, should be considered.

Note This chapter provides information on interest capitalization on fixed assets constructed by proprietary funds. Capitalization of interest on capital assets used in governmental activities is not recorded.

Interest cost is capitalized for assets that require an acquisition period to get them ready for use. The acquisition period is the period beginning with the first expenditure for a qualifying asset and ending when the asset is substantially complete and ready for its intended use. The interest cost capitalization period starts when three conditions are met.

1. Expenditures have occurred.
2. Activities necessary to prepare the asset (including administrative activities before construction) have begun.
3. Interest cost has been incurred.

The amount of interest cost capitalized should not exceed the actual interest cost applicable to the proprietary fund that is incurred during the reporting period. In other words, interest cost that has not been incurred cannot be capitalized. To compute the amount of interest cost to be capitalized for a reporting period, the average cumulative expenditures for the qualifying asset during the reporting period must be determined. In order to determine the average accumulated expenditures, each expenditure must be weighted for the time it was outstanding during the reporting period.

To determine the interest rate to apply against the weighted-average of expenditures computed in the preceding paragraph, the government determines if the construction is being financed with a specific borrowing. If it is, which in the governmental environment is fairly likely, then the interest rate of that specific borrowing should be used. In other words, this interest rate, multiplied by the weighted-average of expenditures on the qualifying assets, would be the amount of interest that is capitalized. If no specific borrowing is made to acquire the qualifying asset, the weighted-average interest rate incurred on other borrowings outstanding during the period is used to determine the amount of interest cost to be capitalized.

As stated above, the amount of interest capitalized should not exceed the interest cost of the reporting period. In addition, interest is not capitalized during delays or interruptions, other than brief interruptions, that occur during the acquisition or development phase of the qualifying asset.

Background

As described earlier in this chapter, the historical cost of acquiring an asset includes the costs incurred necessary to bring the asset to the condition and location necessary for its intended use. If an asset requires a period in which to carry out the activities necessary to bring it to that location and condition, the interest cost incurred during that period as a result of expenditures for the asset is part of the historical cost of the asset.

SFAS 34 states the following objectives of capitalizing interest:

- To obtain a measure of acquisition cost that more closely reflects the enterprise's total investment in the asset
- To charge a cost that relates to the acquisition of a resource that will benefit future periods against the revenues of the periods benefited

Conceptually, interest cost is capitalizable for all assets that require time to get them ready for their intended use, called the *acquisition period*. However, SFAS 34 concludes that in certain cases, because of cost/benefit considerations in obtaining information, among other reasons, interest cost should not be capitalized. Accordingly, interest cost should not be capitalized for the following types of assets:

- Inventories that are routinely manufactured or otherwise produced in large quantities on a repetitive basis
- Assets that are in use or ready for their intended use in the earnings activities of the entity
- Assets that are not being used in the earnings activities of the proprietary activity and are not undergoing the activities necessary to get them ready for use
- Assets that are not included in the statement of net assets
- Assets acquired with gifts or grants that are restricted by the donor or the grantor to acquisition of those assets to the extent that funds are available from such gifts and grants
- Land that is not undergoing activities necessary to get it ready for its intended use

After consideration of the above exceptions, interest should be capitalized for the following types of assets, referred to as *qualifying assets*:

- Assets that are constructed or otherwise produced for the proprietary fund's own use, including assets constructed or produced for the proprietary fund by others for which deposits or progress payments have been made
- Assets that are for sale or lease and are constructed or otherwise produced as discrete projects, such as real estate developments

Amount of Interest to Be Capitalized

The amount of interest cost to be capitalized for qualifying assets is intended to be that portion of the interest cost incurred during the assets' acquisition periods that could theoretically be avoided if expenditures for the assets had not been made, such as avoiding interest by not making additional borrowings or by using the funds expended for the qualifying assets to repay borrowings that already exist.

The amount of interest that is capitalized in an accounting period is determined by applying an interest rate (known as the capitalization rate) to the average amount of the accumulated expenditures for the asset during the period. (Special rules may apply when qualifying assets are financed with tax-exempt debt. These rules are discussed later in this chapter.) The capitalization rates used in an accounting period are based on the rates applicable to borrowings outstanding during the accounting period. However, if a proprietary fund's financing plans associate a specific new borrowing with a qualifying asset, the enterprise may use the rate on that specific borrowing as the capitalization rate to be applied to that portion of the average accumulated expenditures for the asset not in excess of the amount of the borrowing. If the average accumulated expenditures for the asset exceed the amounts of the specific new borrowing associated with the asset, the capitalization rate applicable to this excess should be a weighted-average of the rates applicable to the other borrowings of the entity.

Capitalization Period

As mentioned previously, the capitalization period generally begins when the following three conditions are met:

1. Expenditures for assets have been made.
2. Activities that are necessary to get the asset ready for its intended use are in progress.
3. Interest cost is being incurred.

(The beginning of the capitalization period for assets financed with tax-exempt debt is described later in this chapter.)

Interest capitalization continues as long as the above three conditions continue to be met. The term *activities* is meant to be construed broadly according to SFAS 34. It should be considered to encompass more than physical construction. Activities are all the steps required to prepare the asset for its intended use, and might include

- Administrative and technical activities during the preconstruction phase
- Development of plans or the process of obtaining permits from various governmental authorities
- Activities undertaken after construction has begun in order to overcome unforeseen obstacles, such as technical problems, labor disputes, or litigation

If the proprietary fund suspends substantially all activities related to the acquisition of the asset, interest capitalization should cease until activities are resumed. However, brief interruptions, interruptions that are externally imposed, and delays inherent in the asset acquisition process do not require interest capitalization to be interrupted.

When the asset is substantially completed and ready for its intended use, the capitalization period ends. Interest cost should not be capitalized during periods when the entity intentionally defers or suspends activities related to the asset, because interest incurred during such periods is a holding cost and not an acquisition cost.

Capitalization of Interest Involving Tax-Exempt Borrowings

SFAS No. 62, "Capitalization of Interest Cost in Situations Involving Certain Tax-Exempt Borrowings and Certain Gifts and Grants," amended SFAS 34 where tax-exempt borrowings are used to finance qualifying assets. Generally, interest earned by an entity is not offset against the interest cost in determining either interest capitalization rates or limitations on the amount of interest cost that can be capitalized. However, in situations where the acquisition of qualifying assets is financed with the proceeds of tax-exempt borrowings and those funds are externally restricted to finance the acquisition of specified qualifying assets or to service the related debt, this general principal is changed. The amount of interest cost capitalized on qualifying assets acquired with the proceeds of tax-exempt borrowings that are externally restricted as specified above is the interest cost on the borrowing less any interest earned on related interest-bearing investments acquired with proceeds of the related tax-exempt borrowings from the date of the borrowing until the assets are ready for their intended use.

In other words, when a specific tax-exempt borrowing finances a project, a proprietary fund will earn interest income on bond proceeds that are invested until they are expended or required to be held in debt service reserve accounts. These interest earnings should be offset against the interest cost in determining the amounts of interest to be capitalized. Conceptually, the true interest cost to the fund is the net of this interest income and interest cost. However, this exception to the general rule of not netting interest income against interest expense relates only to this specific exception relating to tax-exempt borrowings and where amounts received under gifts and grants are restricted to use in the acquisition of the qualifying asset.

CAPITAL ASSETS RESULTING FROM CAPITAL LEASE, CLOSE UP TRANSACTIONS

The accounting for capital lease transactions is another area that is conceptually very easy to understand, but when put into practice results in myriad rules that make understanding what is being recorded in the accounting records far more difficult. Here is the concept: Some lease transactions are structured in such a way that it looks more like the government is buying the asset, rather than leasing it. When a lease is treated as a capital lease, the government records it for accounting purposes as if it actually bought the asset, rather than leased it. It records the asset that it is leasing as an asset and records its obligation to make payments under the lease as a liability. What could be simpler? Well, if that is all the reader needs to understand these transactions, feel free to skip the following section and go right to the section on intangible assets. If a little more detail is needed, continue on.

Before starting, some terminology needs to be defined. If a government leases an asset (for example, it leases a copier machine), the government is known as the "lessee." The office supply store or copier company that leased the copier to the government is known as the "lessor." Another term that is important in understanding capital leases is the concept of present value. Present value is a measure of the time value of money. A dollar in your hand today is worth more than a dollar that you will receive say 10 years from now. You can invest the dollar that you have today and at the end of 10 years you will have more than one dollar. Say that you can invest the one dollar today and get a 3% return each year. The interest is compounded, meaning that at the end of year one, you will have $1.03 to invest, which will earn slightly more interest than you were able to earn with the one dollar. For simplicity's sake, at the end of 10 years, by investing the one dollar at 3% interest, you will have $1.35. It is better to have $1.35 in 10 years instead of one dollar in 10 years, reflecting the time value of money. So how much is one dollar in 10 years worth today? It is about 74 cents, which is also known as its present value. In other words, if you invest 74 cents for 10 years, assuming the same 3% interest rate, in 10 years you will have one dollar. Keep this in mind: In determining how much to record for the asset acquired in a capital lease transaction, the government will use the present value of the required lease payments to be made under the lease to compute an asset value. More about this later.

One further matter to keep in mind is that the interest rate used in these calculations is important. The calculations will be different using an interest rate higher or lower than the example 3% interest rate. Sometimes the interest rate is identified in the lease. Other times the interest rate must be discerned from the other terms of the lease or other factors. In these cases, the interest rate is known as the implicit interest rate. If the implicit interest rate cannot be discerned from the lease, another interest rate, called the lessee's incremental borrowing rate, becomes important. This is the rate that the lessee would be required to pay if it went out and borrowed money to directly purchase the asset instead of leasing it.

Accounting for leases is one of the more technically challenging areas in accounting, including governmental accounting.

The following paragraphs describe the accounting and financial reporting requirements for lessees. Essentially, these accounting requirements depend on whether the lease is classified as an operating lease or a capital lease. This classification is made in the same manner by governmental entities as by commercial enterprises. An important difference must be considered, however. The difference is whether the lease is accounted for by a governmental fund, or by a proprietary fund, or in the government-wide financial statements. The accounting and financial reporting requirements differ significantly.

The accounting and financial reporting requirements discussed in this chapter originate with NCGA Statement No. 5 (NCGAS 5), "Accounting and Financial Reporting Principles for Lease Agreements of State and Local Governments." NCGAS 5 directs state and local governments to use the accounting and financial reporting standards of FASB Statement No. 13 (SFAS 13), "Accounting for Leases," including subsequent amendments. NCGAS 5 provides guidance to state and local governments on applying the requirements of SFAS 13 in a manner consistent with that of governmental accounting. In other words, governmental funds need to account for the capital assets and long-term liabilities resulting from accounting for a lease as a capital lease consistent with how capital assets and long-term liabilities are otherwise accounted for by governmental funds. The effect of recording capital leases on the government-wide financial statements must also be considered. The government-wide statements record leases in a manner similar to proprietary funds. The requirements of SFAS 13, as amended, can be applied by proprietary funds and in the government-wide financial statements directly, since these funds and financial statements use the same basis of accounting and measurement focus as commercial enterprises, resulting in identical accounting treatment for these leases.

Note One important consideration in lease accounting for capital leases for governments concerns leases between a primary government and its component units. The accounting differs for blended component units and discretely presented component units.

- *Blended component units.* Capital leases between the primary government and a blended component unit (or between two component units) should not be reported as capital leases in the financial reporting entity's financial statements. The component unit's debt and assets under the lease are reported as a form of the primary government's debts and assets.
- *Discretely presented component units.* Capital leases between the primary government and a discretely presented component unit should be accounted for as usual capital leases under SFAS 13 as described in this chapter. However, related receivables and payables should not be combined with other amounts due to or from component units or with capital lease receivables and payables with organizations outside of the reporting entity. In these cases, governments may consider elimination entries for the lease assets and liabilities, since a double counting of these assets and liabilities results from this accounting treatment.

The accounting for leases is derived from the view that a lease that transfers substantially all of the benefits and risks of ownership should be accounted for as the acquisition of an asset and the incurrence of a liability by the lessee, that is, a capital lease. Other leases should be accounted for as operating leases; in other words, the rental of property.

A lessee accounts for a lease as one of the following:

- Capital lease
- Operating lease

If a lease meets any one of the following four classification criteria, it is a capital lease:

1. The lease transfers ownership of the property to the lessee by the end of the lease term. (To be a capital lease, a land lease must meet this criterion.)

2. The lease contains a bargain purchase option. A *bargain purchase option* is a provision allowing the lessee, at its option, to purchase the lease property for a price sufficiently lower than the expected fair value of the property at the date the option becomes exercisable, and that exercise of the option appears, at the inception of the lease, to be reasonably assured.

3. The lease term is equal to 75% or more of the estimated economic life of the leased property. However, if the beginning of the lease term falls within the last 25% of the total estimated economic life of the lease property, including earlier years of use, this criterion should not be used for purposes of classifying the lease. The *estimated economic life* of leased property is defined by SFAS 13 as the estimated remaining period during which the property is expected to be economically usable by one or more users, with normal repairs and maintenance, for the purpose for which it was intended at the inception of the lease without limitation of the lease term.

Note A good example of the "economic" life of an asset that is being leased would be the life of a personal computer, or PC. While the actual hardware may be expected to function perfectly well for ten years, it would be hard to justify an economic life of more than three to five years, given the rapid changes in PC technology coupled with increasing demands on PC hardware by software packages.

---

4. The present value at the beginning of the lease term of the minimum lease payments, excluding executory costs, equals or exceeds 90% of the excess of the fair value of the leased property. If the beginning of the lease term falls within the last 25% of the total estimated economic life of the lease property, including earlier years of use, this criterion should not be used for purposes of classifying the lease.

Minimum lease payments include only those payments that the lessee is obligated to make or can be required to make in connection with the leased property. Contingent rentals should not be considered part of the minimum lease payments.

In classifying leases as capital and operating and in recording leases, the determination of what are the minimum lease payments under the lease is likely to be an important consideration. Accordingly, SFAS 13 provides some specific guidance in determining what should be considered as part of the minimum payments under a lease.

The payments that a lessee is required to make (or that the lessee can be required to make) in connection with the lease is the basic definition of minimum lease payments. For example, a 60-month lease with a $1,000 required monthly payment would have minimum lease payments under the lease of $60,000.

The following provides some specific examples when the above example is complicated by other factors:

- Executory costs of the lease, such as insurance, maintenance and taxes, which are paid by the lessee are not part of the minimum lease payments.
- If the lease has a bargain purchase option, the minimum rental payments over the lease term, including the payment called for by the bargain purchase option, should be included in the minimum lease payments.
- Minimum lease payments should not include any guarantee by the lessee of debt of the lessor.

In determining the present value of lease payments, the lessee uses its incremental borrowing rate unless the following two conditions are met:

1. It is practical for the lessee to determine the implicit interest rate that the lessor used to compute the lease payments.
2. The implicit rate computed by the lessor is less than the lessee's incremental borrowing rate.

If both of these conditions are met, then the lessee uses the interest rate that is implicit in the lease instead of its incremental borrowing rate in computing the present value of the minimum lease payments. The lessee's incremental borrowing rate is the estimated interest rate that the lessee would have had to pay if the leased property had been purchased and financed over the period covered by the lease.

In applying the above lease classification criteria, it is important to understand the SFAS 13 definition of the lease term. The *lease term* is the fixed, noncancelable term of the lease, plus

- All periods covered by bargain renewal options
- All periods for which failure to renew the lease imposes a penalty on the lessee in such an amount that a renewal appears to be reasonably assured
- All periods covered by ordinary renewal options during which a guarantee by the lessee of the lessor's debt directly or indirectly related to the lease property is expected to be in effect
- All periods covered by ordinary renewal options preceding the date as of which a bargain purchase option is exercisable
- All periods representing renewals or extensions of the lease at the lessor's option

Suffice to say that bargain and regular renewal options are considered in defining a lease's term in determining whether it is a capital lease. However, in no circumstances should the lease term be assumed to extend beyond the date a bargain purchase option is exercisable.

Recording Capital Leases by the Lessee

The following paragraphs provide an illustration of how a lessee would record a capital lease. The recording is also affected by whether the fund that is recording the lease is a governmental or a proprietary fund (or the government-wide financial statements). These differences are also illustrated.

In recording a capital lease, the proprietary fund or the government-wide financial statements record a capital asset in the amount equal to the present value of the minimum lease payments. (However, the amount recorded should not exceed the fair value of the property being leased.) Both an asset and a liability are recorded because a capital lease is accounted for as if the lessee had actually purchased the leased property. In other words, it records the leased property on its books as an asset and records the same amount as a liability, reflecting that the substance of the lease transaction is that the lessee is purchasing the asset from and financing the purchase with the lessor.

Assume that the government leases a van for $400 per month for five years and after the five-year period, the government can purchase the van from the lessor for $1. In this case, the capital lease criteria that a bargain purchase option exists is met. In addition, the lease is arguably for 75% of the economic life of the van, meeting a second lease capitalization criterion. (Although in this case, at least two criteria are met, only one of the four criteria actually needs to be met to require the lease to be accounted for as a capital lease.) Assume that the lessee is unable to determine the implicit interest rate that the lessor used in the lease, and will use its incremental borrowing rate of 6% to perform the present value calculations. The lease term begins June 1 with the first payment due on June 1, with interest paid in advance. The government has a June 30 fiscal year-end.

The $400 monthly payments for five years represent total payments of $24,000 over the life of the lease. The present value of these minimum lease payments using the 6% interest rate is $20,690.

In recording capital leases by a lessee, there are significant differences in the accounts used by governmental funds and proprietary funds. The following illustrates those differences, incorporating the above example.

Governmental fund. In governmental funds, the primary emphasis is on the flow of financial resources, and expenditures are recognized on the modified accrual basis of accounting. Accordingly, if a lease agreement is to be financed from general governmental resources, it must be accounted for and reported on a basis consistent with governmental fund accounting principles.

Capital assets used in governmental activities acquired through lease agreements should be reported only in the government-wide statement of net assets at the inception of the agreement in an amount determined by the criteria of SFAS 13, as amended. A liability in the same amount should be recorded simultaneously in the government-wide statement of net assets. When a capital lease represents the acquisition or construction of a general capital asset, it should be reflected as an expenditure and another financing source, consistent with the accounting and financial reporting for general obligation bonded debt. In this example, an expenditure for capital lease is recorded by the governmental fund for $20,690 with the same amount recorded as another financing source. As each month's lease payment is made, the governmental fund records an expenditure of $400, with a corresponding $400 reduction of cash. Subsequent governmental fund lease payments are accounted for consistently with the principals for recording debt service on general obligation debt.

Government-wide financial statements and proprietary funds. Capital lease accounting for government-wide financial statements and proprietary funds should follow SFAS 13, as amended and interpreted, without modification. All assets and liabilities of proprietary funds are accounted for and reported in the respective proprietary fund. Therefore, transactions for proprietary fund capital leases are accounted for and reported entirely within the individual proprietary fund and also in the government-wide financial statements. Assets and liabilities for capital lease transactions of governmental funds are reported only in the government-wide financial statements.

Using the same van illustration as above, a capital asset would be recorded in the amount of $20,690 and a liability (termed such as "amounts due under capital leases") would be recorded for the same amount. When a $400 monthly lease payment is made, the interest and principal amounts of the payment must be known. Say that $300 of the payment represents payment of the liability and $100 represents interest. When the first monthly payment of $400 is made, cash is reduced by $400, the liability for amounts due under capital leases is reduced by $300, and interest expense of $100 is recorded. Each month a similar entry is recorded, although the breakout of the $400 payment between principal and interest will change as the amount of the outstanding liability is reduced over the life of the lease. That's not all; do not forget that the government recorded a capital asset in the amount of $20,690 with an estimated useful life of five years. Depreciation expense on this asset also needs to be recorded. Assuming no salvage value, the government would record $4,138 of depreciation expense each year for this asset. Note that the estimated life for depreciation purposes does not always equal the simple lease term. In this example, the lease term is over after five years because of the existence of a bargain purchase option at the end of five years. The government may determine that the estimated useful life of the van is seven years and depreciate the van over that period.

The above paragraphs demonstrate the complexities of recording capital leases by governments. Hopefully, they will serve to clarify these concepts for readers of governmental financial statements.

INTANGIBLE ASSETS

Most of the discussion of capital assets provided so far in this chapter relates to assets that you can physically see or touch— what are known as "tangible" assets. There is another group of capital assets that you cannot physically see or touch. These are known as "intangible" assets.

The GASB has recently issued new guidance on accounting for intangible assets. GASB Statement No. 51, "Accounting and Financial Reporting for Intangible Assets" (GASBS 51), which is essentially effective for June 30, 2010, and later fiscal year-ends.

First, GASBS 51 states that all intangible assets included in its scope are considered capital assets, which is why this is being discussed in this chapter. All of the existing accounting rules that apply to capital assets as discussed in this chapter, also apply to intangible assets covered by GASBS 51. What is new under GASBS 51 is the accounting guidance for when a government would recognize (i.e., record as an asset) intangible assets, including those which are internally generated. GASBS 51 also provides guidance as to when amortization of intangible assets should (and should not) be recorded.

The rule of GASBS 51 apply to assets that have all of the following characteristics:

- Lack physical substance
- Nonfinancial in nature
- Initial useful life extends beyond a single report period

Nonfinancial as used above means that it is not in a monetary form (e.g., cash, investments) and does not represent a claim or right to assets in a monetary form, nor is a prepayment for goods or services. These latter points are receivables (such as real estate taxes receivables) or prepaid expenses (such as prepaid insurance), and are not considered intangible assets under GASBS 51.

So what types of assets are intangible assets under GASBS 51? Examples include easements, water rights, timber rights, patents, trademarks, and computer software, among others.

In order for an asset to be recorded as an asset it must be "identifiable," which means it must meet one the following conditions:

- The asset is capable of being separated from the government and sold, transferred, licensed, rented, or exchanged.
- The asset arises from contractual or other legal rights, regardless of whether those rights are separable or transferable.

Even more rules apply if the asset is internally generated, rather than purchased. Internally generated intangible assets require a more difficult decision to determine whether costs related to them should be capitalized as an intangible asset, rather than recorded as an expense. GASBS 51 requires that all of the following conditions must be met before any internal costs are capitalized as an intangible asset:

- The specific objectives of the project and the nature of the service capacity of the intangible asset have been determined.
- The technical or technological feasibility of completing the project have been demonstrated.
- The intention, ability, and presence of effort to complete the project have been demonstrated.

Only outlays incurred after meeting the above requirements should be capitalized. Outlays incurred prior to meeting these requirements would be expensed.

Clearly, the GASB is attempting to impose specific requirements on when outlays (costs) can be recorded as intangible assets. Even more specific requirements apply when the intangible asset involves internally generated computer software. While many of the specifics of these requirements are beyond the scope of this book, the important "take-away" for the reader is that governments do not have carte blanche in recording assets as intangible assets.

The remaining question to be looked at relative to intangible assets is whether they should be amortized. (Amortization is essentially the same as depreciation but is the term used when the related asset does not have a physical existence.) GASBS 51 provides that intangible assets that have definite useful lives should be amortized over those lives. For example, a patent should be amortized over its legal term. Intangible assets that have indefinite lives should not be amortized. For example, a permanent right-of-way easement is used by the GASB as an example of an asset with an indefinite useful life.

Intangible assets with indefinite lives (as well as those that have definite lives and are being amortized) are both subject to tests for impairment, which are discussed in the following section.

One other point on intangible assets is that the above discussion applies when the economic condition measurement focus is used, primarily in the government-wide financial statements and the fund statements of proprietary funds. Governmental funds, which used the current financial resources measurement focus, would record outlays associated with intangible assets as expenditures, rather than assets.

IMPAIRMENTS OF CAPITAL ASSETS

The final topic of this chapter on capital assets concerns asset impairments. The GASB recently addressed this issue with the issuance of Statement No. 42, "Accounting and Financial Reporting for Impairment of Capital Assets and for Insurance Recoveries." This new GASB statement requires governments to write down the asset amounts recorded in the statement of net assets or balance sheet when a capital asset is impaired. While the following paragraphs discuss a technical definition of impairment, it basically means that the usefulness of the asset to the government has significantly and unexpectedly declined.

Some readers may be familiar with the Financial Accounting Standards Board's Statement No. 144, "Accounting for the Impairment or Disposal of Long-Lived Assets" (SFAS 144). While GASBS 42 addresses the same basic topic as SFAS 144, its approach is actually quite different from what is found in the FASB Statement. In SFAS 144, determination of impairment is based on expected cash flows from the asset that is being evaluated for impairment. In the governmental environment, most capital assets do not provide cash flows, nor are they expected to provide cash flows. GASBS 42 presents the GASB's solutions as to how to identify and measure impairment in the governmental environment.

Definition of Impairment

Asset impairment is a significant, unexpected decline in the service utility of a capital asset. The events or circumstances that lead to impairments are not considered normal and ordinary, meaning that they would not have been expected to occur during the useful life of the capital asset at the time that it was acquired.

GASBS 42 provides guidance on what is meant by the term *service utility*. The service utility of a capital asset is the usable capacity that, at the time of acquisition, was expected to be used to provide service. The current usable capacity of a capital asset may be due to normal or expected decline in useful life or it may be due to impairing events, which are discussed in the following pages.

Determining Whether a Capital Asset Is Impaired

There is a two-step process in determining whether a capital asset is impaired.

1. Identifying potential impairments
2. Testing for impairment

Each of these steps is described in greater detail below.

Identifying Events or Circumstances That May Indicate Impairment

The events that may indicate impairment are prominent events, meaning that they are conspicuous or known to the government, and would be expected to have been discussed by governing boards, management, and/or the media. The following are indicators of impairment:

- Evidence of physical damage, such as for a building damaged by fire or flood, when the level of damage is such that restoration efforts are needed to restore service utility
- Enactment or approval of laws or regulations, or other changes in environmental factors, such as new water quality standards that a water treatment plant does not meet and cannot be modified to meet
- Technological development or evidence of obsolescence, such as that related to a major piece of diagnostic or research equipment that is no longer used, because newer equipment provides better service
- A change in the manner or expected duration of usage of a capital asset, such as the closure of a school prior to the end of its useful life. Note that if the government were no longer using the asset, the asset would be evaluated for impairment even if the government decided to sell the asset.
- Construction stoppage, such as stoppage of construction of a building due to lack of funding

Testing for Impairment

If an asset has been identified as potentially impaired by the indicators described above, the second step is to determine if impairment has incurred. GASBS 42 provides that the asset should be tested for impairment if both of the following factors are present:

- *The magnitude of the decline in service utility is significant.* GASBS 42 does not provide any specific methods to evaluate "significant," but does provide the example of expenses associated with the continued operation and maintenance or costs associated with restoration being "significant" in relationship to the current service utility of the asset.
- *The decline in service utility is unexpected.* This means that the restoration cost or other impairment circumstance is not part of the normal life cycle of the capital asset.

If both of these tests are met and the capital asset is determined to be impaired, the government would use the guidance of GASBS 42 in the following section to measure that impairment. If an asset was indicated to be impaired, but does not meet both of these tests, the estimates used in depreciation calculations, such as remaining useful life and salvage value, should be re-evaluated and changed if considered necessary.

Measuring Impairment

To measure the impairment for capital assets meeting the above tests, the government determines whether the impaired capital assets will be used by the government. Impaired capital assets that will no longer be used by the government should be reported at the lower of carrying value or fair value. This also applies to capital assets impaired from construction work stoppage, which are also reported at the lower of carrying or fair value.

For impaired capital assets that will continue to be used by the government, determination of the amount of the impairment (the historical cost that should be written off) is more complicated. Calculation of an impairment loss is beyond the scope of this book. Suffice to say, there are three different methods to calculate impairment that are briefly described below.

Restoration Cost Method

The amount of the impairment is derived from the estimated costs to restore the utility of the capital asset, not including any amounts attributable to improvements or additions. The estimated restoration cost is converted to historical cost either by restating the estimated restoration cost using an appropriate cost index or by applying a ratio of estimated restoration cost over estimated *replacement* cost to the carrying amount of the asset.

Service Units Method

The amount of the impairment is derived from isolating the historical cost of the service utility that cannot be used due to the impairment event or change in circumstances. The amount of the service units impaired is determined by evaluating the service units provided by the capital asset both before and after the impairment.

Deflated Depreciated Replacement Cost Method

The amount of the impairment is derived from obtaining a current cost for a capital asset to replace the current level of service estimated. The estimated current cost is then depreciated (since the capital asset being replaced is not new) and deflated to convert the cost to historical cost dollars.

GASBS 42 generally identifies which method should be used from the various causes of impairment as follows:

- *Impairments from physical damage*—restoration cost method
- *Impairments from enactment or approval of laws or regulations, or other changes in environmental factors or from technological development or obsolescence*—service units method
- *Impairments from a change in manner or duration of use*—deflated depreciated replacement cost method or service units method

Reporting Impairment Losses

GASBS 42 provides that most impairment losses should be considered permanent (requiring a write-down of the asset) unless evidence is available to demonstrate that the impairment will be temporary. Impairment losses (other than temporary impairments) should be reported in the statement of activities and statement of revenues, expenses, and changes in fund net assets, if appropriate, as a program or operating expense, special item, or extraordinary item in accordance with the guidance of GASBS 34. If not apparent from the face of the financial statements, a general description, amount, and the financial statement classification of the impairment loss should be disclosed in the notes to the financial statements. The carrying amount of impaired capital assets that are idle at year-end should be disclosed, regardless of whether the impairment is considered permanent or temporary.

Once an impairment loss has been recorded for an asset, the value of that asset should not be written up in the future if events affecting the circumstances of the impairment change.

Insurance Recoveries

In the governmental fund financial statements, restoration or replacement of a capital asset should be reported as a separate transaction from the insurance recovery. The insurance recovery is reported as another financing source or an extraordinary item, as appropriate.

In the government-wide financial statements (and in proprietary fund financial statements), the restoration or replacement of an impaired capital asset is also reported as a separate transaction from the impairment loss and associated insurance recovery. The impairment loss should be reported net of the associated insurance recovery when the recovery and loss occur in the same year. Insurance recoveries in subsequent years should be reported as program revenue or as an extraordinary item, as appropriate. Insurance recoveries should be recognized only when realized or realizable. If an insurance company has admitted or acknowledged coverage, an insurance recovery would be considered to be realizable.

SUMMARY

The accounting for capital assets by a government includes a number of complex areas. These assets are usually an important part of a government's financial statements and it is important to have a basic level of understanding of its accounting requirements in order to understand a government's financial statements.

CHAPTER 8

Accounting for Pensions and Other Postemployment Benefits

This chapter discusses the accounting for pensions and postemployment benefits other than pensions (OPEBs) by state and local governmental employers. All of the technicalities included in this chapter come down to an attempt to do two things.

1. Match the cost of providing an employee's postemployment benefit (regardless of whether it is a pension or an OPEB) to the time period that the employee works for the government.
2. Provide disclosures about the pension and OPEB plans themselves so that statement readers can see how well funded it is to be able to pay benefits in the future.

As has been seen so far throughout this book, accountants can take pretty simple objectives and devise complex accounting rules to meet those objectives. The problem with understanding pensions and OPEBs, however, is that another group is added to the mix—actuaries. Be forewarned that the complexities that this chapter will attempt to clarify just do not fit well into a book that includes "made easy" in its title.

A Word about OPEBs

One important difference that readers of the first edition of this book will notice in this second edition is the addition of postemployment benefits other than pensions (OPEBs) to this discussion. These are benefits provided, usually upon retirement, that are literally other than the pension benefits. By far, the most common OPEB benefit is health-care insurance for retirees, although the range of benefits is wide and can include dental coverage, eyeglass coverage, legal representation, gym membership reimbursements, and so on. The types of OPEBs are quite varied because governments at various levels negotiate with their employees the various types of OPEB benefits that may be provided.

Previously, governmental employers that provided their employees with OPEB benefits did not follow the rules used for recording pension expenses. With the implementation of GASB Statement No. 45, "Accounting and Financial Reporting by Employers for Postemployment Benefits other than Pensions" (GASBS 45), they now follow accounting rules that are very similar in concept to those previously used by pensions.

The reader might be wondering why, if OPEBs are simply adopting the rules previously used for pensions, has there been such an uprising about governments implementing the requirements of GASBS 45. There are two related reasons. First, the extent of governments' liabilities for these benefits had never been determined and reported in the financial statements. It turns out that using the actuarial methods described in this chapter, governments' obligations for these benefits is huge. The City of New York, for example, was one of the earliest adopters of GASBS 45 and found that their obligation for OPEB benefits exceeded $50 billion. The second reason is that unlike pensions where governments had routinely contributed assets to pensions plans, by far most governments had not put aside any funds in an OPEB plan to pay for these benefits. Governments simply paid the insurance (or whatever benefit) bill for the current year—also known as using a "pay-as-you-go method." Accordingly, governments found that they had huge obligations for these benefits, with no assets set aside to pay them—not a good position to be in. This resulted in a number of public policy debates that in some cases caused governments to actually begin to fund these plans by contributing assets to trust funds devoted to paying these benefits in the future.

To avoid confusing the reader, the accounting and financial reporting requirements for pensions and OPEB benefits are discussed together. GASB deliberately used a virtually identical conceptual framework for its OPEB rules as it had already established for pension plans. (More bad news on the horizon—GASB is beginning to study the current model used for pension and OPEBS to determine whether changes to it need to be made.) Where important differences between the two types of plans exist, these will be highlighted.

One other basic concept should be kept in mind before diving into the details of pension calculations. Pension benefits are paid from the assets of pension plans. Pension plans obtain their assets from two primary sources.

1. Contributions to the plan by the employer and, in some cases, the employees
2. Investment earnings on the assets of the pension plan

Contributions are determined by actuarial calculations. Part of the actuarial assumptions that are used also include an estimate of the investment earnings that the assets of the plan will yield in future years. OPEB plans would work the same way, except that there are generally no assets accumulated to pay the benefits, hence little or no investment earnings, and most employers do not contribute the actuarially determined contribution to the plan.

Accounting and financial reporting for pensions has been an area for which guidance from the GASB was developed over a very long period. Governmental employers are well known as significant users of pensions as important benefits for their employees. Defined benefit pension plans remain an important governmental employee benefit, despite their declining popularity in the private sector. Governments generally pay their employees less than their counterparts in private industry make. However, one factor offsetting these somewhat lower salaries are fairly generous pension and OPEB benefits that retiring employees enjoy at a relatively young age. Accordingly, the accounting and financial reporting for pension and OPEB plan costs and financial reporting by governments for these plans is an important area.

With the issuance of GASB Statement No. 27 (GASBS 27), "Accounting for Pensions by State and Local Government Employers," in November 1994, the GASB filled a void that existed in accounting standards related to accounting for and reporting pension costs. This chapter is based on the guidance contained in GASBS 27, and later in GASBS 45, and provides the details of the requirements for employers accounting for pension and OPEB costs.

The majority of the requirements of GASBS 27 and GASBS 45 relate to governmental employers that have defined benefit plans; however, there is some guidance in the Statement for employers with defined contribution pension plans.

A *defined contribution plan* is defined by GASBS 27 as "a pension plan having terms that specify how contributions to a plan member's account are to be determined, rather than the amount of retirement income the member is to receive." In a defined contribution plan, the amounts that are ultimately received by the plan member as pension benefits depend only on the amount that was contributed to the member's account and the earnings on the investment of those contributions. In addition, in some cases, forfeitures of benefits by other plan members may also be allocated to a member's account. Accordingly, in this type of pension plan there is no guaranteed pension benefit based on an employee's salary, length of service, and so forth.

A *defined benefit pension plan* is defined by GASBS 27 as "A pension having terms that specify the amount of pension benefits to be provided at a future date or after a certain period of time...." In this type of pension plan, it is the amount of the benefit that is specified, rather than the amount of the contributions, which is specified in a defined contribution plan. The defined benefit in this type of plan is usually a function of one or more factors, including age, years of service, and level of compensation.

Similar definitions are contained in GASBS 45 related to defined contribution and defined benefit OPEB plans. In OPEB plans, the defined benefit level may take several forms. For example, the benefits may be specified in dollars (for example, a flat dollar amount provided for health-care insurance) or as a type or level of coverage (for example, prescription drug coverage, or a percentage of health insurance premiums.)

REQUIREMENTS FOR DEFINED BENEFIT PENSION AND OPEB PLANS

The requirements for defined benefit plans can be divided into two basic areas.

1. Measurement of annual pension and OPEB cost and its recognition by the employer
2. Calculation of the amounts disclosed for the unfunded actuarial liability of the plan

The following material addresses these two basic requirements in considerable detail. It is important to keep these two basic objectives in mind, however, not to lose sight of these very basic objectives of GASBS 27 and GASBS 45 when considering the very technical and detailed nature of its specific requirements.

Measurement of Annual Pension and OPEB Cost and Its Recognition by the Employer

The first step in measuring and recognizing annual pension and OPEB cost for a defined benefit plan is to determine what type of plan the defined benefit pension or OPEB plan is. The two main types of defined benefit pensions and OPEBs are

1. Single-employer or agent multiemployer plans
2. Cost-sharing multiemployer plans

The following paragraphs explain how to determine into which of these two categories an employer's defined benefit pension or OPEB plan should be classified.

Single-Employer or Agent Multiemployer Plans

A single-employer plan is fairly simple to identify. It is a plan that covers the current and former employees, including beneficiaries, of only one employer. Note that one employer may have more than one single-employer defined benefit pension or OPEB plan.

For example, a municipal government may have one single-employer pension plan whose members are police officers and another single-employer pension plan whose members are all firefighters. Both of these would be considered single-employer plans as long as the municipal government's employers were the only members of the plan.

An agent multiemployer plan (or agent plan) is a little more difficult to identify. An agent multiemployer plan is one in which more than one employer aggregates the individual defined benefit plans and pools administrative and investment functions. Each plan for each employer maintains its own identity within the aggregated agent plan. For example, separate accounts are maintained for each employer so that the employer's contributions provide benefits only for the employees of that employer. In addition, a separate actuarial valuation is performed for each individual employer's plan to determine the employer's periodic contribution rate and other information for the individual plan, based on the benefit formula selected by the employer and the individual plan's proportionate share of the pooled assets.

For example, a county may have a number of municipalities within it; each municipality provides pension benefits under defined benefit pension plans to its police officers. To be more efficient from an administrative cost perspective and to provide a larger pool of assets for more effective investment, an agent plan may be established at the county level in which each municipality may participate by having its police officers become members of the countywide agent plan. However, each municipality has its own account within the countywide plan, so that their individual proportionate shares of assets and contributions for their own employees can be determined.

Cost-Sharing Multiemployer Plans

A cost-sharing multiemployer plan is one pension or OPEB plan that includes members from more than one employer where there is a pooling or cost-sharing for all of the participating employers. All risks, rewards, and costs, including benefit costs, are shared and are not attributed individually to the employers. A single actuarial valuation covers all plan members regardless of which employer they work for. The same contribution rates apply for each employer, usually a rate proportional to the number of employees or retired members that the employer has in the plan.

For example, a municipal government establishes a cost-sharing multiemployer OPEB plan that covers all of its nonuniformed workers. Also included in the plan are employees of the separate transportation authority, water utility, and housing authority. The OPEB plan has more than one employer, but in this instance, separate accounts are not maintained for each employer. All risks, rewards, and costs are shared proportionately to the number of members that each employer has in the plan. Separate asset accounts or separate actuarial valuations cannot be performed for each employer, which is the primary distinction between this type of plan and the agent plan described above.

Measuring and recognizing annual pension or OPEB cost differs for single-employer (and agent multiemployer plans) and for cost-sharing multiemployer plans. The following describes the measurement and recognition principles for each of these two categories of plans.

Measuring Annual Pension or OPEB Cost—Single-Employer and Agent Plans

For employers with single-employer or agent multiemployer plans, the annual pension cost should be equal to the annual required contribution (ARC) to the plan for the year, calculated in accordance with the requirements of GASBS 27 and GASBS 45. The calculation of the ARC is described in the following sections.

Tip Earlier in this chapter, it was stated that OPEB plans are generally not funded, meaning assets are usually not put into a trust to pay future benefits. Does GASBS 45 change this with the introduction of the annual *required* contribution? The answer is a definitive no. the GASB has no authority to cause governments to fund OPEB plans (or pension plans, for that matter) despite the terminology. As will be seen in the following discussion, the ARC will be more the equivalent of the expense that the government will record in it government-wide (or proprietary fund) financial statements. It does not equal an actual cash contribution into a plan or trust fund.

CALCULATION OF THE ARC

The basic step in calculating the ARC is to have an actuarial valuation performed for the plan for financial reporting purposes. The valuation is performed by an actuary at a specific point in time and determines pension and OPEB costs and the actuarial value of various assets and liabilities of the plan.

The actuarial valuation is generally performed as of the beginning of the fiscal year reported. This makes sense because, as we will see later, both GASBS 27 and GASBS 45 base their calculation of the unfunded actuarial liability of the plan on the same methods used by the actuary to determine the employer's annual required contributions to the plan for the year. For example, where a plan's and an employer's fiscal year ends on June 30, 20X2, the actuarial valuation is most logically performed as of July 1, 20X1, because that actuarial valuation will determine the amount of the contributions to the plan (and/or annual pension cost that is recognized) for the fiscal year that ends on June 30, 20X2.

While the above example would seem to make sense for the financial statement preparer, in recognition that actuarial valuations are themselves costly and time-consuming, GASBS 27 and GASBS 45 permit more flexibility as to when actuarial valuations are performed. GASBS 27 requires that an actuarial valuation be performed only every other year, or biennially.

GASBS 45 is a bit more flexible. A biennial evaluation is required for OPEB plans with a membership of 200 or more. Plans with a membership of fewer than 200 can have the valuation performed triennially, every three years. For plans with less than 100 members, GASBS 45 provides governments with a "do-it-yourself" methodology where the government could calculate the required amounts without obtaining an actuarial valuation. In practice, this methodology is not easy to use and governments with fewer than 100 members may still be inclined to obtain an actuarial valuation. The date of the actuarial valuation does not have to correspond to the employer's fiscal year-end date, but it should be the same consistent date each year (or the same date every other year if performed biennially).

For example, even if an employer has a June 30 fiscal year-end, the actuarial valuation may be performed as of another date, for example, March 31. However, if that is the date selected for the actuarial valuation, that date should be used consistently.

There are two other limitations described for the timing of the actuarial valuation.

1. The ARC reported by an employer for the current year should be based on the results of an actuarial valuation performed as of a date not more than twenty-four months before the beginning of the employer's fiscal year.
2. A new actuarial valuation should be performed if significant changes have occurred since the previous valuation was performed. These significant changes might be alterations in benefit provisions, the size and/or composition of the population of members covered by the plan, or any other factors that would significantly affect the valuation.

PARAMETERS FOR ACTUARIAL CALCULATIONS, INCLUDING THE ARC

GASBS 27 and GASBS 45 do not specify a method for performing actuarial calculations, including the calculation of the ARC. In fact, its provisions are quite broad and flexible as to how the ARC is calculated. The flexibility is achieved by the introduction of a concept referred to as the *parameters*. The parameters are a set of requirements for calculating actuarially determined pension and OPEB information included in financial reports. (This information includes the ARC.)

The ARC and all other actuarially determined information included in an employer's financial report should be calculated in accordance with the parameters.

Before looking at the specific parameters, there are two broad concepts that should be covered.

1. The actuarial methods and assumptions applied for financial reporting purposes should be the same methods and assumptions applied by the actuary in determining the plan's funding requirements (unless one of the specific parameters requires the use of a different method or assumption). For example, if the actuary uses an investment return assumption of 6% for actuarially determining the contribution to the plan, the same 6% should be used in calculating the ARC and the other financial report disclosures.

2. A defined benefit pension or OPEB plan and its participating employer should apply the same actuarial methods and assumptions in determining similar or related information included in their respective reports. For example, continuing the investment return assumption example, if a 6% rate is used by the actuary for the calculations needed for the plan's financial statements, the same 6% assumption should be used by the actuary for the calculations performed for the employer's financial statements, including the funding calculation assumptions, as described in the previous item.

The specific parameters with which the actuarial calculations must comply are as follows:

- Benefits to be included
- Actuarial assumptions
- Economic assumptions
- Actuarial cost method
- Actuarial value of assets
- Employer's annual required contribution—ARC
- Contribution deficiencies and excess contributions

The following paragraphs describe each of these parameters. Again, while these are fairly technical requirements that may be made more understandable by actuaries, the financial statement reader should be familiar with the basic requirements and the terminology used.

Benefits to Be Included

The actuarial present value of total projected benefits is the present value of the cost to finance benefits payable in the future, discounted to reflect the expected effects of the time value of money and the probability of payment. It represents the estimated amount of benefits that are owed to employees and retirees, discounted to be stated in today's dollars. (The previous chapter's discussion of lease accounting includes background on the concept of present value.) Total projected benefits include all benefits estimated to be payable to plan members (including retirees and beneficiaries, terminated employees entitled to benefits who have not yet received them, and current active members) as a result of their service through the valuation date and their expected future service. The benefits to be included should be those pension benefits provided to plan members in accordance with

- The terms of the plan
- Any additional statutory or contractual agreement to provide pension benefits through the plan that is in force at the actuarial valuation date. (For example, additional agreements might include a collective-bargaining agreement or an agreement to provide ad hoc cost-of-living adjustments and other types of postretirement benefit increases not previously included in the plan terms.)

For OPEB plans, determination of the benefits to be included in the calculation is a bit more complicated. In many cases, there is no formal plan document, as you generally find for pensions. In such cases, GASBS 45 instructs that the "substantive" plan provisions be used, which are defined as the plan terms as understood by the employer and the plan members. This is an important concept since some governmental employers mistakenly thought that they had no OPEB liabilities because there was no formal plan. However, GASBS 45 clearly addresses this situation with the introduction of its concept of substantive plan when no formal plan exists.

Note While the above information on calculating the actuarial present value of total projected benefits is presented to provide a complete discussion of the parameters, it should be noted that this amount is not recorded as a liability in the financial statements of the governmental employer.

Actuarial Assumptions

Actuarial assumptions are those assumptions that relate to the occurrence of future events affecting pension costs. These include assumptions about mortality, withdrawal, disablement and retirement, changes in compensation and government-provided pension benefits, rates of investment earnings and asset appreciation or depreciation, procedures used to determine the actuarial value of assets, characteristics of future members entering the plan, and any other relevant items considered by the plan's actuary.

GASBS 27 and GASBS 45 requires that actuaries select all actuarial assumptions in accordance with Actuarial Standards of Practice which are issued and periodically revised by the Actuarial Standards Board. While the details of this standard are beyond the scope of this book, actuarial assumptions generally should be based on the actual experience of the covered group to the extent that credible experience data is available. The covered group represents the plan members included in the actuarial valuations. These assumptions should emphasize the expected long-term trends rather than give undue weight to recent experience. In addition, the reasonableness of each actuarial assumption should be considered on its own merits, while at the same time consistency with other assumptions and the combined impact of all assumptions should be considered.

One actuarial assumption that is unique to the OPEB calculation is the health-care cost trend rate. If the employer is providing health-care insurance to retirees and future retirees, the actuaries must predict how much inflation there will be in the costs of providing health care and related insurance. The reader should not be surprised to see future health-care cost trend (inflation) rates to be in the 3% to 5% range. Readers may be wondering how often these actuaries go to the doctor, because actual health care inflation rates in recent years are often reported at over 10%. The reason is a view of the actuaries that very large health-care inflation rates are unsustainable over the long term as health-care costs would overwhelm the country's gross national product. Accordingly, a lower rate is used, given the very long-term perspective of these calculations.

Economic Assumptions

Economic assumptions used by the actuary are included with the requirements described above for the actuarial assumption parameter. However, GASBS 27 and GASBS 45 provide additional guidance in a specific parameter relating to economic assumptions. The two main economic assumptions frequently used in actuarial valuations are the investment return assumption and the projected salary increase assumption.

1. The *investment return assumption* (or *discount rate*) is the rate used to adjust a series of future payments to reflect the time value of money. This rate should be based on an estimated long-term investment yield for the plan, with consideration given to the nature and mix of current and expected plan investments and to the basis used to determine the actuarial value of plan assets (discussed further below).

2. The projected salary increase assumption is the assumption made by the actuary with respect to future increases in the individual salaries and wages of active plan members; that is, those members who are still active employees. The expected salary increases commonly include amounts for inflation, enhanced productivity, employee merit, and seniority. In other words, this assumption recognizes that a current employee who will retire in ten years will likely be earning a higher salary and perhaps be entitled to a different level of OPEB benefits at the time of retirement, and this higher benefit level has an impact on the amount of pension benefits that will be paid to the employee. (Some of these benefits have already been earned by the employee.)

The discount rate and the salary assumption (and any other economic assumptions) should include the same assumption with regard to inflation. For example, consider a plan that invests its assets only in long-term fixed-income securities. In considering an appropriate discount rate, the actuary will consider the various components of the investment return on long-term fixed-income securities, consisting of "real, risk-free" rate of return, which the actuary adjusts for credit and other risks, including market risk tied to inflation. The inflation assumptions that the actuary uses in this calculation should be consistent with the inflation assumption used for determining the projected salary and other benefit increases.

Actuarial Cost Method

An actuarial cost method is a process that actuaries use to determine the actuarial value of pension and OPEB plan benefits and to develop an actuarially equivalent allocation of the value to time periods. This is how the actuary determines normal cost (a component of the ARC that is described later) and the actuarial accrued liability (the principal liability for benefits that is disclosed, also described later in this chapter).

GASBS 27 and GASBS 45 require the use of one of the following actuarial cost methods:

- Entry age
- Frozen entry age
- Attained age
- Frozen attained age
- Projected unit credit
- Aggregate method

Actuarial Value of Assets

The actuarial value of assets will not necessarily be the same as the value of the assets reported in the pension plan's or OPEB plan or trust's financial statements. Governmental pension plans and OPEB trusts report assets at fair value, which is similar to, but not the same as, the market-related actuarial value for assets prescribed by GASBS 27 and GASBS 45. As used in conjunction with the actuarial value of assets, a market-related value can be either an actual market value (or estimated market value) or a calculated value that recognizes changes in market value over a period of time, typically three to five years. Actuaries value plan assets using methods and techniques consistent with both the class and the anticipated holding period of assets, the investment return assumption, and other assumptions used in determining the actuarial present value of total projected benefits and current actuarial standards for asset valuation.

The reason that other factors are considered by the actuary in valuing assets for purposes of the actuarial valuations is to smooth out year-to-year changes in the market value of assets. Significant year-to-year changes in the stock and bond markets might otherwise cause significant changes in contribution requirements, pension and OPEB cost recognition, and liability disclosures. When consideration of the factors described in the preceding paragraph leads the actuary to conclude that such smoothing techniques are appropriate, there is a more consistent calculation of contributions, costs, and liabilities from year to year.

Employer's Annual Required Contribution (ARC)

As previously mentioned, the ARC is calculated actuarially in accordance with the parameters. The ARC has two components.

1. Normal cost
2. Amortization of the total unfunded actuarial accrued liability

The following paragraphs describe how actuaries arrive at these two amounts.

Normal Cost

The normal cost component of the ARC represents the portion of the actuarial present value of pension and OPEB plan benefits and expenses allocated to a particular year by the actuarial cost method. The list of the actuarial cost methods provided earlier shows the different ways in which an actuary determines normal cost.

Amortization of the Total Unfunded Actuarial Accrued Liability

The total unfunded actuarial accrued liability is the amount by which the actuarial accrued liability for plan benefits exceeds the actuarial value of the assets of the plan. The actuarial accrued liability is an amount determined by the actuary as part of the actuarial valuation. It represents the amount of the actuarial present value of pension and OPEB benefits and expenses that will not be provided for by future normal cost.

GASBS 27 and GASBS 45 have some very specific requirements as to how the unfunded actuarial accrued liability should be amortized. In other words, a portion of the total unfunded accrued liability is added to the normal cost in calculating the ARC. The underlying concept is that since the unfunded actuarial accrued liability will not be paid in the future through normal costs, it must be amortized and paid over a reasonable period so that the plan ultimately has sufficient assets (or the governmental employer records enough of a liability) to pay future pension benefits and expenses. Viewed still another way, amortizing the unfunded actuarial accrued liability will result in higher contributions to the plan, thus eliminating the unfunded actuarial accrued liability over time, resulting in plan assets sufficient to pay the pension benefits and expenses of the plan. Of course in the OPEB world, where most plans are not funded, amortization of the accrued liability will simply result in an increasingly higher liability being recorded on the government employer's financial statements, reflecting that it is not actually funding the ARC amount.

GASBS 27 and GASBS 45 set a maximum amortization period, a minimum amortization period, and requirements for the selection of an amortization method. The maximum acceptable amortization period for the unfunded actuarial accrued liability is thirty years. A minimum amortization period is to be used when a significant decrease in the total unfunded actuarial liability is generated by a change from one of the acceptable actuarial cost methods to another of those methods, or when a change occurs in the methods used to determine the actuarial value of assets. The minimum amortization period in these instances is ten years. The minimum amortization period is not required when a plan is closed to new entrants and all or almost all of the plan's members have retired.

Note This provision is designed to prevent manipulation of the annual pension or OPEB cost. The selection of the actuarial cost method and the valuation methods for the plan's assets are within the control of the plan, its actuary, and perhaps the employer. If one of these two changes resulted in a significant reduction in the unfunded actuarial accrued liability and this whole benefit was recognized by the actuary in one year, this could result in a very significant reduction of the annual pension or OPEB cost in the year that the changes were recognized. The ten-year minimum amortization period for these types of changes reduces the benefit of changing methods solely to manipulate annual pension or OPEB cost amounts.

Amortization Method

There are two acceptable methods to amortize unfunded actuarial accrued liability under GASBS 27 and GASB 45. These are

1. Level dollar amortization method
2. Level percentage of projected payroll amortization method

Level dollar amortization method. In the level dollar amortization method, the amount of the unfunded actuarial accrued liability is amortized by equal dollar amounts over the amortization period. This method works just like a mortgage. The payments are fixed and consist of differing components of interest and principal. Expressed in real dollars (excluding the effects of inflation), the amount of the payments actually decreases over time, assuming at least some inflation. In addition, because payroll can be expected to increase as a result of at least some inflation, the level dollar payments decrease as a percentage of payroll over time.

Level percentage of projected payroll amortization method. The level percentage of projected payroll method calculates amortization payments so that they are a constant percentage of the projected payroll of active plan members over a given number of years. The dollar amount of the pension payments and OPEB benefits generally will increase over time as payroll increases due to inflation. In real dollars, the amount of the payments remains level, because the inflation effect is accounted for by the payroll increases due to inflation.

The amortization calculated in accordance with the preceding paragraphs, when added to the normal cost also described above, is the amount of the ARC for the year.

A contribution deficiency or excess contribution is the difference between the ARC for a given year and the employer's contributions in relation to the ARC. Amortization of a contribution deficiency or excess contribution should begin at the next actuarial valuation, unless settlement is expected not more than one year after the deficiency occurred. If the settlement has not occurred by the end of that term, amortization should begin at the end of the next actuarial valuation.

NET PENSION OR OPEB OBLIGATION

The net pension obligation of a governmental employer is a strictly defined term under GASBS 27 and GASB 45. To avoid getting lost in the details of its calculation, however, a very general way to view the net pension or OPEB obligation is the cumulative amount by which an employer has not actually contributed the ARC to the pension plan or OPEB trust. Thus, its purpose is to highlight where an employer is not making sufficient contributions into the plan for the plan to pay its pension and/or OPEB benefits and expenses.

While a net pension obligation does not indicate that the plan will run out of funds in the near future, it does highlight that it is likely that the employer will need to increase its contributions to the plan in the future for the plan to pay its pension benefits and expenses over the long term. The net pension obligation represents the cumulative difference since the effective date of GASBS 27 between annual pension cost and the employer's contributions, excluding short-term differences and unpaid contributions, other than amounts that have been converted to pension debt. GASBS 27 specifies that when an employer has a net pension obligation, annual pension cost should include one year's interest on the net pension obligation in addition to the ARC.

For OPEB plans, which are generally not funded, recording the difference between what the government actually paid for OPEB benefits in a fiscal year and the ARC for that fiscal year will result in a liability that is recorded by the government, as will be further discussed in the next section. In subsequent years this liability will grow each year until eventually the extent to which the OPEB plan is under funded will be recorded on the governmental employer's financial statements. Note that this is in contrast to having to record the entire unfunded actuarial liability on the government's financial statements all at once. In other words, this liability will creep onto the financial statements over a period of time and does not need to be recorded all at once. Note that the unfunded actuarial liability for OPEB benefits is disclosed in the notes to the financial statements even though it is not immediately recorded as a liability. Upon implementation of GASBS 45, this disclosure is what made users of governmental financial statements take notice of what the government's ultimate estimated liability for these benefits, in current dollars, was expected to be.

RECORDING PENSION- AND OPEB-RELATED ASSETS, LIABILITIES, AND EXPENDITURES/EXPENSES

A large part of this chapter has been devoted to explaining the acceptable means of calculating annual pension and OPEB costs and related assets and liabilities in accordance with GASBS 27 and GASBS 45 for single-employer and agent plans. Following is a discussion of how those financial statement amounts are recorded. It is important to note the differences in accounting between single-employer (and agent multiemployer) and cost-sharing multiemployer plans. Pension and OPEB expenditures made by governmental funds are recognized on the modified accrual basis. The amount recognized as an expenditure is the amount contributed to the plan or expected to be contributed to be liquidated with expendable available financial resources. In the case of unfunded OPEB plans, the expenditure is generally the amount to pay the bill for the cost of the benefits provided in the current year.

On the government-wide financial statements, if the amount of the pension or OPEB contribution recognized for the year in relation to the ARC is less than (or greater than) annual pension or OPEB cost, the difference should be added to (or subtracted from) the net pension or OPEB obligation. A positive year-end balance in the net pension or OPEB obligation should be reported in the government-wide statement of net assets as a liability. In other words, the amount of pension or OPEB expense recognized on the government-wide statement of activities should equal the annual required contribution. If a lower amount was contributed or paid, the difference is reported as a liability on the government-wide statement of net assets. The government-wide statements will basically account for pension and OPEB expenses in a manner similar to proprietary funds, as described in the following paragraph.

Pension and OPEB expenses for proprietary and all other entities that apply proprietary fund accounting should be recognized on an accrual basis. The employer should report pension and OPEB expense for the year equal to the ARC. The net pension obligation should be adjusted for any difference between contributions made and pension expense. A positive year-end balance in the net pension obligation should be recognized as the year-end liability in relation to the ARC. Pension liabilities and assets to different plans should not be offset in the financial statements.

Cost-Sharing Multiemployer Plans

The preceding part of this chapter describes the accounting and financial reporting requirements for governmental employers that participate in single-employer or agent multiemployer plans. The requirements of GASBS 27 and GASBS 45 for governmental employers that participate in cost-sharing multiemployer plans are much simpler. These employers should recognize annual pension or OPEB expenditures or expenses equal to their contractually required contributions to the plan. Recognition should be on the modified accrual or accrual basis, whichever is applicable for the type of employer or for the fund types used to report the employers' contributions. For these types of plans, pension liabilities and assets result from the difference between the contributions required and contributions made. Pension and/or OPEB liabilities and assets to different plans should be offset in the financial statements.

Note   A useful way to view the relationship of a cost-sharing multiemployer plan and its participating employers is that the plan bills the employers for their annual contributions. The employers' handling of these pension or OPEB bills is similar to how they handle other types of bills that they pay, which, of course, depends on whether they follow governmental or proprietary fund accounting.

PENSION AND OPEB DISCLOSURES

These are numerous disclosure requirements relating to defined benefit pension and OPEB plans. The disclosures are somewhat different for single-employer (and agent multiemployer) plans and for cost-sharing multiemployer plans. The disclosures are designed to give the reader of the financial statements information about the funded status of the plans. In other words, how does the actuarial value of the plan's assets compare with the plan's actuarially determined liabilities? Information is also provided as to levels of contributions that the employer government is making to the plan, whether these contributions are equal to the actuarially determined contribution amounts, and how they compare to the total dollar amounts of the payroll for the employees covered under the plan.

In addition to these types of disclosures, three-year trend information is required to be provided by employers participating in single-employer and agent multiemployer plans as required supplementary information to the basic financial statements.

As can be seen from the preceding discussions, there are a great many similarities in the accounting and reporting for defined benefit pension and OPEB plans. The disclosure guidance for pension plans previously was provided by GASBS 27. In determining the disclosure requirements for OPEB plans and benefits, the GASB modified some of the disclosure requirements applicable to OPEB plans under GASBS 45. To bring the GASBS 27 disclosures more in line with those of GASBS 45, yet another GASB Statement was issued, No. 50, "Pension Disclosures—an amendment of GASB Statements No. 25 and 27" (GASBS 50).

While the details of the disclosure requirements are beyond the scope of this book, the reader should be aware of this relatively new statement to avoid confusion in determining the source of the disclosure requirements.

EMPLOYERS WITH DEFINED CONTRIBUTION PLANS

The vast majority of the provisions of GASBS 27 and GASBS 45 relate to defined benefit plans because of the complexity of calculating contributions and the actuarial accrued liabilities for these plans. However, there is some very basic accounting and disclosure guidance contained in GASBS 27 and GASBS 45 that relates to employers that sponsor defined contribution pension plans.

Governmental employers with defined contribution plans should recognize annual pension or OPEB expenditures or expenses equal to their required contributions in accordance with the terms of the plan. Accounting for defined contribution pension plans most closely resembles a governmental employer's accounting for the costs and assets and liabilities of a cost-sharing multiemployer pension or OPEB plan. Recognition should be on the modified accrual basis or accrual basis, whichever applies to the type of employer or the type of fund used to report the employer's contributions. Pension and OPEB liabilities and assets result from the difference between contributions required and contributions made. Pension and OPEB liabilities and assets to different plans should not be offset in the financial statements. Government-wide financial statements would account for defined contribution plans in a manner similar to proprietary funds.

SUMMARY

It is important for readers of a government's financial statements to understand the impact of the existence of pension and OPEB plans on that governmental employer's financial statements. As mentioned at the beginning of this chapter, all of the details inherent in these accounting entries and disclosures focus on recording pension and OPEB costs in the proper accounting period and on indicating the financial well-being of the pension or OPEB plan by clarifying the difference between its assets and its liabilities.

CHAPTER 9

Sundry Accounting Topics

There are several special areas of accounting used by governments that require some study in order to understand the financial statements of governments. These areas involve various asset, liability, revenue, and expense items. While each topic does not warrant its own chapter in this book, collectively these "miscellaneous" items are important in understanding governmental accounting. Specifically, this chapter addresses the following:

- Accounting for investments
- Reporting unrealized gains or losses
- Investment and deposit disclosures
- Compensated absence accruals
- Landfill closure and postclosure care costs
- Pollution remediation obligations
- Derivatives, including interest rate swaps
- Securities lending transactions
- Sales and pledges of receivables and future revenue streams

ACCOUNTING FOR INVESTMENTS

The accounting for investments is the subject of GASB Statement No. 31, "Accounting and Financial Reporting for Certain Investments and for External Investment Pools" (GASBS 31), For purposes of simplicity, let us begin with the accounting for some of the most common investments that a government is likely to have.

Debt Securities

A debt security is one that represents a creditor relationship with another organization. The other organization owes the government funds, evidenced by some type of security. Debt securities are found in the form of bonds and notes. Treasury bills are another form of debt security, as is a collateralized mortgage obligation (CMO) that is issued in equity form but is accounted for as a nonequity investment. Thus, debt securities would include US Treasury securities, US government agency securities, municipal securities, corporate bonds, convertible debt, commercial paper, negotiable certificates of deposit, and interest-only and principal-only strips. GASBS 31 states that certain contracts, specifically option contracts, financial futures contracts, and forward contracts, are not considered debt securities.

Debt securities are reported in the financial statements at their fair value. The term "fair value" is now used instead of the once-common term "market value." The new term indicates that an investment's fair value may be determined even if there is no actual, well-defined market for an investment. Fair value represents the amount at which a financial instrument could be exchanged in a current transaction between willing parties, other than a forced sale or liquidation.

In determining the fair value of a debt instrument, the particular security might not be traded in the marketplace. The government would use market value of a similar security, such as one with the same maturity, interest rate, and credit rating of the issuer, to estimate the fair value of its own debt security.

Equities

The accounting for equities (such as common stocks) is more complicated. GASBS 31 requires that equity securities with readily determinable fair values be recorded at fair value in the financial statements. The fair value of equities is considered to be readily determinable if sales prices or bid-and-asked quotations are currently available on a securities exchange registered with the United States Securities and Exchange Commission, or in the over-the-counter market, provided that those prices are publicly reported by the National Association of Securities Dealers and

Automated Quotations (NASDAQ) systems or by the National Quotations Bureau. Fair value for equity securities traded only in a foreign market is readily determinable if that foreign market is of a breadth and scope comparable to one of the US markets just referred to.

The requirements for equity securities with readily determinable fair values to be reported at fair value also apply to option contracts, stock warrants, and stock rights. The requirements do not apply to restricted stock, because GASBS 31 concludes that the fair value of restricted stock is not readily determinable. Restricted stock refers to equity securities whose sale is restricted at acquisition by legal or contractual provisions, unless the restriction terminates within one year.

Interest-Earning Investment Contract

An interest-earning investment contract is a direct contract that a government enters into as a creditor of a financial institution, broker-dealer, investment company, insurance company, or other financial institution for which the government directly or indirectly receives interest payments. If the investment value is affected by interest rate changes (called participating contracts), the interest-earning investment contracts should be reported at fair value. If the interest-earning investment contracts' redemption terms are not affected by changes in interest rates (called nonparticipating contracts), such as nonnegotiable certificates of deposit, these investments should be reported using a cost-based measure, provided that the fair value of those contracts is not significantly affected by the impairment of the credit standing of the issuer or by other factors.

Mutual Funds

Open-end mutual funds (ones that issue new shares to new investors) should be reported in the financial statements at fair value. A closed end mutual fund (where only a fixed number of shares exist and are traded on an exchange) should be treated as an equity security and reported at fair value if the fair value is readily determinable.

Money-Market Investments

Money-market investments are short-term, highly liquid debt instruments, including commercial paper, banker's acceptances, and US Treasury and agency obligations. Money-market investments should generally be reported in the financial statements at fair value. GASBS 31 provides an exception, however. Money-market investments that have a remaining maturity at the time of purchase of one year or less may be reported at amortized cost, provided that the fair value of the investment is not significantly affected by the impairment of the credit standing of the issuer or by other factors.

Real Estate Held in an Endowment Fund

The GASB recently issued Statement No. 52, "Land and Other Real Estate Held as Investments in Endowments" (GASBS 52), to change the accounting for these types of investments. Endowments are generally funds where the original amount of the principal is required by a donor to be kept intact, and the recipient government is only permitted to spend the investment returns from these assets. Governmental colleges and universities that receive endowments from donors are a good example of an endowment fund in the governmental environment.

Endowments, including permanent funds, previously reported land and other real estate investments at their historical cost. This was inconsistent with how other types of governmental entities (such as pension plans) reported land and other real estate in their financial statements. Accordingly, GASBS 52 requires endowments to report their land and other real estate investments at fair value. Governments are also required to report the changes in fair value as income.

REPORTING UNREALIZED GAINS OR LOSSES

One of the more controversial aspects of GASBS 31 is how changes in fair value of investments from the beginning of the fiscal year to the end of the fiscal year are treated. Say that the fair value of a debt security increases from $100 at the beginning of the fiscal year to $110 at the end of the fiscal year. The government still holds the security at the end of the fiscal year, meaning that it has not sold the security and "realized" the $10 gain. GASBS 31 requires that the "unrealized" appreciation in the fair value of the security be recognized as part of investment income. In other words, there is an impact on a government's statement of activities (or statements of revenues, expenses/expenditures, and changes in fund net assets/fund balance) for unrealized gains or losses in an investment portfolio. Thus in this example, the $10 of unrealized appreciation would be recorded as part of the investment earnings of the government for the year. Keep in mind that declines in the fair values of investments are also reported by governments as decreases in their investment income for the year.

INVESTMENT AND DEPOSIT DISCLOSURES

The GASB recently updated the disclosures required for investments (as well as demand deposits) in the notes to the financial statements of governments not too long ago. Given the recent turmoil in the financial markets, the GASB may have had a crystal ball in requiring certain important disclosures on deposit and investment risk prior to the turmoil. In addition to a discussion of the government's overall deposit and investment policies (such as what types of investments it is authorized to purchase), a government must discuss certain risks that are associated with its investment portfolio. The disclosures discussed are those brought about by GASB Statement No. 40, "Deposit and Investment Risk Disclosures—an Amendment of GASB Statement No. 3" (GASBS 40). The following briefly describes these types of risks.

Custodial Risk

This is the risk that the entity holding a government's deposits or investments (i.e., the custodian) becomes insolvent, resulting in the government losing some or all of its deposits or investments. For example, if a government maintains a checking or savings account at a commercial bank, it is likely to be insured by the FDIC up to $100,000, which has temporarily increased to

$250,000, or in some cases, unlimited coverage. Any amount over the insurance limit would be considered "exposed to custodial risk," and the government would have to disclose the total amount so exposed. There are ways for the government to mitigate this risk by requiring the custodian to collateralize the government's deposits or investments. The same disclosures for custodial risk would apply to the government's investments.

Concentration of Credit Risk

This is the risk that the government's exposure to the credit risk of its investments is concentrated in one or a few issuers. Governments are required to disclose, by amount and issuer, investments (other than those guaranteed by the US government) in any one issuer that represent five percent or more of total investments.

Government financial statement preparers (and readers) should be careful about what investments are actually guaranteed by the federal government as to credit. Certain debt securities may sound like they have a federal guarantee (such as debt issued by the Federal Home Loan Banks) when they actually do not.

Again, remember that credit risk is the risk related to whether the borrower can repay the funds and is not directly related to market risk that may result from changes in the market rates of interest for debt instruments with similar credit ratings.

Interest Rate Risk

The disclosures about interest rate risks are one of the more important disclosures required by GASBS 40. Governments are required to disclose information about the sensitivity of the debt investments to changes in interest rates. Generally, when interest rates rise, the fair value of debt investments declines. Conversely, when interest rates fall, the fair value of debt investments increases. To meet the disclosure requirement, governments are required to present information about the investment maturities of its debt investments (the longer the maturity, the more sensitive to interest rate changes the fair value of the debt investment will be) or information developed about portfolio volatility under various scenarios.

Foreign Currency Risk

If a government's deposits or investments are denominated in a foreign currency, and so are exposed to foreign currency risk, the government discloses the US dollar balances of such deposits or investments, classified by currency denomination and investment type.

COMPENSATED ABSENCE ACCRUALS

This section describes the accounting rules for what the technical accounting literature refers to as "compensated absences." You might know these as vacation and sick leave and teacher sabbaticals.

Governmental entities almost always provide benefits to their employees in the form of *compensated absences*—which is a catch-all phrase for instances where an employee is not at work, but is still paid. Vacation pay and sick leave represent the most common and frequently used forms of compensated absences.

In the past, governmental entities used the guidance of FASB Statement No. 43 (SFAS 43), "Accounting for Compensated Absences," in accounting for and reporting liabilities for compensated absences. One of the objectives of SFAS 43 was the matching of compensation expense with the benefits received from an employee's work. In other words, as an employee works and earns vacation and sick leave that will be paid or used in the future, there should be some recognition that a liability and an expense has occurred during the time that the employee is providing the services. Of course, using the basis of accounting and measurement focus of governmental funds, the liability for compensated absences is generally not recorded by a governmental fund, but is instead recorded only in the government-wide statement of net assets and by proprietary funds. There is no corresponding expenditure in the governmental fund until these amounts are actually paid or when they are due to be paid.

The GASB made some slight modifications to the requirements of SFAS 43 and issued a GASB Statement that addresses
the accounting and financial reporting for compensated absences
for all governmental entities, regardless of the basis of accounting
and measurement focus used. The resulting statement is GASB
Statement No. 16 (GASBS 16), "Accounting for Compensated
Absences." This section summarizes the accounting and financial
reporting requirements for compensated absences, which are
based on the requirements of GASBS 16.

Compensated absences are absences from work for which
employees are still paid, such as vacation, sick leave, and sabbatical leave. GASBS 16's requirements apply regardless of
which reporting model or fund type is used by the governmental
entity to report its transactions and prepare its financial statements. Therefore, these requirements apply to all state and local
governmental entities, including public benefit corporations and
authorities, public employee retirement systems, governmental
utilities, governmental hospitals and other health care providers,
and governmental colleges and universities.

Simply because these requirements generally apply to all
governmental entities does not mean that the presentation of the
amounts in the various types of entities' financial statements
calculated using its guidance will be the same. The amounts calculated as a liability will be the same regardless of the basis of
accounting or measurement focus used by the entity or fund to
which the liability applies. However, the recording of the liability
and recognition of compensation expense or expenditure in
preparing fund financial statements will be different based on
whether the liability relates to a governmental fund (which uses
the modified accrual basis of accounting and the current financial
resources measurement focus) or in the government-wide
financial statements or a fund or entity that uses proprietary fund
accounting (which uses the accrual basis of accounting and the
economic resources measurement focus).

Basic Principle

The underlying principle for accounting for compensated absences is that a liability for compensated absences that are attributable to services already rendered and are not contingent on a

specific event outside the control of the employer and the employee should be accrued as employees earn the rights to the benefits. On the other hand, compensated absences that relate to future services or are contingent on a specific event outside the control of the employer and employee should be accounted for in the period those services are rendered or those events take place.

While this conceptual principle sounds good, to put it into practice the three main types of compensated absences—vacation, sick leave, and sabbatical leave—need to be examined individually to determine when to actually calculate the liability.

Vacation Leave (and Other Compensated Absences with Similar Characteristics)

A liability should be accrued for vacation leave and other compensated absences with similar characteristics and recorded as the benefits are earned by the employees if both of these conditions are met.

1. The employees' rights to receive compensation are attributable to services already rendered

2. It is probable that the employer will compensate the employees for the benefits through paid time off or some other means, such as cash payments at termination or retirement.

In applying this criterion, three different scenarios will arise.

1. The employee is entitled to the vacation pay, and no other criteria need be met. A liability for this amount should be recorded.

    An employer governmental entity would accrue a liability for vacation leave and other compensated leave with similar characteristics that were earned but not used during the current or prior periods and for which the employees can receive compensation in a future period.

2. The employee has earned time, but the time is not yet available for use or payment because the employee has not yet met certain conditions.

Benefits that have been earned but that are not yet available for use as paid time off or as some other form of compensation because employees have not met certain conditions (such as a minimum service period for new employees) are recorded as a liability to the extent that it is probable that the employees will meet the conditions for compensation in the future.

3. The employee has earned vacation benefits, but the benefits are expected to lapse and not result in compensation to the employee.

Benefits that have been earned but that are expected to lapse and thus not result in compensation to employees should not be accrued as a liability.

Sick Leave (and Other Compensated Absences with Similar Characteristics)

A liability for sick leave and other compensated absences with similar characteristics should be accrued using one of the following termination approaches:

- The termination payment method
- The vesting method

Under both methods, a liability is not recorded for sick time earned, which is expected to be taken as time off by employees for illness. This compensation is contingent on the future illness of the employees. Rather, a liability for sick leave is recorded only when actual cash payments for unused leave are expected to be made to employees. The following are descriptions of the two methods of recording a liability for sick leave.

Termination payment method. A liability should be accrued for sick leave as the benefits are earned by the employees if it is probable that the employer will compensate the employees for the benefits through cash payments conditioned on the employees' termination or retirement (referred to as the *termination payments*).

In applying the termination payment method, a liability is recorded only to the extent that it is probable that the benefits will result in termination payments, rather than be taken as absences due to illness or other contingencies, such as medical appointments. The liability that is recorded would be based on an estimate using the governmental entity's historical experience of making termination payments for sick leave, adjusted for the effect of any changes that have taken place in the termination payment policy and other current factors that might be relevant to the calculation.

Note Some governments compensate employees for sick leave at termination based on some reduced payment scheme. For example, the government may have a policy that an employee must have a minimum of ten years of service to be entitled to any termination payment for sick leave, and the termination payment may be calculated based on some fraction of the total unused sick days that the terminating employee has at the date of termination. For example, a government might have a policy that only employees with a minimum of ten years of service will be compensated for sick leave and that compensation will be equal to the compensation for one-third of the total of the unused sick days that the employee has left on termination.

Vesting method. As an alternative to the termination payment method, a governmental entity may use the method described as the "vesting" method. Under the vesting method, a governmental entity should estimate its accrued sick leave liability based on the sick leave accumulated at the balance sheet date by those employees who currently are eligible to receive termination payments, as well as other employees who are expected to become eligible in the future to receive such payments. To calculate the liability, these accumulations should be reduced to the maximum amount allowed as a termination payment. Accruals for those employees who are expected to become eligible in the future should be based on assumptions concerning the probability that individual employees or classes or groups of employees will become eligible to receive termination payments.

Both of these methods should usually produce a similar amount for the liability that a government should record for sick leave and other compensated absences with similar characteristics.

Sabbatical Leave

Determining how or if a liability for sabbatical leave is calculated and reported is based on the nature and terms of the sabbatical leave available to employees. The accounting for sabbatical leave depends on whether the compensation during the sabbatical is for service during the period of the leave itself, or instead for past service.

Some governmental entities permit sabbatical leave from normal duties so that employees can perform research or public service or can obtain additional training to enhance the reputation of or otherwise benefit the employer. In this case, the sabbatical constitutes a change in assigned duties and the salary paid during the leave is considered compensation for service during the period of the leave. The nature of the sabbatical leave is considered to be restricted. In this situation, the sabbatical leave is accounted for in the period the service is rendered. A liability is not reported in advance of the sabbatical.

However, sometimes sabbatical leave is permitted to provide compensated unrestricted time off. In this situation, the salary paid during the leave is compensation for past service. Accordingly, in this situation, a liability should be recorded during the periods the employees earn the right to the leave if it is probable that the employer will compensate the employees for the benefits through paid time off or some other means.

Other Factors Affecting the Liability Calculation

There are two other factors that need to be considered in calculating liability amounts for compensated absences—the rate of pay that is used to calculate the liability and the additional salary-related costs that should be considered for accrual. These two factors are discussed in the following paragraphs.

The liability for compensated absences should be based on the salary rates in effect at the balance sheet date. There is no need to project future salary increases into a calculation that considers that when the vacation or sick leave is actually paid, it is likely to be at a higher rate of pay than that in place at the balance sheet date. On the other hand, if a governmental employer pays employees for compensated absences at other than their pay rates or salary rates (sometimes at a lower amount that is established by contract, regulation, or policy), then the other rate that is in effect at the balance sheet date should be used to calculate the liability.

As for salary-related payments, an additional amount should be accrued as a liability for those payments associated with compensated absences. These amounts should also be recorded at the rates in effect at the balance sheet date. Salary-related payments subject to accrual are those items for which an employer is liable to make a payment directly and incrementally associated with payments made for compensated absences on termination. These salary-related payments would include the employer's share of social security and Medicare taxes and might also include an employer's contribution to a pension plan.

Financial Reporting Considerations

The accounting and financial reporting for compensated absences for state and local governments must take into consideration the differences between the governmental fund and the proprietary fund and government-wide financial statement accounting basis and measurement focus with respect to

- Fund long-term liabilities and government-wide financial statement long-term liabilities
- Current liabilities and noncurrent liabilities

The accounting and financial reporting differ on whether the liability is recorded in the government-wide financial statements or a proprietary fund or in a governmental fund. The differences are not in how the amount of the liability is calculated. The difference in the accounting and financial reporting relates to where and how the liability is recorded.

For governmental funds, the long-term portion of the liability for compensated absences is one that is recorded only in the government-wide statement of net assets. Consistent with the modified accrual basis of accounting and the current financial resources measurement focus, the long-term portion of the compensated absence liability will not be liquidated with the expendable available financial resources of the governmental funds to which it relates and, accordingly, is not recorded in the fund.

For proprietary funds and for the government-wide financial statements, the accounting and financial reporting for recording the liability for compensated absences resembles more closely that used by commercial enterprises. The total applicable compensated absence liability is recorded in the government-wide financial statements and in the proprietary funds, and the corresponding amount of the liability that must be accrued is recorded as an expense.

LANDFILL CLOSURE AND POSTCLOSURE CARE COSTS

Yes, the GASB has even stuck its nose into the accounting matters related to your local town garbage dump, or as those in the know call it, a municipal solid waste landfill. Actually, the accounting rules make a lot of sense in that they attempt to match the cost of landfill closure and postclosure care costs with the time that the landfill is being used.

The GASB issued Statement No. 18, "Accounting for Municipal Solid Waste Landfill Closure and Postclosure Care Costs" (GASBS 18), in part in response to requirements promulgated by the US Environmental Protection Agency (EPA). Landfill operators are obligated to meet certain requirements of the EPA as to closure and postclosure care. The postclosure care requirements extend for a period of thirty years. Landfill operators also may be subject to state and local laws and regulations. Governments are required to recognize the liability for these closure and postclosure costs as the landfill is being used, so that by the time the landfill becomes full and no longer accepts waste, the liability for closure and postclosure care costs is recorded in the financial statements of the governmental entity that operates the landfill and is responsible for these requirements.

A municipal solid waste landfill is an area of land or an excavation that receives household waste. What makes a landfill "municipal" is not the ownership of the landfill, but the type of waste that is received by the landfill—municipal waste means household waste. Landfills operate in many different ways. Their operating methods, along with their closure and postclosure care plans, are filed with regulatory bodies. Many landfills operate on a "cell" basis, where the total landfill is divided into sections that are used one at a time. Each cell can then be closed when it reaches capacity and the waste is then received by the next cell that is put into use. After each cell (or the entire landfill, if it is operated as one large cell) is filled to capacity and no longer accepts waste, a final cover is applied. Sometimes even when the landfill is operated as a number of cells, the final cover is not applied until the entire landfill is filled to capacity and no longer accepts solid waste. At or about the time that waste is no longer accepted by landfill, there are various *closure* costs that are incurred, including the installation of the final cover. Separate from the closure costs are the *postclosure* care costs (these are the ones that last for thirty years) that involve collecting and disposing of the leachate and the natural gas that emit from the landfill over this period of time.

The following costs are included in the definition of the estimated total current cost of closure and postclosure care costs:

- *The cost of equipment expected to be installed and facilities expected to be constructed near or after the date that the landfill stops accepting solid waste and during the postclosure period.* Equipment and facilities that are considered as part of these costs are only those that will be used exclusively for the landfill. This may include gas monitoring and collection systems, storm water management systems, groundwater monitoring wells, and leachate treatment facilities.
- *The cost of final cover expected to be applied near or after the date that the landfill stops accepting waste*
- *The cost of monitoring and maintaining expected usable landfill area during the postclosure period.* Postclosure care may include maintaining the final cover, monitoring groundwater, monitoring and collecting methane and other gases, collecting, treating, and transporting leachate, repairing or replacing equipment, and remedying or containing environmental hazards.

The purpose of the preceding list is not to make the reader an expert in landfill operations, but to give a sense of the types of costs that are included in the estimated current cost of closure and postclosure care costs, because this is the amount that will provide the basis of the liability that is recognized, as explained in the remaining paragraphs of this section.

The true impact of applying the requirements for recognizing a liability for closure and postclosure care costs is seen in the government-wide financial statements and proprietary funds. This is because as the liability is recorded proportionally each year for total estimated current costs, a corresponding expense is recorded in the statement of activities or statement of revenues, expenses, and changes in fund net assets. This results in the matching of the proportional estimated total cost of closure and postclosure costs with the period benefited by the landfill's use (i.e., the period during which it accepts household waste). These costs would not be accrued under this methodology by governmental funds.

Here is an overview of how the calculations work. For landfill activities reported in proprietary funds and for reporting in the government-wide financial statements, a portion of the estimated total current cost of closure and postclosure costs is recognized as an expense and as a liability. Recognition begins in the period that the landfill begins accepting waste, continues during the subsequent period that it accepts waste, and is completed by the time that the landfill stops accepting waste. The estimated total current cost is assigned to the period proportionately based on the landfill's use. Accordingly, some measure of the landfill's capacity used each period is compared to the landfill's total capacity.

An example should make this much clearer. Say that the estimated total current cost of closure and postclosure care of a landfill is $1 million. The landfill's total capacity is one million cubic yards. In the first year that the landfill is used, 100,000 cubic yards of waste (10% of the landfill's total capacity) is put into the landfill. An expense and liability of $100,000 (10% of $1 million) is recorded. Say that the second year of operation was a busy one and an additional 200,000 cubic yards of waste is deposited into the landfill, meaning that the landfill is now 30% full. The liability that should be recorded at the end of year two is $300,000 (30% of $1 million). Since a liability was already recorded for $100,000 at the end of year one, an additional liability of $200,000 (along with a corresponding expense of $200,000) is recorded in year two. Note that year two's financial statements show a liability of $300,000 and an expense of $200,000 for this landfill's closure and postclosure costs. The reason that the calculation is done on the cumulative amount of the landfill used is that the estimated total current cost should be reviewed and adjusted as appropriate. Say that at the end of year two, the estimated total current cost of closure and postclosure has been revised to $1.2 million due to inflation in the price of some the materials needed. Now the government should have a liability of $360,000 recorded at the end of year two. This means that expense in year two needs to be recorded for $260,000 in order to bring the liability up to the correct amount. After the landfill is closed, disbursements to pay for closure and postclosure care costs would reduce the estimated total current cost of the closure and postclosure care costs. In addition, after closure, the remaining estimated current cost amount would be adjusted (with corresponding increases or decreases to expense) to reflect updated estimates of what the total current costs of closure and postclosure care actually will be.

As mentioned earlier, this accounting method is used in the government-wide financial statements and by proprietary funds. Governmental funds would report closure and postclosure care costs in the year that the liability is actually incurred, which is basically when they expend the funds to pay for the closure and postclosure care costs. A landfill whose activities are recorded in a governmental fund would still have the liability and expense calculations performed as in the example, but the amounts would be recorded only in the government-wide financial statements. When the closure and postclosure care costs are incurred, the governmental fund would record an expenditure for the costs incurred.

Pollution Remediation Obligations

Beginning with calendar year-end 2008 financial statements, governments will need to implement new requirements about recording obligations to remediate (clean up) pollution that are required by GASB Statement No. 49, "Pollution Remediation Obligations" (GASBS 49).

The new requirements relate obligations for cleanup or site assessment of existing pollution. They do not relate pollution prevention or control obligations with relating to current obligations, nor to future pollution remediation activities that are required when an asset (think nuclear power plant) is retired.

Recording an obligation for pollution remediation under GASBS 49 is a two-step process. First, the government determines whether an "obligating event" has occurred that would require it to record a liability for pollution remediation. If an obligating event has occurred, the government must then determine how much of a liability will be recorded.

Since the liability that may be recorded under GASBS 49 is for pollution remediation activities, it is important to know what GASBS 49 considers to be pollution remediation activities. These are as follows:

- Precleanup activities, such as the performance of a site assessment, site investigation, corrective measures feasibility study, and the design of a remediation plan.
- Cleanup activities themselves, such as the containment, removal, disposal or neutralization of pollutants and site restoration.
- External government oversight and enforcement-related activities, such as work performed by an environmental regulatory authority dealing with the site and chargeable to the government.
- Operation and maintenance of the remedy, including required monitoring of the remediation effort.

Not every pollution remediation will involve all of the above activities. Rather, these are broad categories of activities that may be required.

GASBS 49 is very specific in defining "obligating events," which are as follows:

- The government is compelled to take pollution remediation action because of an imminent endangerment.

- The government violates a pollution-related permit or license.
- The government is named, or evidence indicates that it will be named, by a regulator as a responsible party, or potentially responsible party, for remediation, or as a government responsible for sharing costs.
- The government is named, or evidence indicates that it will be named, in a lawsuit to compel participation in pollution remediation.
- The government commences or legally obligates itself to commence pollution remediation.

There is a lot more specific information in GASBS 49 about these obligation events, a discussion of which is beyond the scope of this book. The above list should be enough to give the reader a flavor of those events which might prompt the recording of a liability.

One important question that the reader may be asking, however, is whether the government is required to conduct an active search for pollution and then determine whether there is an obligating event. The answer to that is really no. A government should determine whether an obligating event has occurred when the government "knows or reasonably believes" that a site is polluted. Note that the term "government" is used, not the "government's accounting department." Accordingly, financial statement preparers are likely to require some outreach to the various branches/departments of the government to determine the total population of sites that the government as a whole knows or reasonably believes to be polluted.

If an obligating event has occurred, a government's next step is to calculate the amount of the liability that should be recorded. Amounts have to be "reasonably estimable" under GASBS 49 in order for a liability to be recorded. GASBS 49 provides certain benchmarks (like stages) in the pollution remediation process to require governments to determine whether amounts are reasonably estimable for each stage or benchmark. In other words, a government cannot simply take the position that they cannot reasonably estimate the total cost of the remediation, therefore they do not have to record any liability. The remediation efforts need to be broken down into components, and as certain benchmarks are reached, an estimate of the remediation liability should be evaluated.

The real fun of GASBS 49 starts when estimating the liability for the pollution remediation and its components. An expected cash flow method is required to be used, in which various probabilities are assigned to different levels possible cash flows and then a weighted-average of the expected cash flows and probabilities is taken to arrive at the amount of the estimate of the liability. As new benchmarks are met, or when new information about the expected outlays becomes known, the liability should be adjusted to reflect the new circumstances.

The liability that is described above is what would be recorded in the government-wide financial statements and proprietary fund financial statements (i.e. those statements where the accrual basis of accounting and economic resources measurement focus are used). Except in certain circumstances described in the next paragraph, the liability is established by recording an expense for the amount of the liability recorded. Governmental funds would not record a liability until it actually incurs the pollution remediation costs, which would be at the same time that it records an expenditure.

So under what circumstances would an expense not be charged when a pollution remediation liability is recorded? What if the pollution remediation effort would require the purchase of heavy construction equipment that would ordinarily be recorded as a capital asset? Should that equipment be recorded as an asset, or should it be expensed? For the most part, the portion of the liability related to that equipment is going to be recorded as an expense, not an asset. GASBS 49 provides some very limited opportunities to record assets (also known as capitalizing the expenses) instead of expenses. Pollution remediation outlays should be capitalized only for the following circumstances:

- To prepare property in anticipation of a sale.
- To prepare property for use when the property was acquired with known or suspected pollution that was expected to be remediated.

- To perform pollution remediation that restores a pollution-caused decline in service utility that was recognized as an asset.
- To acquire property, plant, and equipment that have a future alternative use.

Clearly, these four circumstance are fairly narrow (and have additional limitations detailed in GASBS 49), which will result in most pollution remediation outlays being recorded as expenses.

As with many other governmental accounting standards, GASBS 49 is conceptually simply—record a liability for pollution remediation obligations—yet implementation of the concept leads to many technicalities and complexities.

DERIVATIVES, INCLUDING INTEREST RATE SWAPS

Derivatives and interest rate swaps are complicated areas that, as was stated for pension accounting, are difficult to describe in a book that includes "made easy" in its title. Obtaining an understanding of derivatives and interest rate swaps is really beyond the scope of this book. However, the following paragraphs describe recent activities of the GASB in their area. Derivatives, including interest rate swaps, are proprietary fund statements of net assets recorded at fair value on the government-wide statement of net assets.

The GASB issued Technical Bulletin No. 2003-1, "Disclosure Requirements for Derivatives Not Reported at Fair Value on the Statement of Net Assets" (GASBTB 2003-1), which currently requires various disclosures related to derivatives that are not reported at fair value on a government's statement of net assets. It does not provide any accounting guidance for recording derivatives.

In June 2008, the GASB issued Statement No. 53, "Accounting and Financial Reporting for Derivative Instruments" (GASBS 53), which provides accounting and financial reporting requirements for derivatives, that will essentially be in effect for fiscal year-ends of June 30, 2010, and thereafter. Since the implementation of GASBS 53 is imminent, the following discussion will be based on the requirements of GASBS 53, which essentially incorporates similar disclosure requirements that are currently effective under GASBTB 2003-1.

By far, the most common type of derivative instruments used by governments are interest rate swaps. By means of entering into an agreement with another party, governments can effectively "swap" a variable interest rate on debt that it has issued for a fixed interest rate. Of course, the rate of interest on the debt does not actually change. What happens is that the other party will pay the government the interest payments approximately equal to the variable rate interest payments that the government has to pay the actual bondholders of its debt. In return, the government pays the other party payments based upon a mutually agreed-upon fixed rate. In order for the transaction to work, the other party and the government are making certain "bets" as to the direction of interest rates, which is why they are interested in entering into this type of agreement. This example is very simplified and in actuality, most swaps are more complicated.

Other types of derivatives that governments sometimes use include instruments called commodity swaps, interest rate locks, options, swaptions, forward contracts, and futures contracts. Details of all these types of transactions are beyond the scope of this book. It is enough for the reader to know that these types of instruments are considered derivatives.

One significant feature of GASBS 53 is that the recognition and measurement provisions of GASBS 53 should not be applied to financial statements using the current financial resources measurement focus. This means that the financial statements of governmental funds would not recognize derivative financial instruments on the balance sheet in accordance with the requirements of GASBS 53. For purposes of applying GASBS 53, the statement of net assets refers only to government-wide, proprietary fund, and fiduciary fund financial statements.

Scope

GASBS 53 defines a derivative instrument as a financial instrument or other contract that has all of the following characteristics:

- *Settlement factors.* A derivative instrument has (1) one or more reference rates (including indexes or underlyings) and (2) one or more notional amounts (sometimes called the face amount) or payment provisions or both. GASBS 53 describes a reference rate as a specified interest rate, security price, commodity price, foreign exchange rate, index of prices or rates, or other variable (including the occurrence of nonoccurrence of a specified event such as a scheduled payment under a contract). GASBS 53 provides the following examples of reference rates:

  - A security price or security price index
  - A commodity price or commodity price index
  - An interest rate or interest rate index
  - A credit rating or credit index
  - An exchange rate or exchange rate index
  - An insurance index or catastrophe loss index
  - A climatic or geological condition (such as temperature, earthquake severity, or rainfall), another physical variable, or a related index

  Common reference rates are the London Interbank Offered Rate (LIBOR), the Securities Industry and Financial Markets Association (SIFMA) swap index, the AAA general obligations index published by Municipal Market DATA, or a commodity pricing point.
  The notional amount is the number of currency units, shares, bushels, pounds, or other units specified in the derivative instrument. The notional amount and reference rate are key factors of a derivative instrument's settlement payment.
- *Leverage.* It requires no initial net investment or an initial net investment that is smaller than would be required for other types of contracts that would be expected to have a similar response to changes in market factors. An interest rate swap is an example of leverage, in that an interest rate swap generally requires no initial net investment.
- *Net settlement.* Its terms require or permit net settlement, it can readily be settled net by a means outside the contract, or it provides for delivery of an asset that puts the recipient in

a position not substantially different from net settlement. In the interest rate swap example above, the government and the third party wouldn't actually transfer the gross amounts of the payments to each other. Rather, only the net amount which would be either due to the government or due to the third party, depending on the changes in interest rates, would be paid, usually on a monthly basis.

Recognition and Measurement of Derivative Instruments

GASBS 53 provides that derivative instruments should be reported on the statement of net assets and should be measured at their fair value. Fair value should be measured by the market price if there is an active market for the derivative instrument. If a market price is not available, a forecast of the expected cash flows may be used, provided that the expected cash flows are discounted. Formula-based methods and mathematical models are also acceptable means of determining fair value.

The real complexities of GASBS 53 come into play in determining how changes in the fair value of derivative instruments from period to period are presented in the financial statements. The determination of how changes in the fair value of derivatives are reported in the financial statements is based upon whether or not the derivative instrument meets the criteria to be considered a hedging derivative instrument.

- Changes in the fair values of investment derivative instruments (i.e., a derivative that is entered into primarily for the purpose of obtaining income or profit, or a derivative that does not meet the criteria of a hedging derivative instrument) should be reported within the investment revenue classification in the "flow of financial resources" statement—the statement of activities, statement of revenues, expenses and changes in fund net assets, or statement of changes in fiduciary net assets.
- Changes in fair value of hedging derivative instruments are recognized through the application of hedge accounting. In hedge accounting, changes in the fair values of derivatives are reported as deferred inflows or deferred outflows (i.e., deferred debits and credits) on the statement of net assets.

Clearly, the determining whether a derivative instrument meets the criteria to be considered a hedging derivative instrument is critical to determining the proper accounting for changes in the fair value of these instruments as changes in the fair values of hedging derivative instruments are only recorded on the "balance sheet" while changes in the fair values of investment derivative instruments flow through the "income statement." A significant part of GASBS 53 is devoted to setting the criteria that must be met to qualify a derivative for hedge accounting.

Hedging Derivative Instruments

GASBS 53 provides that a hedging derivative instrument is established if both of the following criteria are met:

1. The derivative instrument is associated with a hedgeable item (described below). Association is established by consideration of the facts and circumstances of the derivative instrument, including whether

   a. The notional amount of the derivative instrument is consistent with the principal amount or quantity of the hedgeable item.
   b. The derivative instrument will be reported in the same fund, if applicable, as the hedgeable item.
   c. The term or time period of the derivative instrument is consistent with the term or time period of the hedgeable item.

GASBS 53 defines hedgeable items as those that expose a government to identified financial risks that can be expressed in terms of exposure to adverse changes in cash flows or fair values. Hedgeable items can be all or a specific portion of

1. A single asset or liability, for example, an entire bond issue or a specific portion of a bond issue.
2. Groups of similar assets or similar liabilities. If similar assets or similar liabilities are aggregated and hedged as a group, all of the individual assets or individual liabilities in the

group are required to be exposed to the same indentified financial risk that is being hedged.
3. An expected transaction

Since the determination of whether or not a derivative instrument is considered an effective hedge has a significant impact on the treatment of changes in its fair value on a government's activities statement, determining whether a hedge is effective or not comprises a significant portion of GASBS 53's discussions and requirements.

The two basic methods to determine whether or not a derivative instrument is an effective hedge are categorized as the consistent critical terms method and the quantitative method, which is really comprised of several different quantitative methods.

- *Consistent critical terms method.* The consistent critical terms method, as defined by GASBS 53, evaluates effectiveness by qualitative consideration of the critical terms of the hedgeable item and the potential hedging derivative instrument. If the critical terms of the hedgeable item and the potential hedging derivative instrument are the same, or similar in certain circumstances as, the changes in cash flows or fair values of the potential hedging derivative instrument will substantially offset the changes in cash flows or fair values of the hedgeable item.
- *Quantitative methods.* GASBS 53 specifies three quantitative methods that may be used to evaluate effectiveness: the synthetic instrument method, the dollar-offset method, and the regression analysis method. Quantitative methods other than those specifically described in this statement also may be used to evaluate effectiveness, provided that they meet certain criteria.

Application of any of these methods to determine hedge effectiveness is well beyond the scope of this book. These calculations are probably some of the more difficult ones found in any GASB Statement. As usual, what is important is to understand the basic concept. What is important to understand is that in order to record changes in the fair value of derivatives as deferred assets or deferred liabilities on the statement of net assets, the purpose of the derivative must be to hedge a related item.

For example, in the interest rate swap discussed at the beginning of this section, the government is attempting to hedge increases in interest rates by entering into the interest rate swap agreement. What the consistent critical terms method and the quantitative methods are used for is to determine if the derivative is effective enough in providing this hedge against interest rate increases to qualify for reporting changes in the fair value of the derivative as deferred assets or liabilities. All of the rest of the discussion is simply more specifics as to what a hedge really is and how to apply the various calculations to determine the hedge's effectiveness.

Disclosures

GASBS 53 has many specific disclosure requirements for derivative instruments, which are summarized in the remainder of this section. This information is provided not because the reader will be preparing governmental financial statements. Rather, reading and (somewhat) understanding some of the matters that are required to be disclosed provides insight into various risks and other features that are inherent in derivatives.

Summary Information

Governments are required to provide a summary of their derivative instrument activity during the reporting period and balances at the end of the reporting period. The information disclosed should be organized by governmental activities, business-type activities, and fiduciary funds. The information should then be divided into the following categories—hedging derivative instruments (distinguishing between fair value hedges and cash flow hedges) and investment derivative instruments. Within each category, derivative instruments should be aggregated by type (for example, receive-fixed swaps, pay-fixed swaps, swaptions, rate caps, basis swaps, or futures contracts). Information presented in the summary should include

1. Notional amount
2. Changes in fair value during the reporting period and the classification in the financial statements where those changes in fair value are reported.
3. Fair values as of the end of the reporting period and the classification in the financial statements where those fair values are reported. If derivative instrument fair values are based on other than quoted market prices, the methods and significant assumptions used to estimate those fair values should be disclosed. However, if the fair value is developed by a pricing service, there is no requirement to disclose significant assumptions if the pricing service considers those assumptions to be proprietary and, after making every reasonable effort, the pricing service declines to make that information available. This fact, however, should be disclosed.
4. Fair values of derivative instruments reclassified from a hedging derivative instrument to an investment derivative instrument. There also should be disclosure of the deferral amount that was reported within investment revenue upon the reclassification.

Hedging Derivative Instruments

The following note disclosures are provided for all hedging derivative instruments:

- *Objectives.* For hedging derivative instruments, governments should disclose their objectives for entering into those instruments, the context needed to understand those objectives, the strategies for achieving those objectives, and the types of derivative instruments entered into.
- *Terms.* For hedging derivatives instruments, governments should disclose significant terms, including

  - Notional amount
  - Reference rates, such as indexes or interest rates
  - Embedded options, such as caps, floors, or collars
  - The date when the hedging derivative instrument was entered into and when it is scheduled to terminate or mature

- The amount of cash paid or received, if any, when a forward contract or swap (including swaptions) was entered into.

- *Risks.* For hedging derivative instruments, governments should disclose, if applicable, their exposure to the following risks that could give rise to financial loss. Risk disclosures are limited to hedging derivative instruments that are reported as of the end of the reporting period. Disclosures required by this paragraph may contain information that also is required by other paragraphs. However, these disclosures should be presented in the context of a hedging derivative instrument's risk

  1. *Credit risk.* If a hedging derivative instrument reported by the government as an asset exposes a government to credit risk, the government should disclose that exposure as credit risk and disclose the following information. These credit risk disclosures do not extend to derivatives that are exchange-traded, such as futures contracts. For those derivatives, disclosures for amounts held by broker-dealers is evaluated by applying the custodial credit risk disclosures found in Statement No. 3, "Deposits with Financial Institutions, Investments (including Repurchase Agreements), and Reverse Repurchase Agreements," and No. 40, "Deposit and Investment Risk Disclosures."

     a. The credit quality ratings of counterparties as described by nationally recognized statistical rating organizations—rating agencies—as of the end of the reporting period. If the counterparty is not rated, the disclosure should indicate that fact.
     b. The maximum amount of loss due to credit risk, based on the fair value of the hedging derivative instrument as of the end of the reporting period, that the government would incur if the counterparties to the hedging derivative instrument failed to perform according to the terms of the contract, without re-

    spect to any collateral or other security, or netting arrangement.

    c. The government's policy of requiring collateral or other security to support hedging derivative instruments subject to credit risk, a summary description and the aggregate amount of the collateral or other security that reduces credit risk exposure, and information about the government's access to that collateral or other security.

    d. The government's policy of entering into master netting arrangements, including a summary description and the aggregate amount of liabilities included in those arrangements. Master netting arrangements are established when (1) each party owes the other determinable amounts, (2) the government has the right to set off the amount owed with the amount owed by the counterparty, and (3) the right of setoff is legally enforceable.

    e. The aggregate fair value of hedging derivative instruments in asset (positive) positions net of collateral posted by the counterparty and the effect of master netting arrangements.

    f. Significant concentrations of net exposure to credit risk (gross credit risk reduced by collateral, other security, and setoff) with individual counterparties and groups of counterparties. A concentration of credit risk exposure to an individual counterparty may not require disclosure if its existence is apparent from the disclosures required by other parts of this paragraph, for example, a government has entered into only one interest rate swap. Group concentrations of credit risk exist if a number of counterparties are engaged in similar activities and have similar economic characteristics that would cause their ability to meet contractual obligations to be similarly affected by changes in economic or other conditions.

2. *Interest rate risk.* If a hedging derivative instrument increases a government's exposure to interest rate risk, the government should disclose that increased exposure as

interest rate risk and also should disclose the hedging derivative instrument's terms that increase such a risk. The determination of whether a hedging derivative instrument increase interest rate risk should be made after considering, for example, the effects of the hedging derivative instrument and any hedged debt.

3. *Basis risk.* If a hedging derivative instrument exposes a government to basis risk, the government should disclose that exposure as basis risk and also should disclose the hedging derivative instrument's terms and payment terms of the hedged item that creates the basis risk.

4. *Termination risk.* If a hedging derivative instrument exposes a government to termination risk, the government should disclose that exposure as termination risk and also the following information, as applicable:

   a. Any termination events that have occurred
   b. Dates that the hedging derivative instrument may be terminated
   c. Out-of-the-ordinary termination events contained in contractual documents, such as "additional termination events" contained in the schedule to the International Swap Dealers Association master agreement

5. *Rollover risk.* If a hedging derivative instrument exposes a government to rollover risk, the government should disclose that exposure as rollover risk and also should disclose the maturity of the hedging derivative instrument and the maturity of the hedged item.

6. *Market-access risk.* If a hedging derivative instrument creates market-access risk, the government should disclose that exposure as market-access risk.

7. *Foreign currency risk.* If a hedging derivative instrument exposes a government to foreign currency risk, the government should disclose the US dollar balance of the hedging derivative instrument, organized by currency denomination and by type of derivative instrument.

- *Hedged debt.* If the hedged item is a debt obligation, governments should disclose the hedging derivative instrument's net cash flows based on the requirements established by Statement No. 38, "Certain Financial Statement Note Disclosures," paragraphs 10 and 11.
- *Other quantitative method of evaluating effectiveness.* If effectiveness is evaluated by application of a quantitative method not specially identified in GASBS 53, governments should disclose the following information. However there is no requirement to disclose information that a pricing service considers to be proprietary and after making every reasonable effort the pricing service declines to make available. This fact, however, should be disclosed.

  - The identity and characteristics of the method used
  - The range of critical terms the method tolerates
  - The actual critical terms of the hedge

Investment Derivative Instruments

For investment derivative instruments, GASBS 53 requires governments to disclose their exposure to the following risks that could give rise to financial loss. Risk disclosures are limited to investment derivative instruments that are reported as of the end of the reporting period. Disclosures required by this section may contain information that also is required by other sections. However, these disclosures should be presented in the context of an investment derivative instrument's risk

1. *Credit risk.* If an investment derivative instrument exposes a government to credit risk (that is, the government reports the investment derivative instrument as an asset), the government should disclose that exposure.
2. *Interest rate risk.* If an investment derivative instrument exposes a government to interest rate risk, the government should disclose that exposure consistent with the disclosures required by GASBS 40, paragraphs 14 and 15. Further, an investment derivative instrument that is an interest rate swap is an additional example of an investment that has a fair value that is highly sensitive to interest rate

changes as discussed in GASBS 40, paragraph 16. The fair value, notional amount, reference rate, and embedded option should be disclosed.

3. *Foreign currency risk.* If an investment derivative instrument exposes a government to foreign currency risk, the government should disclose that exposure consistent with the disclosures required by GASBS 40, paragraph 17.

SECURITIES LENDING TRANSACTIONS

Governments, particularly large ones, sometimes enter into transactions in which they loan securities in their investment portfolios to broker-dealers and other entities in return for collateral that the governmental entity agrees to return to the broker-dealer or other borrower when that entity returns the borrowed security. The GASB issued Statement No. 28 (GASBS 28), "Accounting and Financial Reporting for Securities Lending Transactions," to provide accounting and financial reporting requirements for these types of transactions.

Securities lending transactions are defined by GASBS 28 as transactions in which governmental entities transfer their securities to broker-dealers and other entities for collateral—which may be cash, securities, or letters of credit—and simultaneously agree to return the collateral for the same securities in the future. The securities transferred to the broker-dealer or other borrower are referred to as the *underlying securities.*

The governmental lender in a securities lending transaction that accepts cash as collateral to the transactions has the risk of having the transaction bear a cost to it, or it may make a profit on the transaction. For example, assume that the governmental lender of the securities invests the cash received as collateral. If the returns on those investments exceed the agreed-upon rebate paid to the borrower, the securities lending transaction generates income for the government. However, if the investment of the cash collateral does not provide a return exceeding the rebate or if the investment incurs a loss in principal, part of the payment to the borrower would come from the government's resources.

Of course, the situation is different if the collateral for the transaction is not in the form of cash, but instead consists of securities or a letter of credit. In this case, the borrower of the security pays the lender a loan premium or fee in compensation for the securities loan. In some cases, the government may have the ability to pledge or sell the collateral securities before being required to return them to the borrower at the end of the loan.

During the recent turmoil in the financial markets, securities received as collateral in securities lending transactions have received greater attention, since rapid declines in the market value for this collateral may put the government at risk of loss in the event of nonperformance by the securities "borrower."

Governmental entities that lend securities are usually long-term investors with large investment portfolios. Governmental entities that typically use these transactions include pension funds, state investment boards and treasurers, and college and university endowment funds. Governments that enter into securities lending transactions are usually long-term investors; a high rate of portfolio turnover would preclude the loaning of securities because the loan might extend for a period beyond the intended holding period. At the same time, securities lending transactions are generally used by governmental entities that are holders of large investment portfolios. There are several reasons for this, such as the degree of investment sophistication needed to authorize and monitor these types of transactions, as well as the existence of enough "critical mass" of investments available to lend to allow the governmental entity lender to earn enough profit on these transactions to have an acceptable increase in the overall performance on the investment portfolio. In addition, many lending agents are not interested in being involved with securities lending transactions for smaller portfolios.

GASBS 28 requires the following basic accounting treatment for securities lending transactions:

- The securities that have been lent (the underlying securities) should continue to be reported in the balance sheet.
- Collateral received by a government as a result of securities lending transactions should be reported as an asset in the balance sheet of the governmental entity if the following collateral is received:

  - Cash is received as collateral.

- Securities are received as collateral, if the governmental entity has the ability to pledge or sell them without a borrower default.

- Liabilities resulting from these securities lending transactions should also be reported in the balance sheet of the governmental entity. The governmental entity has a liability to return cash or securities that it received from the securities borrower back to the borrower when the borrower returns the underlying security to the government.

For purposes of determining whether a security received as collateral should be recorded as an asset, governmental lenders are considered to have the ability to pledge or sell collateral securities without a borrower default if the securities lending contract specifically allows it. If the contract does not address whether the lender can pledge or sell the collateral securities without a borrower default, it should be deemed not to have the ability to do so unless it has previously demonstrated that ability or there is some other indication of the ability to pledge or sell the collateral securities.

Securities lending transactions that are collateralized by letters of credit or by securities that the governmental entity does not have the ability to pledge or sell unless the borrower defaults should not be reported as assets and liabilities in the balance sheet. Thus, in these two cases only the underlying security remains recorded in the balance sheet of the lending governmental entity.

The obvious result of applying the requirements of GASBS 28 is the "grossing-up" of the governmental entity's balance sheet with an asset for the collateral received and a corresponding liability, which are both in addition to the underlying security, which remains recorded as an asset. This effect can be quite large when the governmental entity has a large investment portfolio and an active securities lending program.

In determining the amount of collateral received by the governmental entity lender, generally the market value of securities received as collateral is slightly higher than the market value of the securities loaned, the difference being referred to as the margin. The margin required by the lending government may be different for different types of securities. For example, the governmental entity might require collateral of 102% of the market value of securities loaned for lending transactions involving domestic securities, and it might require collateral of 105% of the market value of securities loaned for lending transactions involving foreign securities.

The preceding discussion focuses on the accounting and financial reporting requirements of GASBS 28 relative to grossing-up a government's balance sheet. GASBS 28 has a similar effect on a governmental entity's operating statement—amounts will be grossed-up, but there is generally no net effect of applying the requirements of the statement.

GASBS 28 requires that the costs of securities lending transactions be reported as expenditures or expenses in the governmental entity's operating statement. These costs should include

- *Borrower rebates* (These payments from the lender to the borrower as compensation for the use of the cash collateral provided by the borrower should be reported as interest expenditures or interest expense.)
- *Agent fees* (These are amounts paid by a lender to its securities lending agent as compensation for managing its securities lending transactions and should be reported along with similar investment management fees.)

In either of these cases, these costs of securities lending transactions are not netted with interest revenue or income from the investment of cash collateral, any other related investments, or loan premiums or fees.

When the above requirements are applied, investment income and expenses are effectively grossed up for the interest earned on the collateral securities received by the lending governmental entity (or on the invested cash received as collateral), and expenditures or expenses are increased for a similar amount representing the amounts that would be paid to the securities borrower in compensation for holding the collateral asset, as well as the investment management expenses relating to securities lending transactions.

Sales and Pledges of Receivables and Future Revenue Streams

Governments have sometimes sold or pledged their interests in receivables (such as a tax lien sale) or sold or pledged their interests in future revenues (such as payments states and certain localities have received under the master settlement agreement with tobacco companies). The GASB issued Statement No. 48, "Sales and Pledges of Receivables and Future Revenues and Intra-Entity Transfers of Assets and Future Revenues" (GASBS 48), to address the accounting issues inherent in these types of transactions.

This is a fairly specialized accounting topic and the requirements will be briefly summarized so that the reader can be aware of the accounting questions that are addressed when these types of transactions occur. The financial reporting question addressed by GASBS 48 is whether the transaction in question should be regarded as a sale or as a borrowing resulting in a liability.

GASBS 48 establishes criteria that governments must use to determine whether the proceeds received in these types of transactions be reported as revenue or as a liability. The criteria that should be used to determine the extent to which a transferor government either keeps or gives up control over the receivables or future revenues is based upon its continuing involvement with those receivables or future revenues.

GASBS 48 requires that a transaction be reported as a collateralized borrowing unless its specific criteria indicating that a sale has taken place are met.

- If it is determined that a transaction involving receivables should be reported as a sale, the difference between the carrying value of the receivables and the proceeds should be recognized in the period of the sale in the statement of activities. This amount is really the government's gain or loss on the sale of its receivable, based on what it receives compared to the amount that the receivable was recorded at on its books.
- If it is determined that a transaction involving future revenues should be reported as a sale, the revenue should be deferred and amortized, unless specific criteria are met.

If the conditions of sale are not met, then the transaction is recorded as though the government is simply borrowing the proceeds from the transaction, using the receivables or future revenues as collateral. In this case, a liability would be recorded for the amounts received from the transaction.

SUMMARY

The topics covered in this chapter are important for a broad understanding of governmental accounting and financial reporting.

CHAPTER 10

Upcoming Developments in Governmental Accounting

Accounting principles, including governmental accounting principles, are not a static group of rules or requirements. The GASB has a continuous agenda of new projects to study that will result in a constantly evolving set of accounting principles to be used by governments. Why are new accounting standards necessary? There are a number of reasons, but consider just a few.

- Some accounting areas are not covered by an existing authoritative statement, often resulting in a diversity of accounting practices being used, which makes financial statements among different governments less comparable.
- New types of transactions, such as derivatives, either come into being or become more widely used, often resulting in the need for new accounting guidance.
- Actions by other standards setters, such as the FASB, may result in the need to clarify or set requirements for similar areas in the governmental accounting environment.
- Abuses by entities of "loopholes" in accounting principles may point to the need for a new standard or standards revisions.

Whatever the reason, to understand governmental accounting it is useful to keep an eye on whatever areas the GASB is currently concerned with. Some of the GASB's projects have broad impacts on virtually every government preparing financial statements. Other projects are more narrowly focused and do not affect a large number of governments. This chapter will provide an overview of the current projects on the GASB agenda, with a focus on those that will impact the largest number of governments.

PENSION (AND OPEB) ACCOUNTING—REVISITED

The original accounting model developed by the GASB for defined benefit pensions (and later "copied" for use with postemployment benefits other than pensions, OPEBs) was based upon a GASB statement issued in 1994. Since that time, and with its reconsideration during the more recent developments for OPEBs, the GASB believes that it is time to evaluate these accounting and reporting requirements to see if they need to be updated.

Some of the areas where the GASB is looking to reexamine the current requirements are

- Are there better ways to match the cost of providing these benefits to employees to the period during which they provide service to the government?
- What factors should be considered in projecting the benefit obligation for plan members?
- How should the discount rate that is used to calculate the present value of benefits be determined? Some actuaries believe that it might be appropriate to use a risk-free (i.e., very low) discount rate, which would greatly increase the amount calculated as a pension or OPEB obligation.
- Should there be additional requirements for pension cost recognition for employers with cost-sharing multiemployer plans?

As this book goes to press, the GASB has issued an Invitation to Comment on these and other areas. A final standard (if any) for these matters is likely to be at least a couple of years away.

One matter resulting from OPEB implementation that may see some more immediate GASB action deals with issues related to the frequency and timing of actuarial valuations and the use of the alternative measurement method for small plans. The GASB has this narrow project on its agenda and may issue a statement on this narrow area prior to revisiting the entire accounting model for pensions and OPEBs.

Voluntary Reporting of Service Efforts and Accomplishments

The GASB has had long-running research projects regarding the reporting performance information that is beyond the financial reporting information contained in the financial statements, or even comprehensive annual financial reports. Service efforts and accomplishments (SEA) reporting is meant to provide information to help determine the degree to which a government was successful in helping to maintain or improve the well-being of its citizens by providing services. SEA reporting is also sometimes referred to as performance measurement reporting.

Some commentators (notably the Government Finance Officers Association, or GFOA) believe that SEA reporting is outside the scope of the GASB and that it should not be providing any standards (even if they are voluntary) on reporting of this information.

The GASB has issued a Request for Response to obtain views on a framework for SEA reporting that it has developed. It is impossible to predict where this project will end up in terms of what the voluntary guidelines will look like, or even whether they will actually be issued. It is fairly safe bet that whatever is issued will result in guidelines that will be voluntary, not mandated.

Bankruptcy Accounting

The GASB has an item on its agenda to address accounting and financial reporting issues for governments that have been granted protection from creditors under Chapter 9 of the United States Bankruptcy Code.

In a typical bankruptcy, a government is relieved from certain debt obligations, so the accounting question arises as to how to account for the debt reduction. Other areas are the accounting for legal and other direct costs of the bankruptcy and, for governments not expected to continue operations, the requirements for reporting assets at remeasured values.

Financial Reporting Entity

The GASB is reexamining GASB Statement No. 14, "The Financial Reporting Entity" to determine its effectiveness, including its provisions for reporting fiduciary activities. This project will involve taking another look at the requirements for including certain legally separate entities within the reporting government's financial reporting entity. It will also examine how effectively component unit information is displayed, including the concepts of blended and discretely presented component units.

Accounting for Public/Private Partnerships

The GASB calls this project "service concession arrangements," but the underlying reason for its being on the agenda is the growing use of public/private partnerships, which can admittedly involve a wide range of arrangements. Here are some of the arrangements that the GASB provides as examples of public/private partnerships:

- A hospital authority transferring its assets, liabilities and hospital operations to a not-for-profit hospital system through a lease and management agreement, with the hospital authority's ongoing operations being limited to issuing conduit debt for the not-for-profit hospital system and serving as a "pass-through" for governmental grants.
- A university leasing land to a third-party developer for construction of a dormitory building, with the building being leased back to the university or the units being leased directly to university students and faculty by the developer.
- A state leasing a portion of its turnpike system to a private consortium in exchange for an up-front payment.
- A state entering into an agreement with a private consortium to build and then operate a tollway in exchange for an up-front payment.

One of the fundamental questions that the GASB is addressing is whether the related asset in these types of arrangements should remain on the books of the government. The GASB has tentatively concluded that control over the use of the property is a key determiner in deciding who reports the property as an asset.

Other accounting topics that will be studied are the accounting for back-loaded payments and payment holidays and whether there were recognizable intangible assets inherent in certain types of these arrangements where a government operator has a right to access another organization's property.

Fair Value Measurements

The Financial Accounting Standards Board has recently released its Statement No. 157, "Fair Value Measurements," somewhat prompting the GASB to add a project to its agenda addressing the same area. The GASB's current research project is to review and consider alternatives for the further development of the definition of fair value, the methods used to measure fair value, and potential disclosures about fair value measurements. Specific areas included are the fair value measurement of alternative investments, such as private placements and hedge funds, real estate investment trusts, state land trusts, and partnership interests.

SUMMARY

Keeping abreast of future changes in governmental accounting and financial reporting is necessary for even the casual reader and user of governmental financial statements. This chapter attempts to provide a broad overview of the more important projects that are currently on the GASB's technical agenda. About the only thing that we can be sure of is change, and readers are cautioned that any of the preliminary conclusions discussed in this chapter are all subject to change by the GASB. In addition, new accounting issues might arise that would require a quick response by the GASB, so there could be areas that are addressed in the near future that are not included in this chapter because they are not yet known